NATIONAL INSTITUTE FOR SOCIAL WORK

RESIDENTIAL CARE

A Positive Choice

*Report of the Independent Review
of Residential Care*

Chaired by Gillian Wagner, OBE, Ph D

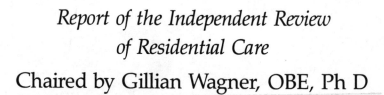

LONDON
HER MAJESTY'S STATIONERY OFFICE

EC 4/94
AJSN/2
WM 860

Contents

[iii]

Throughout the Report references to evidence received are indicated thus:

E = formal evidence

P = personal letters

H = personal letters received in direct response to the Committee's appeal on Thames Television's Help programme.

Introduction

The Independent Review of Residential Care was commissioned in December 1985 by the Rt. Hon. Norman Fowler, Secretary of State for Health and Social Services 'to review the role of residential care and the range of services given in statutory, voluntary and private residential establishments within the personal social services in England and Wales; to consider, having regard to the practical constraints and other relevant developments, what changes, if any, are required to enable the residential care sector to respond effectively to changing social needs; and to make recommendations accordingly.'

This Report, *A Positive Choice*, is written not only for politicians, policy makers and practitioners in the field of residential care; it is addressed to a far wider audience, for the quality of residential services provided by all three sectors affects, directly or indirectly, almost the whole population. Unlike the NHS, residential services command little popular support, and public interest is only normally aroused if there is thought to be financial mismanagement or if another scandal is given headline treatment.

The Review was set up at a time when there was wide agreement that residential services, particularly in the statutory sector, were in a demoralised state, too often used as a service of last resort and seen to be of low status. (It is worth noting in this context that the residential sector is largely staffed by women and a majority of its largest group of users, the frail elderly, are also women). The Committee had been at work for six months when the Audit Commission published its report *Making a Reality of Community Care* in December 1986 charging the Government with wasting money and with allowing the private residential care sector to expand in a manner inimical to the development of care in the community—and for a full year before the appalling disclosures made in the report of the Nye Bevan Lodge Enquiry

[1]

shocked the public.

When we formulated guidelines for organisations wishing to submit evidence we were working from the premise that, with suitable modification and adjustments, the sector, as it was constituted, could be adapted and improved to meet changing needs. It was after we had asked service users, their families and those who had direct responsibility for caring for them, for their views that we came to see our task in a different light. We realised that seeking to take account of consumer views would add to its complexities. We would be seeking views from people of widely differing age ranges and widely differing needs. This proved to be a matter of some difficulty to us when we came to write the Report, wanting to establish general principles and yet wishing to recognise the differing social needs of children, adults and very old people.

Using every possible means including a television appeal we asked elderly people in residential care and their relatives, and those who cared for them, to let us have their views, promising confidentiality to those who wrote. On our visits we talked with children in care and people with severe disabilities in residential establishments. We note with regret that we failed effectively to reach people with mental handicap and mental illness.

It was reassuring to learn that there were people who had found residential establishments where they were respected as individuals and felt secure and well cared for. Evidence of this came from all three sectors—statutory, voluntary and private. But alongside this came disturbing evidence, again from all three sectors, of an insensitivity to the rights of individuals and examples of cruelty causing both mental and physical suffering to the residents. None of us who read those letters could remain unmoved by the depth of unhappiness and despair revealed by their writers.

Letters from those working in residential establishments referred to the low esteem in which they were held, low morale among staff, the lack of training and of knowledge about the philosophy of residential work or of what constitutes good or bad practice. One respondent ended by saying whoever 'had the idea of setting up a Review of Residential Social Work should have a medal.'

The cumulative weight of the consumer evidence added to our consideration of the research reviews, reinforced our early realisation that to concentrate solely on the role of residential care as traditionally defined would not only entrench a system of caring that still carried within itself the stigma of its workhouse origins; it would do nothing to protect the rights or enlarge the choice of the user.

In *A Positive Choice* we seek to promote a fundamental change in the public perception of the residential sector and of its place in the spectrum of social care. We believe that residential services can no longer be considered in isolation but need to be seen as part of the continuum of care in the community: they must aim to provide a service of excellence; the complex and often stressful nature of the work needs to be recognised and staff must have proper support and training; there must be greater diversity in the services provided. The view of the Association of Directors of Social Services that 'there is an increasing need for organisational coherence which sets residential care in the context of a spectrum of care networked according to the needs of individual clients' is one with which the Committee are in full agreement.

No situation remains static. The projected rapid growth in the numbers of elderly and aged, the expansion of private residential care, the dramatic decrease in residential provision for children coupled with the equally dramatic increase in cases of child abuse, were all part of the background against which the Committee deliberated. We believe that giving primacy to the views and wishes of the service users will, inevitably, alter the context in which residential services operate. We believe that people should be able to make a positive choice between different models of care when they can no longer cope with life unaided. At present, they are too often presented with a stark choice between remaining in the community and moving into residential care. We believe that if needs for services and accommodation are looked at separately, however, the range of possible choice for each individual can be vastly expanded. Given this power of choice, there will in time be a change in the fundamental dynamics of the relationship between client and professional which could lead society into a more positive understanding of the needs of its most dependent members.

We draw attention to the fact that our recommendations apply to all three sectors—statutory, voluntary and private. We note that they would also affect the housing, education and health services. When Sir Roy Griffiths was appointed by the Government late in 1986 to review the way in which public funds are used to support community care policy, we were able to exchange views with him from time to time during our deliberations.

The Committee was set up with a membership representing many different aspects of the residential services, which has given us the opportunity to make radical suggestions as to the way in which we should hope to see those services developing into the twenty-first century. It is not possible to promulgate far-reaching principles and at the same time to foresee their final results and thus to evaluate their costs with any kind of precision. Added to this, Sir Roy Griffiths' review will be completed at about the same time as our own. It follows that a lot more detailed work will have to be done if the recommendations we have outlined are to be implemented. It is our hope that our Report will prompt further discussions, that time will be given to working out the implications of 'a positive choice', and that financial support will be forthcoming to enable our recommendations to be carried forward.

The Committee was fortunate in having the benefit of reviews of research as well as of a considerable number of vivid and moving personal letters which greatly influenced our thinking. The research, which we were able to commission at an early stage (thanks to the advice of Mr Peter Barclay, chairman of the Barclay Committee), enabled us to appreciate the historic, economic and moral context in which residential services developed. This research, published as Volume II of the Report, gave us the necessary background against which to formulate our proposals for a new and broader view of the scope of residential services. We thank Dr Ian Sinclair for his work as editor, Professor R A Parker who contributed the introductory chapter (which we were enabled to commission by a grant from the Joseph Rowntree Memorial Trust), and all the contributors for the speed with which they produced their papers. Each of them subsequently attended a meeting of the Committee at which their findings and conclusions were discussed with great frankness.

We are grateful to the many organisations and individuals who responded to our questionnaire and sent us formal evidence; also to all who wrote personal letters, either as residents, relations, friends, visitors or staff. The letters have been surveyed by Elma Sinclair and no one reading her account can fail to be affected by the immediacy with which they convey the thoughts and feelings of those involved in the residential experience. The Committee is indebted to Elma Sinclair, not only for her work on the personal evidence, but also for her comprehensive analysis of the formal evidence; these are published together as Appendix I to this Report. We thank Mr Sidney Wilkinson for help in sifting the written evidence and Dr Roger Clough who produced for us at short notice a paper on 'Scandals in Residential Centres'.

We made several visits as a group which were very helpful to us but must have been taxing for our hosts. We would like to record our gratitude to the Social Services Departments of Birmingham, Bradford, Clwyd, Coventry and Warwickshire who made us welcome, and to the Directors of the Royal National School for the Blind in Leatherhead and of Pengwern Hall near Rhyl who entertained us when we were in their areas. During our residential visits we took the opportunity to meet and talk with both residents and staff. The Committee met either at the National Institute for Social Work or at the Thomas Coram Foundation as a full working group on some 30 occasions. We also held two longer residential sessions at Cumberland Lodge, Windsor.

The Review was based at the National Institute for Social Work, which we thank for its support during the past two years. We pay tribute to the Principal, Mary Sugden who first attended as an observer and subsequently became a member of the Committee, and to Daphne Statham, her successor, who has taken a constructive interest in our deliberations. Chris Payne, of the Institute's academic staff, was a valued professional adviser. Roger Toulmin, as secretary of the Committee brought patience and expertise to producing a coherent document from the sometimes conflicting views of Committee members. We should also like to extend particular thanks to Elizabeth Blackaby for her help with the drafting of the final Report. Anne Whitehouse and her successor Pamela Graham were both supportive members of the Secretariat.

Let no one have any illusions. A Committee can only make recommendations. Unless society at large feels the same sense of burning indignation as the Committee at the way in which the present system can devalue the lives of some of the people most in need of help and support—despite the dedicated work done by so many—recommendations will remain recommendations. Adjustments and modifications will be made but public inertia will ensure that the system with all its weaknesses will remain essentially unaltered.

We should have liked to have had the opportunity of discussing our ideas with many other interested bodies but our remit was very wide and time did not permit. The Committee is unanimously and solidly behind its recommendations, and we must look to others to continue the debate.

GILLIAN WAGNER

CHAPTER ONE

Making Residential Care a Positive Choice

1. People who move into a residential establishment should do so by positive choice, and living there should be a positive experience. These are the two fundamental requirements for the proper functioning of all residential services.

2. As a Committee we are united in the view that residential services have much to offer, and our aim is to promote their contribution. At the same time, we could not fail to be aware of much bad residential practice, in which vulnerable and relatively powerless residents, who have few if any available alternatives, are subject to control by staff, behind closed doors, in establishments which are regarded by the general public as an undesirable alternative to ordinary living. Such situations can result in miserable lives for residents and behaviour by staff which is the very opposite of caring.

A Positive Choice

3. We believe it to be essential that a person entering a residential establishment should so so by positive choice, since the quality of life in a residential establishment will depend quite crucially on the consent and cooperation of those who share it. An important implication of this is that there need to be real and valid alternatives on offer, from which potential residents may make their choice. An older child, for example, may wish to choose between a community establishment and a fostering placement, and a handicapped adult between a residential community and living in an ordinary house; an elderly person will wish to consider the pros and cons of residential care as

against intensive domiciliary support. In all cases the alternatives need to be attractive enough to constitute valid potential choices; thus, there is no valid choice if old people are driven into a residential establishment because domiciliary services are skimpy, or if they remain precariously in their own homes because the residential services on offer are of poor quality.

4. The choice needs to be a real decision, not simply an expression of personal preference to be accorded limited weight in a judgement to be reached by those in authority. This is not to deny the importance of professional expertise and the value of impartial assessment, but these are better employed in identifying the alternatives and helping to illuminate the choice between them, than in support of the attitude 'We know better than you do what is best for you'. To give this power of choice to the consumer is important because it changes the fundamental dynamics of the relationship between client and professional, and on a wider scale, between the dependent person and society.

5. By a positive experience we mean residential care which is actively aimed at providing every resident with the highest quality of life of which they are capable and, indeed, a better life than would be open to them in any other environment; we know the best residential establishments already make this their aim, and we believe that all should do so. There must be diversity in residential care. Its excellence will depend on providing appropriate care for differing groups of users and varying purposes. For example, there must be provision for meeting the needs of elderly people for long-term residence without unnecessary loss of independence, of deprived children for a stable and supportive environment, of those who are mentally ill or handicapped for asylum and pathways to independence, and of relatives for relief from caring without rejection of the cared for.

6. It would, however, be naive to ignore the important qualifications to the basic principle of choice. First, we have to recognise that there are people who, in differing degrees and for different reasons, are incapable of deciding for themselves; they include babies, people with severe mental handicaps, some people subject to mental health disorders and some confused elderly people. While every effort must be made to take account of their wishes, decisions may well have to be made on their behalf. But where their wishes can be ascertained, however inarticulately expressed, they should not be lightly overriden.

7. Second, there are those whose behaviour or need for

personal care is such that their continued presence outside residential care is no longer supportable. Thus, some children may need to be contained at times of crisis—a function which, on occasion, only a residential establishment can provide—and some handicapped or elderly people reach a point when their needs are beyond the resources of their informal carers, and it is necessary to find alternative support systems. In such cases the definition of the person seen as the client, customer or service user may need to be broadened to include the family and even the community. How should the needs not only of the potential resident but also of the informal carers be met? How does one take account of the protection or assurance the local community requires in the face of bizarre or anti-social behaviour? Faced with such questions, choice is no longer the simple process of a potential resident choosing from alternative services, it becomes a process of negotiation of which the key feature has to be honesty in analysing the comparative needs of the parties involved.

8. In the course of negotiation, there may well be lessons to be learned, and alternative solutions may emerge. In the end, one or more of the parties may be a loser in the sense that the outcome may not coincide with their personal choice; but the process, if successful, will lead to a positive consensus, and will provide a sounder basis for the ensuing package of services, whether residential or not.

9. Positive choosing does not end with the decision over admission. Whether a package of services is provided in their own home or in a residential setting, the process of having positive choices, of the consumer being in control as far as possible, and of negotiation in relation to the needs and wishes of others, must continue. Having choice and being involved in negotiation, even where choice is restricted, can be a positive and rewarding experience for everyone involved.

The Context and the Task

10. The needs which residential provision has to meet are changing. The reduction in capacity of the large hospitals for the severely mentally handicapped and chronic mentally ill has led to fears about the quality of life of their former residents, who may become homeless, or overburden their families or enter prison. A

heightened awareness of the prevalence of physical and sexual abuse of young children has been added to the longstanding public concern with juvenile delinquency and deprivation. Meanwhile, the numbers of very old people in England and Wales have increased dramatically since the beginning of the century and will continue to grow into the next; with this increase comes a rise in the numbers who are mentally or physically frail, in the burdens on the carers who look after them and in the numbers who are frail and live alone. A growing number of frail elderly people among ethnic minority communities also have special needs, as do children from these same communities who for one reason or another come into local authority care. Thus, changes which have major implications for residential provision are occurring for different reasons and over varying timescales but are apparent in most or all groups of user.

11.   Although the needs highlighted by these changes are widely agreed, the appropriateness of residential services to meet them is not. Arguments have been put to us that residential provision for children should be virtually eliminated through the creative use of fostering, family centres and other forms of community support; that residential provision for mentally handicapped people has mistakenly combined arrangements for accommodation and for care, and that many of the residents in old people's homes do not need or want to be there. However, others have suggested that many adolescents prefer a residential establishment to the complex demands of fostering (a choice endorsed by many parents of children in care), and that this is particularly appropriate for some deprived children e.g. to keep large families together or after fostering breakdowns. It is also argued that the growth of the private residential sector, particularly for older people, is evidence of the need and demand for it. The personal evidence on these issues was divided, the majority writing movingly of their experience of good care now or in the past, but others of their suffering in bad or unsympathetic environments.

12.   It is a matter of great concern to us that so little residential provision has yet been made, or even detailed planning undertaken, for the special needs of the children, the elderly, and other vulnerable people of ethnic minority communities. While we have been made aware of one or two pioneering schemes, evidence about the general position has been hard to come by. We address these issues to the best of our ability in the course of

this Report, but do not feel that we have been able to deal with them either comprehensively or satisfactorily. We have, however, formed the strong impression that ethnic minority communities are almost without exception particularly ill-served by the residential sector and that special provision for them in all its forms is everywhere inadequate and in many places virtually non-existent. We regard this as a matter of great concern, and see an urgent need for local authorities to review with representatives of ethnic minority communities their special needs for residential and other forms of social care.

Outline of the Report

13. Throughout this Report, we emphasize that residence must be seen as an element in a range of community care services; one of our primary aims will be to promote a fundamental change in the public perception of the residential sector and of its place in the wider spectrum of social care. Thus, in considering the definitions of residential care suggested to us, we seek to move away from current models of provision into a new and broader view of the scope of residential services. With this in mind, we survey briefly the range of housing provision and of support services, and the possible permutations between them. It is a corollary of this approach that housing and support need to be looked at separately in relation to each person's particular circumstances, before they are brought together in the form of possible solutions to individual need.

14. Within the wealth of options which such an approach opens up, the needs and wishes of the user must be paramount. All decisions about whether and how to have recourse to residential services must come, in the last analysis, from the user—or in cases where the user is not competent to reach this decision, from the person who can most appropriately make the decision on their behalf. It is important to stress that we make this claim in the context of a multi-cultural society and would expect this cultural diversity to be fully reflected in the range of choice offered.

15. To make such choice a reality, a number of conditions have to be met. First there must be a range of valid options, and information and advice about them must be readily accessible. Whatever new resources may become available, they should not be tied up in conventional models of provision but should be used

to finance individual packages of care. This in turn requires mechanisms of service delivery which will employ the skills of social workers in new ways, with users having clear and effective avenues for complaint and review, and access to the courts as a last resort. We see this as requiring legislative change, but urge in the first instance the full implementation of existing legislation.

16.   Parallel with changes in methods of service delivery, we see the need for a shift in the role of social services departments, with the main emphasis moving from provision of their own residential services to the planning and coordination of services of all kinds in the interests of the user. This planning and coordination should embrace the full range of facilities offered by the voluntary and private sectors, and secure the involvement of community health and education services in appropriate cases.

17.   When the focus of the Report shifts to life in residential settings, our primary concern is for the quality of the experience enjoyed by each individual. We are strongly opposed to anything which tends to create or maintain an artificial distinction between people who receive services in their own home, and those who elect for an integrated package of accommodation and support in a residential setting. Wherever feasible, common standards and principles should apply to both groups. With this in mind we make specific proposals for ensuring the right of people living in residential setings to enjoy personal privacy, security of tenure and financial autonomy.

18.   All residential establishments without exception need to have their own internal procedures for self-evaluation and performance review; in the absence of these, external inspection will be inadequate to maintain standards of care, let alone improve them. At the same time, we recognise the need for the same system of registration and inspection to apply across the statutory, voluntary and private sectors.

19.   We see it as an essential condition of good residential practice that people providing services should see themselves, first and foremost, as there to serve the interest of the users. Barriers to good practice are identified and principles underlying good practice stated and discussed. To enable service providers to practice in accordance with these principles, certain support systems are needed. These include adequate staffing levels; clear recruitment and selection criteria and procedures; sound management and supervision in the workplace; an integrated career structure and conditions of service for all levels of staff; career

planning for each individual, and workforce planning as a whole. There should be continuing provision for staff development and training at the workplace, and opportunities for qualifying training.

20. Finally we consider in more detail how these general principles can be applied to improving accommodation and services for people with particular needs—children, adults with a mental handicap or who are mentally ill, people with alcohol or drugs problems, and elderly people who are mentally infirm.

CHAPTER TWO

The Spectrum of Housing and Services

What is Residential Care?

1. We were much concerned during the earlier stages of our discussions with considering the boundaries of residential care, and how these might influence the course of our Enquiry. This led us to question the extent to which people needed to change their existing accommodation in order to receive the services which they might require. By examining the relationship between, on the one hand, accommodation, and on the other, services, we begin to question many current assumptions and policies. In this chapter we first discuss some of the definitions and descriptions of residential care provided by the formal evidence; then the relationship between different types of accommodation and service provision, and finally the policy implications resulting from this.

2. The Social Care Association (SCA) wrote in the course of their evidence to us:

> It is our view that the following components of care are common to all residential experience:
>
> It is place based...
> It is purpose based, and the experience should be positive...
> It is an organised experience...
> It is an experience of inter-dependent living...
> It is influenced by staff and residents...
> It may involve separation from people, places or objects to which the person is attached.
> (E111: para 24).

3. This was one of the few examples we received which made an attempt to define residential care by identifying the qualities and characteristics found in all types of establishment. The dearth

of examples in our evidence perhaps demonstrates the difficulty of defining such a wide spectrum of provision. Drawing on the SCA definition, two important points may be stressed. The fact that residential care is said to have a purpose and to be organised implies that complete freedom of action for residents is not possible; if this is the case, the balance of their freedom with the organisation and aims of the home is plainly a crucial task in which both staff and residents must be involved and their needs and preferences need to be taken into account.

4. People who spoke of residential care in this conventional sense commonly contrasted it with 'care in the community'—although they often urged the need for links between the two. Others pointed to new forms of community provision such as 'core and cluster' developments and unstaffed hostels and suggested that these, too, needed to be taken into account either as forms of residential care or as close alternatives to it. Thus the National Council of Voluntary Organisations (NCVO) Advisory Group on Residential Care described two main groups of alternatives to traditional services, arguing that both residential projects and home-centred care must be provided if the needs of individuals are to be met without damaging their right to be treated with dignity and respect, and allowing them to retain as much independence and sense of self-worth as possible:

> A range of residential projects which may or may not be registered with the local authority and which provide some or all of the elements found in residential care: accommodation, board, and personal care/emotional/support. These projects are typically run by a housing association or voluntary organisation and include sheltered housing for elderly people, hostels, group homes, and other forms of supported housing for people with a mental handicap or single homeless people who have previously lived in institutions such as ex-prisoners or former patients of psychiatric hospitals.

> Other key components of what is known as 'community care', i.e. services which support an individual living at home either alone or in the care of a relative. These services include meals on wheels, home helps, intensive home care schemes which provide personal care provision, and services which aim to support the 'informal' carers of disabled people such as care attendant schemes. (E90: para 1.2)

5. MIND similarly urged the expansion of innovatory forms of accommodation in place of the type of care provided within

residential care homes. It expressed concern that recent legislation, in particular the Registered Homes Act 1984, laid emphasis
on 'the provision of segregated "inward-looking" communities
or care homes, which are sufficient in themselves'.

> This is in contrast to the innovatory forms of care pioneered by the
> voluntary sector shared housing movement. Here the emphasis is
> on the provision of ordinary housing accommodation with support
> put into the house as appropriate. The essential feature of this
> support is to ensure that people are able to maintain their
> accommodation, whilst also developing links and relationships
> within the surrounding community. The intention is that residents
> become as integrated as possible, taking full advantage of all the
> services and facilities that are available to 'ordinary' people along-
> side whom they will be living. This after all is true 'community
> care'. (E151: Part II, para 1.5)

6. The ever-widening variety of such provision was brought
out by the National Federation of Housing Associations who gave
us a list of projects including very sheltered housing; schemes
designed to provide appropriate care for members of ethnic
minority groups; schemes providing support and skills training
for single homeless people, many with problems of mental
illness, alcohol and drugs; community based housing for patients
from long-stay hospitals; small schemes for mentally handicapped people; and housing and care schemes for adults with
physical disability, some in mixed communities with able-bodied
people. The NFHA criticised the legislation and the recommendations of 'Home Life' for their traditional view of residential care
as 'provision for physically dependent people who need long
term support... Yet the components of residential care, i.e.
accommodation, personal care and board do not have to be
provided in an institutional setting. Residential care is the
provision of both housing and care, including board, by one
organisation for (or, in the case of the voluntary sector by two
organisations working in partnership). It is therefore essential
that residential care is seen in its broadest sense, encompassing
the wide variety of voluntary sector projects.' (E153: para 2.3)

7. This line of argument was carried even further by the
Campaign for People with Mental Handicaps which argued that
the traditional concept of residential care should be discarded in
favour of the dual concepts of housing and support services:

> The main implication will be that the need of people with mental
> handicap for housing will be recognised and will no longer be seen

as separate from and different from the housing needs of other citizens. Instead their housing needs will be met from within the existing range of options open to the population in general. Clearly, this does not mean that people with mental handicaps will have unlimited choice. None of us has that. But it does mean that they will have choices that would be considered 'typical' or 'ordinary' within the housing market.

Many of the structures and features of residential services have a profound impact on their users. Not having a proper tenancy agreement, being moved along a 'continuum' of services which forces you to move home every so often, living in special buildings away from ordinary residential neighbourhoods—all these common experiences of people with mental handicaps using residential services are devaluing, stigmatising and set people apart from the rest of society. (E100: page 3)

We found this, initially, a challenging concept but over the months it grew upon us and came to influence us considerably, to the point where we now urge that all service providers should begin to look at people's requirements in a new way by distinguishing between need for accommodation and need for support services.

8.   The boundaries of what constitutes residential care are constantly shifting with the emergence of new forms of provision; some of these, such as Very Sheltered Housing, Core and Cluster Schemes, and multiple fostering are expressly designed with a view to combining the benefits of what have hitherto been considered separately as 'residential care' and 'care in the community'. We were very conscious also of establishments outside the social service field, such as Boarding Special Schools and Probation Hostels, providing elements of residential care. We would in many ways have liked to include them in our review but to have done this was not within our formal terms of reference, and would have greatly complicated our task. Reluctantly we decided against doing so, while hoping that what we have written in this Report will be found relevant and helpful by those who live and work in these establishments.

Accommodation and Services

9.   In keeping with the concept of looking separately at housing and support services, we now describe briefly the

spectrum of housing provision and the range of personal social services, before bringing them together to consider various modes of group living within a residential setting.

10.   Most people, adults and children alike, live at home. Home, whether owner-occupied, privately rented or rented from the local authority, is seen to be part of normal housing provision. Leaving one's own home can be painful and it is now taken for granted that whenever possible other measures are preferable to breaking up a family or removing someone from their home. Homelessness or inadequate housing is not infrequently a precipitating cause of admission to a residential establishment. By contrast, an appropriate solution to a person's housing problem, coupled with support services, may on occasions enable recourse to residential care to be avoided.

11.   Thus in old age the advantages of 'staying put' in a long-familiar living environment and of a supportive neighbourhood are not to be despised. This is particularly true with the onset of forgetfulness and mild confusion in old age. In a much-loved home, these can often be contained; whereas an abrupt move to a strange environment may precipitate a steep and irreversible decline. The various schemes for staying put, offering both home improvements or adaptation and personal social services in the home, are comprehensively described by Hedley Taylor in 'Growing Old Together; elderly owner-occupiers and their housing' (Policy Studies in Ageing No. 6, 1986). We would like to see similar provision made more widely available for long-standing tenants of rented accommodation. A move to a totally strange environment is particularly traumatic for elderly people of a different culture and race, whose native language may not be English, and whose dietary preferences may not be met away from their own family or community.

Ordinary Housing

12.   Ordinary housing is playing an increasingly valuable role in enabling people with special needs to retain, or develop, the maximum degree of independence. We have seen young people with mental handicaps living together in flats or terraced houses, learning the skills of independent living; similarly, people recovering from a mental illness can derive mutual support, and help one another to come to terms with continuing problems,

through living together in small groups. Supporting staff may either live in with them, or be on call from a centre close at hand, as in a 'core and cluster' development. Some people with physical handicaps have told us that ordinary housing, suitably adapted, and with the necessary supporting services, is the *only* form of provision wholly acceptable to them.

13. For children, life in a foster home provides an experience of family living. We received evidence (E81: Children's Family Trust) of extended forms of fostering where 'large family groups' in ordinary housing offer the same degree of normal living. When young people are coming to the end of their time in local authority care an experience of independent living becomes vital to the achievement of a satisfactory adult life. We were given examples of both staffed and unstaffed houses providing experience of this kind, and as we make clear in a later chapter, we believe that the National Association of Young People in Care (NAYPIC) is justified in its view that much more provision is needed for young people entering adult life. (E148)

14. Those elderly people who make a timely move into accommodation designed for disability or old age—the owner-occupied bungalow, and the 1 or 2 bedroom flats which many local authorities and housing associations reserve for tenants without dependants—are better off in several important ways. First, their home environment is one in which they can look forward to being able to 'manage', without the upheaval of major adaptations or conversion, almost indefinitely. Second, where the move is also from a relatively isolated situation into an established community, this will make it far easier to provide a home help, meals-on-wheels or community nursing services as and when they are needed.

Sheltered Housing

15. Most housing authorities and associations provide a limited amount of sheltered housing; and developments of this type are increasingly being offered, for those who can afford them, by private developers also. The dwelling units are purpose-built, to designs which emphasise ease of access of management and a resident warden is on hand. A limited range of communal facilities may also be provided, for residents who wish to use them. Sheltered housing has been commended to us as a valuable

resource for meeting the needs of frail elders from minority ethnic communities. Services offered should take into account the particular culture from which such elders come and thus provide continuity with their previous pattern of daily living. Similarly, sheltered housing can offer the benefits of independent living to mentally ill and physically and mentally handicapped people.

16.   For elderly people there is some evidence that a move into sheltered housing is not infrequently followed by a second move into a residential establishment, because of the difficulty of maintaining and increasing the levels of support which become necessary. Wardens, by reason of their terms of employment and workload, can often give only limited support, and when they are absent the cover needed is not always available. We would hope that all providing agencies can follow the lead given by developments taking place in all sectors, which now provide the appropriate levels of service to enable people to remain where they are for as long as they wish.

17.   The strong demand for sheltered housing is surely here to stay—particularly among elderly people. It may reflect to some extent however the inadequacy of support services to people in their own homes, rather than a real preference for a sheltered way of life. For the foreseeable future, wardens in sheltered housing will represent an essential element in the provision of community care services, and their role should be strengthened. In a local authority context the warden is usually an employee of the housing department, and thus is not necessarily in a privileged position to secure assistance from community health or social services. Local authorities should consider whether it would be better for them to be first-line representatives of social services rather than occupying a somewhat isolated position within housing departments. It is essential that wardens should receive some formal training, and we should like to see the available training schemes further developed across all three sectors. Wardens may not have the job of providing social care, but it is important that they should be in a position to procure services.

Very Sheltered Housing

18.   A number of housing authorities, social services departments, voluntary bodies and private providers have pioneered 'very sheltered' accommodation or 'extra care' housing develop-

ments for those whose need for care exceeds what can practically be provided in a person's own home or in ordinary sheltered housing. Both elderly and physically handicapped people have benefited, as have groups with mental illness or mental handicap. The characteristic of such developments is that residents continue to occupy their own self-contained accommodation, with the basic facilities for leading an independent existence, but a range of caring services is available on site, together with provision for communal meals and recreation. All residents receive the level of personal care they need, and make as much or as little use of the communal facilities as they choose. (These communal facilities may often double as a day centre for the benefit of residents round about.) In practice, very sheltered housing can provide frail elderly residents with a level of care equivalent to that given by the traditional residential home, combined with a greater degree of continued privacy and independence than the latter can usually offer.

Services to Meet Needs

19.   The personal social services required by people, according to their ages, disabilities and circumstances who may be living in their own homes or in residential establishments, should all have the common aim of ultimately enabling people to meet their needs as individuals. The services are too many to describe in detail, but generally they are intended to meet one or more of the following needs:

—practical assistance in daily living; this includes the provision of food, warmth, clothing, environmental supports and assistance with personal care like washing, dressing, bathing and going to the toilet.

—practical advice and help in coping with day-to-day problems, and counselling when needed.

—specific teaching and guidance in order to acquire new abilities and skills or to reinforce existing ones; these are often included as part of programmes of rehabilitation for people with severe physical or learning disabilities, for people who have been incapacitated as a result of mental illness and for young people as part of their preparation for leaving care.

—specialised programmes of care, assessment, treatment and rehabilitation, which aim to produce substantial changes in individuals' functioning so that they can live more freely, independently and with integrity.

—control and containment, but only in the interests of child care or where individuals are at risk of endangering themselves and others.

20.   We stress that none of these categories of need requires as a necessary condition that the individual be placed in a special setting in order to receive the services indicated. In every case— including the last one—it is possible to conceive of many alternative forms of service delivery; for example, a young offender might be put under strict curfew or supervised within a 'tracking' scheme instead of being placed in a community home. However, for specific purposes and under certain circumstances it will be desirable to deliver some of these services as part of an integrated programme of accommodation plus personal social services. There are, after all, limits to the community's ability to tolerate, cope with or effectively provide for every individual circumstance. There are also some services that are considered to be effective only when delivered as part of an integrated set of living arrangements, e.g. as a residential therapeutic community.

21.   We believe that the basic principles governing the identification of the need for and delivery of different types of services should be that:

(i) nobody, young or old, should be expected to change their permanent residence simply in order to obtain the services, including health care, which they need; these should be made available to them in or within reach of their own homes;

(ii) people who do change their accommodation, for whatever reasons, and move into a residential or semi-residential facility in whatever setting should continue to have access to the full range of community support services which they would have received had they still been living in their own homes; including being able to have a GP of their own choice, community nursing, and other services. We regret that there are crucial shortfalls in some of these services at the present time; but this does not alter the principle. We should not have the situation, described in some of the personal evidence sent to us, where admission to a residential home has resulted in people actually being deprived of these basic facilities and services. This is tantamount to reducing their status as citizens by virtue of the fact of their going into residential care;

(iii) where accommodation and services are combined they should have a clearly defined purpose and should be fully integrated, philosophically and organisationally into the wider spectrum of service provision to which they relate.

Bringing the Two Together: Group Living

22.   We use the term 'group living' to denote those arrangements whereby accommodation and services are integrated to enable groups of people with some identified assumed or real common needs to live interdependently. For young people unable to live with their parents, we argue in a later chapter that some form of group living is an essential element in any comprehensive scheme of community care. For adults with a mental handicap, or those recovering from mental illness, group living may represent a stepping-stone from full institutional care to greater independence in ordinary housing; alternatively, such adults may prefer the extra support and companionship of living with a group of similar residents on a more permanent basis. For some elderly people, privacy may equate with loneliness, independence with insecurity or inability to cope, and for such, the experience of group living offered by a residential establishment may well be the preferred solution.

23.   At a more abstract level, the formal evidence called for group living to meet four main requirements. First, there were those who would choose group living (as opposed for example to very sheltered housing), and who should have this option available to them. Second, there were those whose need for specialist provision could only be met on the basis of group living; they included a few people with very rare and disabling conditions, but the majority were said to need some form of training, therapy or rehabilitation which made specific use of group living. Third, various forms of short-term care might often be more easily made available on a residential basis including assessment, crisis accommodation, convalescence and respite care. Finally, some evidence claimed that residential care was

necessary simply because of the shortage of relevant domiciliary
services.

24.   In looking at these requirements, we would stress that
group living within a residential setting is not and should not be
seen as the only resource available for those in need of care, nor
even as the last resort in extreme cases. For almost every condition, a range of alternative provision exists and some form of
group living should be seen as one valid option among others.

25.   Hotels, lodgings and boarding houses, provide a combination of accommodation and basic services. There has been a
substantial increase in the use of these forms of accommodation
in recent years for homeless families, who are given 'bed and
breakfast', and for patients discharged from psychiatric and
mental handicap hospitals. Such an existence, however, can in no
way be construed as 'ordinary living' and failure to provide the
support services needed causes unnecessary suffering. That there
should be so many homeless families and single people living in
such conditions is a disgrace which the Government should take
urgent steps to remedy.

Implications for Policy

26.   The distinction which we make between accommodation
and services has many implications for the funding and allocation
of resources across the housing, social services and health
services. Little, however, will be achieved unless national
housing policies first ensure adequate housing stock. Separating
accommodation from services means that they can be charged for
separately even where residence is deemed to be integral to the
services provided. Financial arrangements should not hamper the
development of flexible and varied forms of accommodation, nor
should the social security system favour the development of
private residential care at the expense of other services.

27.   Housing and social services will need to agree and
administer jointly policies for the allocation of supported
housing. Primary health care services will need to be made available to people in residential establishments on the same basis as
if they were living in their own home. Attention will also have to
be given to the development of new social worker roles (which we
describe more fully in the next chapter) to facilitate the process

whereby people will be able to receive individualised packages of accommodation and services.

Recommendation

The role of wardens in sheltered housing should be strengthened, and they should receive formal training; local authorities should consider whether wardens should be employed in social services rather than housing departments.

CHAPTER THREE

Enlarging and Safeguarding Choice

The Rights and Needs of Individuals

1. We wish to ensure that people who begin to need assistance in order to care for themselves are able to exercise a positive choice over the combination of accommodation and personal services which they require. In order to do this it is necessary that:

(i) they have adequate information about options;

(ii) there are realistic alternatives to choose from;

(iii) they have help if necessary in making choices;

(iv) the initial choice should be tested by a trial period with an option to return to the previous situation if possible, or to another setting;

(v) the chosen service should be reviewed at appropriate intervals;

(vi) in order to guard against their being overwhelmed by the power of the service providers they have ways to appeal against inadequate, inappropriate or enforced services.

2. There is a responsibility on local authorities to produce information but information about all services needs to be more widely disseminated. We think that the primary source of information on matters so important to the individual citizen should be one which is universally available, objective and impartial. We should therefore like to see the Public Library service in each locality coordinate, and periodically update, a comprehensive outline of the help available from the social services and housing departments, the community health services, voluntary organisations and private agencies. An abstract of this information could be made available to the general

public through post offices, doctors' surgeries, clubs, churches and other places where people congregate. We recognise that this will have resource implications.

3. In making this recommendation we do not overlook the invaluable role of the Citizens Advice Bureaux, who already hold much of this information and make it available to those who seek their help. Some local authorities also offer a comprehensive information and advice service through a network of neighbourhood advice centres run by themselves or voluntary agencies. But we believe that people seek the help of a Citizens Advice Bureau or a neighbourhood advice service once they have perceived that they have a problem; and we do not wish information about basic community services to be seen in terms of problems. It should quite simply be available to everyone, on the same matter-of-fact basis as information about train and bus times, church services, local tourist attractions, or forthcoming events.

4. We believe that for a substantial majority of adults—as well as for some young people—obtaining this information will be sufficient to enable them to make up their minds about a preferred solution. The remainder will need more detailed information and advice, either because of complexities in their situation or because they find difficulty in using the information they have received. For them the Citizens' Advice Bureau or neighbourhood advice centre seems the obvious resource and we would hope to see the Public Library service referring on to them any members of the public with whose queries they could not readily deal.

5. Of those who seek additional information and advice in this way we would, again, expect the majority to be enabled to identify a preferred solution to their problem but there will remain a small number who, after all possible information and advice have been given, still need help in making up their minds. Whether their problems are caused by a multiplicity of needs or by conflicting pressures, such people will be right to turn to the social services department for help.

Ensuring a Positive Choice

6. As already explained, we see the concept of 'residence plus care' as embracing a multitude of permutations between different models of accommodation and of supporting services. It

follows that the positive choice which we wish to see exercised in all cases will seldom be simply one of applying for admission to a residential establishment. Individuals and their families should have available to them the skills of a nominated social worker (who could be either a field or residential worker) whose primary responsibility is to act as their agent, and who should be trained in the individual assessment of needs and in the imaginative creation of a package of services designed to meet them. Existing legislation provides for varying forms of user representation, but only for people with specified needs; we would wish to see the general application of such provision. We see the task of such a social worker as working out, with the user and his or her family, friends and neighbours, the services which are needed and can be found, or created, to allow the user to live in the way he or she most wants. For some this will mean staying in their present accommodation with services provided there; for others it may mean a move to other forms of accommodation such as sheltered housing or foster accommodation, while yet others may opt for group living in a residential setting.

7.   Sometimes the nominated social worker may have to do little more than ensure that the individual has clear and realistic information about resources; for others, some services may need to be created, and yet others may need help in making decisions between the options available. In many instances the choices will involve not only users, but relatives, friends and neighbours. A nominated social worker should always be appointed where a prospective user has no relative and is deemed to be unable to exercise effective choice or give effective consent. Nominated social workers, therefore, need also to be skilled in assisting users and those who make up their human environment to reach decisions when interests conflict or where disabilities seem to make the choice one of lesser evils. They must be skilled in working with individuals, families and community networks and will need the time to undertake this work at the pace required by users, if users are to exercise their rights to choose. This work, in our view, is as complex and demanding as any other specialised social work task. This means that case loads must be restricted and this will have staffing implications.

Impediments to Choice

8.   At critical points in their lives many people find it difficult to assess their own needs and make a positive choice. Those facing the greatest difficulties are those already disadvantaged by their poverty, race or gender. Their access to information and their ability to secure resources for themselves or their relatives are likely to be the most restricted. The barriers they face will be difficult to remove because they derive from deeply held social attitudes, expectations and differences in power. People may have low expectations of the level and range of services to which they are entitled or their ability to influence an agency's decisions; agencies may have similarly low expectations of people's abilities to make informed choices or to use power effectively. The imbalance in power between agencies and users becomes entrenched and difficult to change.

9.   The powers vested in all social service agencies are remarkably wide. Statutory agencies in particular may exercise the functions of counsellor, gatekeeper, professional assessor, landlord, provider of care, monitor of quality, recipient of complaints and, sometimes, court of appeal. Most agencies exercise their responsibilities with humanity and in the interests of their clients, but more is required to alter the balance of power between providers and users.

10.   Individual social workers and their agencies have to work within severe resource constraints which reduce the range and availability of services. This results in their having to focus more on the means of rationing limited resources than of increasing access to information in order to enhance choice.

11.   In addition to facing the constraints on their own budgets, social service agencies have had to bear the consequences of financial pressures in the health service, in education and social security. Further, their ability to influence policy and practice is not as strong as is sometimes supposed. It is evident that hospitals often require the early discharge of patients, which in turn puts pressure on social service agencies to admit people to residential establishments. These factors produce a tendency to limit the information available to prospective users about the different forms of community care and to restrict access to it. When, for example, a social service department knows that all its residential establishments are full, the residential option is likely to feature less prominently among the services offered than when

establishments are less than fully occupied.

12.   Other factors influence the extent to which information is made available to users. Policies can result in their consciously withholding or restricting information about services provided elsewhere, because of negative attitudes towards them. Examples brought to our notice include local authorities refusing to give information about private care, voluntary organisations championing one particular form of provision to the exclusion of others, and private agencies which fail to see the need for working in partnership with statutory services.

13.   Finally, barriers arise from the multiplicity of roles played by social workers and the failure to identify conflicts which exist between them. For example social workers are expected at one and the same time to act as agent for users and their families, as representative of their employer, and as custodian of resources. The social worker can be reduced to being powerless to carry out any of these responsibilities effectively, unless there is clarity about which is primary at any given time.

Assessment

14.   Assessment has three aspects: assessment of the capabilities and disabilities of the individual, of the services which need to be provided in order to compensate for such disabilities, and of eligibility for existing limited services. Initial assessment must be based on a judgement of the minimum quality of life to which everyone is entitled simply by virtue of their citizenship, and which income maintenance payments are designed to ensure. If this assessment should indicate that such a minimal quality is not being reached, then further assessment needs to be undertaken to ascertain what services would effectively compensate for this lack. The outcome of such an assessment would establish eligibility for compensatory services, ranging from a few hours of domiciliary care assistance to admission to a residential establishment.

15.   Unfortunately, the compensatory services are presently limited in scope, and it may therefore be necessary to assess further whether a particular individual meets the local criteria for their provision, on the basis either of rationing or of means testing. The nominated social worker is thus working with the criteria specified by the service providers to determine eligibility,

and at the same time acting as the agent of the potential user to procure the services of which she or he is in need. Nevertheless, assessment should be needs-led rather than resource-led, and the nominated social workers must regard themselves as primarily the agent of the user, and be recognised as such by the management of the providing agencies.

16. As explained in the paper 'Costs and Residential Social Care' in Volume II of this Report, experience suggests that the best results are achieved where social workers have direct control over financial resources and are accountable for their use of them. We recommend that local authorities should develop systems of delegated budgeting whereby nominated social workers can exercise direct control over financial resources. Controlling money frees the imagination, and individual social workers have been shown to exercise great resourcefulness and ingenuity in devising comprehensive packages of service within the resources available. When overall resources are tightly stretched, as they are at present, then the more effectively such resourcefulness can be mobilised, the better the provision that will be available all round. Systems of rigid centralised authorisation or control will not prove compatible with the flexibility and responsiveness to individual need at which we are aiming.

17. It is also our view that social workers should remain in touch with users whom they have assisted, or be available to them at their request. This is necessary because some of the packages of service which are created need to be continuously maintained. Carers take holidays, become sick or want a change and so the package will need to be altered. Furthermore users' needs may change and the services will have to be increased, altered or reduced accordingly. This applies to all users whether they live at home, in sheltered accommodation or in a residential setting. As and when needs change, either users or carers should be able to call a review. We are particularly concerned with those residents who are unable to exercise effective choice or give effective consent; where a general practitioner judges this to be the case, we recommend that it be a statutory requirement that a review be held at least every six months.

18. We have stressed the advantages of nominated social workers having delegated authority over resources, but equally we stress the necessity for a clear system of accountability as well as the provision of support, supervision and in-service training. They will be doing a difficult and stressful job, often with users

whose problems seem insoluble and who may not always be easy to work with. It is essential that they themselves are managed by senior officers who understand and are in sympathy with the demands of the job.

Complaints and Appeals

19.   However much good will is put into devising a system of service delivery which is truly user-oriented, the possibility of undue pressure being put upon users or of a failure to offer valid alternatives will remain. In order to provide some built-in protection for users' rights we consider that each residential services provider must have a clear and well-publicised complaints system to which users can turn when they are dissatisfied with a decision reached in their case, or when the service previously agreed on is not giving the results they had expected and wished. Complaints systems can vary greatly in detail but if they are to be effective three essential elements are required: a person to whom to complain who is readily accessible; someone to investigate with the means to ascertain the full facts; and a means of adjudicating with authority.

20.   The Local Authority Associations have recommended a complaints procedure and we recommend its speedy adoption. This, with the final avenue of appeal to the local government Ombudsman, will suffice to resolve the great majority of disagreements in the public sector; we recommend that private and voluntary providers should establish comparable procedures.

21.   Some users will require assistance in presenting their complaints. We therefore recommend that the services of an advocate or personal representative be made available to them. The advocate would need to be someone entirely independent of those providing the service; a possible approach would be to recruit a panel of advocates and it may well be helpful if one or more were legally trained. In some rare cases service providers may fail to take up or resolve complaints which are considered so serious that they should be pursued through the courts. These may be allegations of ill-treatment or serious breaches of contract.

22.   We are most concerned to ensure that appropriate services are available, particularly to those who are reliant on state provision. This is not to advocate providing whatever services people demand, but we see the need for a means

whereby the discretion exercised by the providers of care services can, in. the last resort, be questioned. We recommend that a statutory duty is placed on local authorities to propose a package of services, enabling a person to remain in their own home if that is their choice and it is reasonable for them to do so. Failure to uphold that duty could then be challenged in the courts if necessary. Where access to a package of services is limited to finance provided through the social security system, then an appeals system already exists through the social security tribunals.

The Case for a Community Care Allowance

23.   We considered ways in which users of any community services might exercise a stronger influence over the allocation of resources. We have been much attracted by the idea of issuing Community Care Allowances to people with special needs, to be used by them to procure care services of their choice. The allowance could be used either to recruit help in the home, or to procure admission to a particular residential establishment or—if preferred—could be banked with the area social services office where a nominated social worker could assemble a package of care services.

24.   The advantages of Community Care Allowances can thus be summarised:

  (i) they encourage consumer choice;

 (ii) the outcome is likely to be more satisfying to users, and possibly more economical, where community care options are viable;

(iii) they encourage flexible provision of community care, and remove the perverse incentive of the existing residential care allowance to force into residential care people who could manage more independently.

We are attracted by the advantages of a system of Community Care Allowances, and we recommend that it should be studied more closely in relation to costs, eligibility and assessment.

Recommendations

A statutory duty should be placed on local authorities to propose a reasonable package of services, enabling a person to remain in their own home if that is their choice and it is reasonable for them to do so.

Anyone for whom residential provision might be an option should have available to them the skills of a nominated social worker to act as their agent; a nominated social worker should always be appointed where a prospective user has no relative and is deemed unable to exercise effective choice.

Local authorities should develop systems of delegated budgeting whereby nominated social workers can exercise direct control over financial resources.

Further study should be given to a system of Community Care Allowances, which would enable people with special needs to procure care services of their choice.

Each local authority should have a clear and well-publicised complaints procedure, and comparable measures should be taken by private and voluntary agencies.

People who require assistance in presenting their complaints should have the services of an advocate or personal representative who is entirely independent of those providing the service.

There should be a statutory review every six months for those residents who are unable to exercise effective choice or give effective consent.

The Public Library service in each locality should coordinate, and periodically update, comprehensive information on the range of services available.

CHAPTER FOUR

Group Living—
Rights, Risks and Responsibilities

1. It is clearly one of the major principles of good residential practice that residents should have as much control over their own lives as possible, maintaining normal lifestyles and exercising choice. In particular, it is our view that residents are entitled to be involved in all decisions which affect their daily lives. It is one of the tests of the quality of care to check to what extent such basic principles are in evidence.

2. It is true that some residents cannot, or are not permitted to, exercise this right; they include young children, people with severe mental handicaps and confused elderly people. Confused old people who start to wander are likely to be brought back. Children may be confined to the premises, or have limitations placed on their dress or bedtime. People with mental handicaps may not be able to travel unaccompanied: their options are limited by the perception of staff and others as to the extent to which they are able to make meaningful choices, or may put themselves or other people at risk if some control is not exercised. As the law stands, however, the residents are under no legal constraint, and the adults in question are technically to be considered lucid, capable and independent. Yet their rights are diminished *de facto*, and at present there is no system for acknowledging this loss of rights.

3. The problem is equally acute for staff, who often feel caught between conflicting forces. On the one hand they wish to give residents choice and control over their own lives, and they are aware that their authority to restrain or control the residents in their care is limited to that normally exercised within a family or by a member of the public in the event of unacceptable behaviour. Yet on the other hand they know that people in many cir-

cumstances are often placed is residential establishments for the purpose of closer support and supervision, and expectations are put upon the staff that residents will be contained and controlled.

4. In short, residents' control over their own lives is constrained in the interests of themselves and others without any system of monitoring, and staff are placed in the false position of controlling residents' lives without having the specific authority to do so. What is more, because this process is unacknowledged, the necessary distinctions are not made between the legitimate diminution of rights and that which is designed for staff convenience or ease of institutional management. We think it is time to face these issues explicitly and honestly.

5. We recommend that every resident should have all the rights of a citizen of their age, and should be assumed to be lucid, capable and independent in terms of making choices about their lives and controlling their own lifestyle, unless there are overriding reasons to the contrary. We recommend that, in all cases where rights are denied or diminished, the following safeguards be applied:

   (i) there should be explicit grounds recorded and sanctioned at the appropriate level of management, as should be the precise means of restraint involved;

   (ii) their duration should be as short as possible, perhaps during crises or pending training to make use of the right;

   (iii) wherever residents cannot argue lucidly on their own behalf, the measures taken should be agreed with a near relative or other guardian with the sole role of guarding the resident's interests;

   (iv) the measures should only be agreed within the context of giving residents maximum feasible choice and control, including the taking of considered risks where this will maintain or encourage independence;

   (v) any emergency denial of rights should always be recorded and reported to management for retrospective sanction;

   (vi) a regular review should take place (as recommended in the previous chapter) of every resident whose rights have at any time been diminished or denied.

6. Such a system would protect residents in that it would make explicit the actual rights which were being diminished or denied—so that the measures taken could be acknowledged,

questioned and appealed against if necessary—and in consequence would make it clear that other rights were unaffected. It should also eliminate any unacceptable methods of control or restraint which are at present being employed, including the misuse of drugs for the purpose of controlling behaviour. At the same time it would give protection to staff, who would know what authority they had, and the limits to that authority; it would give them backing when taking risks, and the security of knowing the limits to their responsibilities.

A Contract of Accommodation and Services

7. If we have argued above that it is necessary and realistic to recognise that the rights of some residents have to be curtailed, and have suggested an orderly framework within which this can be done, it is equally necessary to ensure that the freedoms of other residents are not infringed needlessly or heedlessly, through institutional pressures or in the interests of administrative convenience. There is a constant need to guard against people in residential establishments becoming institutionalised.

8. Central to this is the principle of upholding the individual resident's right to personal independence. The most effective means for this, in our view, will be a written contract of accommodation and services between the resident (or their agent) and the provider. Such a contract will need to specify the rights of the individual with regard to such matters as:
  —privacy
  —a trial period
  —continued occupation of a specific room
  —financial automony.
together with the services to be provided, periodic assessment and reviews, and access to complaints procedures.

Privacy

9. Privacy, in the residential context, is partly a matter of design and partly of practice: the right to a room of one's own where one may live as one pleases, and the right to privacy respected by staff. The possession of a personal key, carries with it the power to withdraw into the privacy of one's own room;

only the senior responsible person present should hold a duplicate key, and sanction its use to verify the resident's well-being.

10. We would not expect that all residents would wish to avail themselves of this right; there will be many for whom privacy is of less importance than the ability to summon help at any time, and a few whose infirmity of body or mind plainly precludes it. Only the person in charge should take the decision that a resident's condition and special needs do not permit of their having a personal key; this decision should normally be taken after consultation with the resident and in agreement with any close relatives, and it should be subject to the safeguards (including regular review) outlined in paragraph 5 above.

11. Inevitably, consideration of privacy leads us to the vexed question of the sharing of rooms. For an elderly person accustomed to living in their own home, there is something all but derisory in the notion of 'a positive choice for residential care' if this is to entail sharing sleeping accommodation with one or more strangers. Most local authorities have plans to minimise the number of shared rooms, both in their own residential homes and in voluntary and private homes registered with them; but at the present rate of progress a significantly high number of shared rooms are likely to remain well into the twenty-first century. We find this prospect wholly unacceptable.

12. We believe that no one should be required to share a bedroom with another person as a condition of admission; we realise that it may take longer to provide choice for the present occupants of shared rooms, some indeed may not desire it; but as and when the present occupants cease to require them we would wish to see most shared rooms converted for single occupancy, except for the small number required for married couples and others who express the wish to share. Accordingly, we recommend that in new residential homes as from 1st January 1990 out of every ten rooms there should only be two double rooms, and that in existing homes the same requirement should apply as from 1st January 1995. Furthermore, from these dates rooms should only be shared where the occupants have made a free and considered option for this, either before admission, or as an expression of affinity with another resident, or in cases of advancing infirmity where mutual support in a shared room enables two residents to manage more successfully than either could do on their own.

13. We recognise that this process will require significant

additional capital funding in all sectors, with particular implications for local authorities' loan sanction requirement; there will also be considerable revenue impact as per capita costs increase. But we believe these financial facts have to be faced, as it is simply not tolerable to leave things as they are at present.

Security

14. When elderly people move into residential establishments run by local authorities, known generally at Part III accommodation, they lose their entitlement to Housing Benefit; many residents are also required to relinquish their pension books and receive what amounts to pocket money in exchange. They also lose whatever security of tenure they enjoyed previously in their own homes. We consider that every adult person entering a residential establishment with a view to an extended stay should be entitled to an appropriate trial period, for example two months, during which nothing would be done to dispossess them of their previous accommodation. *'Home Life'* (Chapter 2) sets out the need for each residential establishment to make available to prospective long-stay residents a prospectus detailing the terms and conditions on which accommodation and care are offered. We endorse this, and further recommend that if the resident wishes to stay on at the end of the trial period, their acceptance of the terms and conditions should be deemed to constitute a contract, binding on both sides, of the kind discussed in paragraph 8 above.

Financial Autonomy

15. Financial autonomy is the necessary counterpart of security of tenure. For residents capable of managing their own affairs, the requirement to surrender their pension or allowance book, and receive back a weekly sum in 'pocket money', is surely unnecessary, inconsiderate and demeaning. In our view all residents of a residential establishment should be entitled to retain their pension or allowance book and be entitled to a rent book or its equivalent; to collect their own pension, and to pay from it the

agreed sum for accommodation and services or—if they wish—to use the normal 'agent' or 'appointee' procedure to enable someone else to do this for them. When this responsibility is undertaken by the person in charge, or the proprietor of the establishment then the strictest accountability should be observed. Furthermore we are strongly of the opinion that in the assessment of their rent commitment, residents should be eligible for Housing Benefit on the same basis as everyone else.

16.   At present there are significant anomalies in the financial arrangements for individuals between the local authority and the private and voluntary sectors. The result is a capital disregard for residents in local authority residential establishments set at £1,250 compared to £3,000 in the private and voluntary sectors. Clearly such a discrepancy should have no place in a mixed economy of residential provision intended to be determined primarily by user choice. Furthermmore, the differences in the levels of weekly personal allowances (presently £7.90 in local authority residential establishments and £9.25 in private and voluntary residential establishments) also need readjustment. We recommend that the higher level of capital disregard and of personal allowance should apply in all cases.

17.   The safeguards for personal independence which we advocate are neither idealistic nor impractical; they are already being put into effect successfully in a number of places. For example, Coventry decided some years ago that all new residential provision for elderly people should be in the form of independent self-contained flatlets, and already has several such units in operation; and Warwickshire is engaged in converting existing old people's homes along the same lines. For a variety of reasons, these new units are officially designated 'Very Sheltered Housing' but this should not obscure the fact that they represent a new and preferred form of long-stay residential provision.

18.   The safeguards in this chapter have been expressed primarily in terms of the elderly, but we wish to make it clear that they are equally applicable to other adults in residential settings, such as mentally ill and physically or mentally handicapped people, and to children and young people of an age and at a stage of development to benefit from them.

Recommendations

Every adult person entering a residential establishment with a view to an extended stay should be entitled to a trial period during which nothing would be done to dispossess them of their previous accommodation. At the end of the trial period, acceptance of the terms and conditions of the residential establishment should constitute a contract binding on both sides.

No one should be required to share a bedrom with another person: in new residential homes as from 1990, and in existing homes as from 1995, there should be only two double rooms for every ten rooms.

Each resident should be entitled to a personal key for their own room.

All residents capable of arranging their own affairs, should be entitled to retain their pension or allowance book, and to pay from it the agreed sum for accommodation and services. Residents should be eligible for Housing Benefit in the assessment of their accommodation commitment.

The differing levels of capital disregard and of personal allowance in the local authority, voluntary and private sectors should be brought into line at the higher levels.

CHAPTER FIVE

Residential Provision as a Community Resource

1. Where accommodation and personal care are combined to produce group living, each establishment has a role to play in its community, both as a centre contributing to the range of local social care services and through the interaction of the residents and life outside. Expecting managers and staff to adopt a perspective on their work that includes and emphasises what might be termed 'external relations', adds a further dimension to the demands already placed on them. Throughout the Report we maintain that residential work is complex, and this aspect of it is not least so in expecting much in the way of enlarged horizons, insight and tact.

2. Many local authorities and voluntary organisations are responding creatively to local needs, by adapting what have in the past been single function establishments (*e.g.* long-stay children's homes or homes for elderly people) for use as multiple service agencies. For example, many children's homes have become resource centres bringing together a wide range of family services, day care and residential provision. There are also examples of elderly persons' homes being used for the organisation, administration and delivery of a wide range of domiciliary services in addition to providing respite and day care.

3. Whilst, in principle, we support these developments, as they clearly offer considerable scope for encouraging the flexible responses to needs that we are striving to establish, we do not do so without reservations. We have been concerned that some resource centres may have been developed as much to cut costs as to create more community-oriented services. For example, there is evidence that some children's centres are being expected to discharge too wide a range of functions. Re-organisation of services under one roof can sometimes be seen as an invasion of

existing resident's rights e.g. where access to a home-care organiser's office can only be obtained by walking through the residents' lounge. Such examples give sufficient indication of the need for these centres, if they are to achieve their goals, to be carefully planned and managed.

Day Care in Residential Establishments

4.   In deciding how day care facilities can most appropriately be organised within a residential establishment, much obviously depends upon its primary purpose and the needs of its residents. At best, offering day care can bring a breath of fresh air into a comparatively static situation, but at worst it can be experienced as an invasion that destroys all illusion of homeliness. Management of multiple purpose centres is a highly skilled undertaking which requires specific training. The strains on staff are increased when they are given responsibilities for people on a day care basis, and appropriate training is again required. Where residential establishments incorporate day care it is important that the facilities used for day care are quite distinct from those used by residents. Where new centres are being built the need to have separate facilities for residential and day care purposes should be incorporated into the design. We have seen an outstanding example of this in Colwyn Bay where residential and day care facilities are on different floors, though day care facilities are shared by residents.

5.   In everyone's interests a balance has to be struck; on the one hand, there are residents' needs and management must safeguard their right to privacy and their own space; on the other hand, there are the requirements of day users for welcome, attention, care, stimulation and choice of activity. Ensuring that day care is a positive experience, as distinct from a merely 'minding' operation, will further tax staff energies and skills. They therefore need to be assured that in this sector of their work, as in others, they will have the cooperation of colleagues from fieldwork and health services. Some combined residential and day provision will need to be planned and delivered jointly by health and social services.

Respite Care and Services for Informal Carers

6. Our evidence reflected—and we feel that this cannot be said too often—how vast is the scale of informal caring (mainly by women) at the present time. By comparison, the contribution of residential care, important as it is, appears very small indeed. As the NCVO Advisory Group on Residential Care wrote:

> The vast majority of people from the four main clients groups live at home, either by themselves or with a caring relative. It has been estimated that perhaps three times as many bedfast and severely disabled elderly people are living at home as in all institutions put together. Similarly, as long-stay hospitals close, people with a mental handicap or mental illness are being left in the care of relatives. . .

> Residential establishments will never be able to cater for all those in need of care and support, and most people do not wish to move from their own homes in order to receive adequate levels of support. Providing these services at home may, in addition, be far more cost-effective than housing in residential care. But the needs and wishes of 'informal' carers should always be taken into consideration when planning these services, for the danger is that their goodwill and efforts could well be exploited. (E90:, para 3.5)

It would almost seem more appropriate to speak of reviewing the role of residential care in relation to informal carers, rather than the other way round.

7. The critical need to 'care for the carers' is now generally recognised; less so, perhaps, is the extent of the back-up potential that is latent within residential services. To start with, we urge a fresh look at the basis on which respite care is provided. The concept of respite care has several purposes and forms. For the individual, respite care provides a change of surroundings and can offer an opportunity for assessment, attention to health problems and active rehabilitation of many kinds. It may also serve to familiarise them with a residential setting and help to prepare them for eventual admission if this should be decided upon. For carers it provides a welcome relief from the burden of caring, and an opportunity to recharge their batteries.

8. Respite care may be provided on a regular or on an ad hoc basis, either by admitting the individual into a residential setting or by placing a relief carer in the home. It is important that arrangements should be made around the needs of the people concerned; these needs will include both those of the individual

and of the carer and it must be recognised that these interests may conflict. There may be occasions when respite care has to be strongly urged for the benefit of one or the other, or of both.

9.   We believe that the community care services should use every means available to contact as many as possible of the informal carers in their area, so as to find out what support of all kinds they may need. Even where it appears that they require no regular support, it will still be important to enquire whether the carers ever have a holiday, since if they do not, the whole caring arrangement should be regarded as potentially 'at risk'—of undue stress, of sudden breakdown, of damage to the mental and physical health of the carer, and consequent danger to the person cared for. Ideally, all informal carers should have the opportunity of at least two weeks respite from their task each year.

10.   We have all come across cases where a planned period of respite care has precipitated an unplanned admission because the informal carer refused to take the person back. We do not see this as an intrinsic risk in offering respite care but rather as an inevitable consequence of leaving a problematic situation to fester for too long.

11.   The positive attitude of those actually providing the respite care will make acceptance that much easier both for the individual and for the carer who may be anxious or over-conscientious. Much good can stem from the partnership between care staff and informal carers—they have in common both experience and expertise. Carers should be encouraged to see the residential establishment as a source of concern and of help for themselves in their own right, which willingly takes a share in the task of caring, and as an information resource able to point them in the right direction for any counselling, support groups and additional services that could help them continue to give care without undue cost to their own wellbeing. The risk of breakdown is always present in informal caring arrangements and needs to be taken seriously by all concerned. The more informed residential staff become about the likely breaking points, the more timely and appropriate their advice and support can be.

Relinquishing the Caring Role

12.   Parents caring at home for a son or daughter with a physical or mental disability have to face the challenge of relinquishing

the caring role. As the Voluntary Council for Handicapped
Children wrote to us:

> Although the majority of disabled school leavers live with their
> natural parents, we recommend that their right to move on to
> greater independence should be recognised like any other member
> of the community. . .Thus a young person may move from the
> parental home to a staffed group home or other supported residen-
> tial provision, then to a minimally or unstaffed group home and
> hence to ordinary housing with or without friends and with support
> from social services departments as appropriate. (E186: p4)

We are in general agreement with this view, though we believe
that the best option for the young person may be to remain in a
group home and for staff, rather than the young person, to move
in and out as required.

13.   Similarly, the relatives of a person afflicted with a disabling mental illness may have to ask themselves whether, at
some cost to their own feelings, they should encourage them to
leave home for a treatment setting where they may gradually
learn to cope with their problems and with the world around
them. In this context residential care assumes a doubly beneficial
aspect—it relieves the carers of a burden which would otherwise
have no end, and enables the handicapped person to attain the
highest degree of personal independence of which they are
capable. The provision of long-term supportive accommodation
for this purpose needs to be greatly expanded.

Keeping in Touch

14.   A residential establishment is a part of its local community and the people who live in the establishment are full and
equal members of that community, and should have every opportunity to enjoy its leisure, educational and other facilities. We see
each resident as bringing strengths into the group, not of self
only, but of self plus family, friends, neighbours and advisers.
They should be free to invite and receive relatives and friends as
and when they choose, taking due account of the practicalities of
group living. Staff should ensure that residents are enabled to
keep whatever patterns of contact they choose to have with their
families and friends. For most residents continuity of personal
relationships is important; this is most easily achieved in establishments which are situated in the residents' own locality—in

our view a potent argument for small scale highly localised residential services. Where it is desirable or necessary for a person to move to another neighbourhood, work by staff may be needed both to maintain established relationships and to assist the formation of links with the new community.

15.　　Regard must be paid to the diversity of family patterns deriving from the differing ethnic and cultural traditions of particular minority communities; this most frequently arises in inner city areas but is by no means exclusive to them. All local authorities in which there are ethnic minorities should seek to follow the example of those—such as the London Borough of Hackney—which make the effort to identify and meet the particular needs of members of such communities living in residential settings, for instance by ensuring wherever possible a match between the ethnic composition of the staff group and the residents. A valuable source of knowledge about residents' particular interests and needs can be tapped by employing members of the relevant communities as consultants to particular establishments.

Volunteers

16.　　A residential establishment should make clear in its prospectus the part played by volunteers in contributing to the quality of residents' lives and to the residential environment as a whole. Residents themselves will introduce many volunteers in the persons of their informal social networks, and their participation in a resident's life will be that of any friend, neighbour or relative. There is also another route by which people in the community become participants: the tradition of volunteering is of long standing and the range of voluntary contribution has, if anything, increased in recent years as people have more surplus time at their disposal and seek to use it in constructive ways. Whilst we have no wish to decry or discourage the contribution that volunteers can make to life in a residential setting, we would sound a note of caution against the assumption that volunteers *per se* are a good idea and can therefore be imposed.

17.　　A residential establishment is a natural target for impulsive offers of help from well-meaning people in its neighbourhood. MSC Community and Youth Training Programmes often approach residential services, as do schools, with the commendable objective of giving young people a taste of social care work.

The terms of acceptance of such offers should be clearly understood: volunteers should be invited in only if residents wish, and it can be demonstrated that they are likely to enlarge the areas of choice, freedom and independence. To seek ways of deploying volunteers because they are available is to put things the wrong way round; rather, staff should find out from residents whether they have needs or interests which could best be met by effecting an introduction to someone with similar interests from outside. Local volunteer bureaux and councils of voluntary work usually act as clearing houses and match volunteers to need, or the neighbourhood 'grapevines' or a card in the newsagent's window often produce the looked-for response.

18. Fund raising is a traditional function of voluntary groups, though it is not without paradox. In some circumstances notions of 'charity' can contradict important values and objectives, such as making residential establishments more ordinary and less stigmatising places, and enabling residents to be as self-supporting as others in the community. It is therefore important that residents be involved in planning any fund raising exercise from the outset and that its objectives—whether or not they relate directly to improving their own amenities—have been discussed and agreed with them.

19. The Volunteer Centre in its evidence helpfully differentiated between person-centred and task-centred voluntary roles:

> The person centred volunteer, whether attached to the establishment or a member of a community group, is someone with whom individual residents have significant personal relations. The relationship is pre-eminent as an end in itself, and may be a substitute for absent members of the resident's nuclear or extended family. . .

> The task centred volunteer is someone who is in contact with individuals or groups of residents for limited tasks only. These tasks take precedence over the forming of relationships although tasks may provide the starting point for relationships. The young volunteer who enters an establishment to help in an adult education class, or the community group which takes a number of residents on an outing are examples. (E108, para 7a)

We would not wish to prejudge which role should be given greater emphasis because so many factors need to be considered. We know from experience that volunteers can very helpfully meet residents' needs for friendship and support where these are otherwise lacking, and it is now suggested in some quarters that volunteers might equally helpfully carry out some practical tasks in order to free paid staff to devote more time to giving residents companionship and counselling. Obviously any such developments would raise some delicate political issues as, in any case, there is always the risk that volunteers will be seen to be used as substitutes for paid staff.

20.   Working with volunteers should be an item of discussion at staff and residents' meetings, and staff should be helped to understand the volunteers' role. Once their offer of help has been accepted, or they have been purposely recruited, volunteers need to experience satisfaction if they are to make a commitment to continuing involvement. They need to know what is expected of them, to see the value of what they do, and to feel that they and their contribution are welcomed by individual residents or by the group as a whole. It is important that they are properly supported and supervised, and given training where appropriate. Issues of role boundary and team working should be paid particular attention in both staff and volunteer training.

Recommendations

Where residential and day care are provided in the same establishment, the facilities for each should be quite distinct.

Statutory and voluntary agencies, should use every means available to contact informal carers in their area, so as to find out what services they may need.

The provision of long-term supportive accommodation to enable people with disabilities to leave the parental home needs to be greatly expanded.

There should be a match between the ethnic composition of the people in a residential establishment and the staff group. Advice on special needs should be sought from representatives of the relevant ethnic communities.

The help to be contributed by volunteers should be clearly understood and accepted by themselves, residents and paid staff; they should be properly supported and supervised, and given training where appropriate. Residents should always be involved from the outset in any voluntary fund-raising activity.

CHAPTER SIX

Ensuring the Quality of
Residential Services

1. We start from the assumption that residential care within personal social services will continue to be provided by local authorities, voluntary organisations and private agencies. We would not seek to limit this diversity. Singly each sector has its characteristic strengths and weaknesses; together they could offer the users maximum choice. To realise this potential, however, would require of each sector both a reappraisal of their individual role and a readiness to work in closer partnership.

Local Authorities

2. The largest sector within our remit consists of establishments provided by local authorities. Its present range of facilities represents services developed over the past forty years. Homes for the elderly are in some cases large houses adapted for their present use, but in the main they are purpose-built establishments housing 40 to 50 people. The more recent of these have been designed or adapted for living in smaller groups. Large children's homes and many community homes with education (CHEs) have now disappeared, but numbers of family group homes built in the 1950s and subsequently are still in use, often with specialised functions. Although a number of hostels and assessment centres built in the 1960s and 1970s have been closed, some remain. Hostels for people with mental illness or mental handicap were set up in response to policies for developing care in the community; more recently 'core and cluster' units have been established.

3. The fact that local authorities are responsible for the full range of personal social services for children, families, people

with disabilities and elderly people means that they are uniquely placed to use their residential provision as one element in the totality of their caring services. It should not even be necessary to speak in terms of 'links with the community'—residential establishments should so clearly be a part of the community they exist to serve.

4. Unfortunately this is by no means always the case, although there is a steady shift towards smaller, more domestic and more localised residential services, which permit people to remain in their own localities. In this respect the potential ability of social service departments to draw on local council housing stock is a considerable advantage. The biggest problem for local authorities in terms of buildings may well prove to be that they find themselves encumbered with residential establishments for elderly people that are over-large by today's standards. Where these remain in use, we should like to see them progressively adapted to provide fewer residents with better accommodation on the model of very sheltered housing.

Voluntary Organisations

5. The voluntary sector has a long and impressive record of identifying areas of social need and deprivation and of developing specialist services in response, particularly in relation to services for children, where the major children's voluntary organisations set up national networks of residential homes. Over the last two decades these organisations have re-thought their policies—partly in response to changing patterns of child care, partly in response to the fact that local authorities make less use of their residential facilities—and are meeting children's needs in a variety of non-residential ways. Voluntary organisations have the freedom to choose where to work, so they can be flexible and innovative, and some of the best practice and latest thinking may be found in the voluntary sector.

6. Other voluntary residential services—which originally consisted largely of single homes for the elderly, with local management committees—have now been developed to meet a range of different needs; for example, the Cheshire Homes for people with physical handicaps and the Richmond Fellowship for people with mental illness. Some organisations have also

developed supportive networks for relatives of the users of their services.

7.   The most recent development has been the involvement of housing associations, particularly in the setting up of sheltered accommodation, supported housing, and core and cluster systems. We particularly welcome this development since it reflects our wish to see people in suitable accommodation where care services can be provided as necessary.

Private Sector

8.   There has long been a small number of private homes catering for the needs of the elderly, but in the last decade there has been a huge increase in the amount of residential provision available, with the private sector now providing more places for elderly people than local authorities. This is partly because of the growing numbers of elderly people, and partly because of funding through supplementary benefits which for the first time has given many people of pensionable age real choice in this field. Private homes vary considerably in size; some belong to corporate organisations, but the great majority are small businesses using a wide variety of adapted premises, often run by their proprietors. Many private homes are sited in older premises and are numerous in and around seaside towns. In part, this reflects the wishes of people retiring to these areas, but it can also change the nature of these neighbourhoods, and put pressure on local health and other support services.

9.   Although the majority of residents in the private sector are elderly, the number of homes for people with mental illness and mental handicap is growing steadily, often run by nurses or social workers from mental hospitals and mental handicap hospitals or community-based services. Recent developments also include high quality sheltered and very sheltered housing, which we welcome as providing further choice for the consumer.

The Balance of Provision

10.   It will be seen that all three sectors contribute different facilities and their very diversity increases consumer choice. It is our view that there should continue to be a blend of provision

from all three sectors. We have, however, noted the idiosyncratic nature of much of the growth and contraction of residential services, and the resultant uneven spread of provision. For example, Warwickshire Social Services Department has closed all its children's homes, whilst other authorities are contemplating opening new ones to cope with the increased number of abused children. We recommend that local authorities should take the lead in the strategic planning of services within their boundaries. The different roles, responsibilities and catchment areas of the three sectors will, of course, present difficulties, but planning should help to increase collaboration, identify shortfalls in services and develop a more appropriate balance of provision.

11.   We have noted the range and diversity of provision, but we need also to note some weaknesses. Overlong chains of command and bureaucratic procedures make for rigid, impersonal services. This is a danger in local authorities, in major voluntary organisations and in large private companies. Smaller organisations need to be on their guard against losing contact with developments in good practice. In the private sector, whilst the larger agencies have built-in support and monitoring systems, most of the smaller establishments are worryingly short of external support.

12.   Recent abuses in residential establishments have been well publicised, with private proprietors accused in the press and on television of exploitation and mistreating residents; but Roger Clough's paper 'Scandals in Residential Centres', commissioned by the Committee, was a stark reminder that reports of neglect and abuse in residential centres go back for more than thirty years. After examining reports of different types of residential centres, including two reports in 1987 on homes for elderly people in Camden and at Nye Bevan Lodge in Southwark, Clough writes:

> The reports show what can and does go wrong in residential establishments. The answer is not only in exhortation, not only in planning to avoid past mistakes, it lies in understanding the complexities of residential work and of the systems in which people work and live—and then working out the best system to promote the well-being of the residents.

Registration and Inspection

13.   The system of registration and inspection attracted a great deal of criticism in our written evidence. There was seen to be a failure on the part of registration authorities to address themselves to the central issues of the quality of care and an undue emphasis upon the physical features of care establishments. It was in the latter sphere that there was evidence of inflexibility, particularly in relation to users other than the elderly. The evidence highlighted inconsistencies between different registration authorities, was critical of the skills and experience of registration officers, and suggested that authorities often required of voluntary and private establishments standards higher than they themselves maintained in the establishments for which they had direct responsibility.

14.   We need to see these criticisms in some historical perspective. The new legislation came into operation only in January 1985 so that a very short period had elapsed when we received our evidence. Registration authorities had given low priority to this sphere of their responsibilities prior to the 1984 Act. There were a number of reasons for this, some of them related to financial constraints, others to the weakness of the previous legislation; but is quite clear that in a number of authorities, the process of inspection had been severely neglected. (Elsewhere— and especially in those areas where the private sector had been developing steadily over many years—some constructive collaborative arrangements had been established.) There were also differences of opinion between the Government and the local authority associations about the cost of the additional responsibilities under the new legislation. The stance adopted by the Government was that manpower and other resource costs had to be met from fee income. Initially, fees were fixed at a level quite unrelated to the resource required and had to be revised drastically after little more than a year; we understand that a further substantial increase is now in prospect.

15.   It was surely unfortunate that these developments coincided with a sharp reduction in local authority financial sponsorship of individual residents in voluntary establishments. As increasing numbers of people found their way into voluntary and private establishments with the aid of social security benefits, it was understandable that hard-pressed local authorities should decide to scale down their own payments for this purpose; but

the change has had a major impact upon some voluntary organisations and has disrupted collaborative arrangements of long standing.

16. Against this background, we have had to take into account the independent reviews of residential care in the London Boroughs of Brent and Camden, with their disquieting revelations of chronic mismanagement, staff shortages and poor standards of care, followed by the truly horrific abuses described by the Inquiry into Nye Bevan Lodge in the London Borough of Southwark. These reports have profoundly affected our Committee, as we believe they have public opinion generally. It is plain that in all these London Boroughs, local authority residential care management proved ineffective over long periods to improve standards or prevent abuses. We recognise that the inner areas of London and other large cities have their own special problems, but some of the letters we received from residents, relatives and staff in residential establishments conveyed a disquieting impression that situations of this kind could arise almost anywhere.

17. We find the conclusions urgent and inescapable, first, that local authority residential establishments should be registered and inspected regularly, in the same way as those in the private and voluntary sectors; second, that to ensure independence and impartiality, no service providing agency should undertake the inspection of its own establishments; and third, that national guidelines should be drawn up for the inspection of residential establishments in all three sectors which, while allowing for legitimate local diversity, should pay equal attention to matters relating to standards of accommodation, quality of life, and the qualifications of management and staff. We recommend accordingly.

18. We see these recommendations as applying equally to children's establishments. At present voluntary children's homes are inspected periodically by the Social Services Inspectorate. Community homes with education are inspected jointly by the Schools and Social Services Inspectorates. Local authority and private children's homes are not at present subject to regular inspection, although under the Children's Home Act 1982, (yet to be implemented) a private children's home where any child in care is resident would be required to register with the local authority. The Government have recently announced that they 'propose to consult on the possibility of rationalising the current

registration arrangements so as to make them fully comprehensive' (The Law on Child Care and Family Services, Cm 62, para 81). We welcome this announcement as timely, not least as it provides a forum in which our recommendations on inspection could also be discussed.

19.   We should like ways to be found of building into the task of inspection an element of 'peer review'. This could be provided by a panel of suitable persons with current or very recent residential experience, drawn from all three sectors—local authority, voluntary and private—who could act as independent assessors or observers. A single assessor would probably be considered sufficient for visits which were considered fairly routine. In cases of importance (by reason of the size of the establishment) or difficulty (by reason of doubts about standards) it may seem desirable to have two assessors, one with local authority experience and the other with a private or voluntary sector background. Assessors could receive a fee for their services, and precautions would be needed to avoid any conflict of interest. Thus, a local authority assessor would not be involved in the inspection of an establishment belonging to his employing authority, nor would voluntary or private panel members be deployed on any inspection in which they had a personal interest. We recommend that consideration be given to a system of peer review along these lines.

Self-evaluation and Performance Review

20.   We emphasise, however, that we do not recommend inspection as an end in itself, still less as a sufficient answer to the problems of maintaining and improving standards of care; rather we see it as creating the necessary framework within which positive measures for improving standards can be initiated, and their success evaluated. For such measures to succeed, we identify three pre-requisites:

(i) as already noted, every residential establishment should have a written brochure or prospectus setting out its aims and objectives, its basic values and principles, and the range of services offered. Such a prospectus is required to provide the basis for each resident's contract with the management; but it is equally essential in order that inspection may be effective: an establishment without declared aims cannot be held to account for failing to achieve them.

(ii) to complement the prospectus, there needs to be a detailed statement of the means by which the aims and objectives are to be achieved. It is important that this statement should reflect the expressed wishes and views of residents and of all levels of staff, preferably jointly arrived at, since staff cannot be held to account for failing to meet expectations on which they have not been consulted and of which they may be unaware.

(iii) there must be provision for a periodic performance review in which the establishment's aims, its methods and its success in achieving them are evaluated at least annually; this again is a process in which residents, their relatives and other regular visitors, and staff at all levels need to be involved and their views recorded.

21. This threefold system of self-evaluation need not be sophisticated, so long as it is conscientiously implemented. We recommend local authorities, the major voluntary organisations and the independent bodies representing private proprietors to promote the adoption of such a system in residential establishments with which they are involved. We do not think any new establishment should be registered which has not drawn up a system of self-evaluation at least in outline, and the operation of the system should be a major focus of inspections.

Loopholes and Anomalies

22. We have been impressed by the unanimity of the advice tendered to us, that small private residential homes caring for three or fewer people, which are at present excluded from the provisions of the Registered Homes Act, should be brought within the scope of some measure of regular inspection and control. We see no reason to dissent from this view, although we would not wish the full mechanisms of registration and inspection to be brought to bear on such small establishments, which we see as having more in common with fostering or boarding-out arrangements than with larger residential establishments. We

recommend that provision be made for the preliminary vetting of small homes caring for three or fewer people, and for periodic visits to ensure that the residents are well cared for. Where, however, a number of small residential homes in the same neighbourhood are operated by one proprietor, providing for a total of four or more residents, then the full requirements of the Act should apply.

23. It is perhaps not widely known that residential establishments operating under Royal Charter are at present exempt from the requirements of the Registered Homes Act. We do not know whether this situation came about by inadvertence or by design, but we see it as an anomaly and we recommend that it should be ended as soon as possible.

24. We do, however, have much sympathy with the case made by the Social Welfare Committee of the Catholic Bishops' Conference of England and Wales, who have reported to us that some religious communities caring for their own members who have become elderly or infirm, are being obliged to seek registration under the Registered Homes Act. On the understanding that a community is only providing a home for its bona fide members and is not taking in new residents for the purpose of giving them accommodation and care, we are agreed that it should be treated rather as an extended family than as a residential home, and we recommend that it should not be subject to the requirements of registration and inspection.

Continuity of Care

25. We have received from Age Concern Scotland a copy of their paper 'The Case for Change: Regulating Standards in Private & Voluntary Residential Care and Nursing Homes in Scotland', in which they argue that the distinction between residential and nursing homes should be abandoned as no longer useful or appropriate, and that a single registration and inspection system should be instituted for all establishments providing accommodation and care. We think such a development would make it much easier to ensure continuity of care in one setting as residents' disabilities increase, and we recommend that it should be given serious consideration in relation to England and Wales.

Recommendations

Local authorities should take the lead in the strategic planning of residential services within their boundaries.

Local authority, voluntary and private residential establishments should be subject to the same system of registration and inspection.

The DHSS should draw up national guidelines for the inspection of residential establishments, and should give equal attention to standards of accommodation, quality of life and the qualifications of management and staff.

To ensure independence and impartiality, no agency should undertake the inspection of its own residential establishments.

As an adjunct to inspections, consideration should be given to appointing panels of independent assessors from all three sectors.

Local authorities, voluntary organisations and the representatives of private proprietors should promote systems of self-evaluation and performance review in all residential establishments; no new establishment should be registered which is not prepared to adopt such a system.

Small private establishments caring for three or fewer people should be subject to preliminary vetting and to periodic visits; but where one proprietor operates a number of such homes, in the same neighbourhood, providing for a total of four or more residents, then the full requirements of the Registered Homes Act should apply.

Residential establishments operating under Royal Charter should be brought within the scope of the Registered Homes Act.

Religious or secular communities, which continue to provide a home for members who have become old or infirm, should not be deemed to be within the scope of the Registered Homes Act.

Serious consideration should be given to a unified registration and inspection system for residential and nursing homes, to facilitate continuity of care.

CHAPTER SEVEN

Principles of Practice

1. Our evidence has included many statements from residents and their families which express considerable satisfaction with the quality of services received. Such statements are made about local authority, private and voluntary establishments, no one sector appearing superior to another. However the letters of complaint include some that are extremely disturbing. We have also read a number of official reports of enquiries into allegations of inadequate care and ill-treatment (referred to in the preceding chapter), and we can only conclude that there are wide variations in the quality of provision throughout the services as a whole.

2. It is not our intention in this chapter to lay down specific practice techniques but to identify underlying principles or values which should inform all aspects of residential practice. These principles have been the basis of many of our deliberations and we discuss them here, not to provide a code of practice, but as a statement of our convictions.

3. During the course of our discussions we identified five inter-related principles, which taken together form the basis of good practice, *viz*:

Caring —this should be personal, and residents should feel valued, safe and secure;

Choice —each resident's right to exercise choice over their daily life should be respected;

Continuity —This includes both consistency of care from staff, and the maintenance of links with a resident's previous life;

Change —for residents, the opportunity for continued development; for staff, a commitment to respond to changing needs;

Common values—ensuring that practice is based on a shared philosophy and values.

[60]

It is true that what we have to say has been said many times before; the question remains, why has it not been consistently translated into practice. It is important to continue stating these basic principles as they provide the yardsticks against which services and practice can be tested and evaluated. The challenge is to ensure that they are applied sensitively, in accordance with the needs of particular individuals, and in line with the opportunities and constraints of group living.

Caring for People Individually

4.   Most caring experiences are reciprocal, embodying close personal relationships which are frequently bound up with powerful and often ambivalent feelings of commitment, warmth, love, guilt, anxiety, frustration, anger and sometimes sexuality. The ability to care for others as paid helpers is based on personal experiences of being cared for and caring; every person's capacity to be cared for is similarly rooted. This has to be recognised, understood and actively worked with by carers and cared for alike, if they are to be able jointly to make caring a positive and constructive experience. Caring is about treating people individually; thus a residential establishment where individuality is respected at all times and in all circumstances is by definition a caring one.

5.   Serious shortcomings in caring are conveyed by this letter, from a relative:

> It has always been rather sad to see him clad in clothes other than his own (which are well labelled and all co-ordinating). To see him eat, using old, worn second-grade cutlery, drink from a plastic cup, all presented on a rather grotty tray, can be so upsetting and served to add salt to a wound for me or his wife when visiting, after spending a life together since the age of seventeen. Having enjoyed all the niceties of life in their home together, these standards are humiliating and degrading . . . My father is happy, clean and well fed. I would certainly not wish to ridicule this Home. My comments have fallen on deaf ears. We pay our money, and can't take our choice. (H50)

We recognise that this letter also raises issues of resources.

6.   Safety is an important aspect of caring. For example, children with past damaging experiences have a particular need to feel safe. Caring for them in residential establishments requires

that they know that they will be protected from physical violence, including their own; that their belongings are safe and they themselves are not allowed to steal; that they will be protected from sexual intrusion, from undue expectations of giving or receiving love, and situations which are beyond them. The needs of an old person for safety in a residential establishment may be met very differently, but in all cases the nature of group living has to be taken into account.

Enabling People to Make Choices

7.   It is emphasised throughout this Report that choice about life-style is as important to people living in residential settings as it is to anyone else. Any restrictions on individual choice should be imposed only when it is clearly proved that a resident is incapable of exercising this basic human right. Residential staff thus need to be constantly asking themselves how they can respect and extend the range of choices open to their residents. For some whose lives have previously been restricted, the experience of group living can itself bring an enlargement of choice.

8.   As a general principle, the more personal a matter is, the more free should be the choice. Adults should be free to choose in matters of relationships, physical care, personal space and food. It is also important to make clear where limits and restrictions exist, but to keep general rules to a minimum. Thus, if a resident plays a radio late at night, upsetting others, the answer should not be to make a rule prohibiting the playing of radios after 10 pm. Rather, it is better to help residents to negotiate arrangements between themselves. In such ways people will learn how to live with and respect one another, and to make responsible choices which do not cause offence or harm.

9.   In the past the inability of residents to choose and therefore to express their individuality has been one of the main criticisms of residential care. Some of our correspondents clearly think that institutionalisation is inevitable and look to more radical solutions in order to be able to choose freely. For example, a young man paralysed after a swimming accident writes:

> It would be essential that each person's flat is their own, to do with as they see fit, to decorate in any way they choose and to have any

visitors at any time they choose. The staff must have absolutely no say in this whatsoever. The emphasis of the entire establishment should be of staff depending on the residents for their job and not the residents depending on the staff for anything other than 'hired muscle'. (P103)

10. Others, however, certainly feel that even whilst living within a residential environment they have as much freedom of choice in their daily lives as they want. For example:

—In this home there are no restrictions. You are free to come and go as you please (P12)

—. . . . probably among the best of its kind. The matron and the permanent staff are all very good, responsive to suggestions and trying all the time to help the residents (P16)

—A relative writes:— I have always been consulted about drugs and alternative methods of care (do you want her to go into hospital? etc) I have always been immediately informed when things have gone wrong eg; another resident hit her on one occasion. The staff are friendly and open and my daily visits are welcomed (P17)

Achieving Continuity

11. A move into a residential environment not only means that home life is disrupted but many other aspects of life also. The links between past, present and anticipated future may all be broken. To minimise the effects of these disruptions and to restore some continuity is thus a vital part of the planning which needs to go into their move into a residential setting and into their life there.

12. The continuity which comes from having consistent attention from staff whom an individual can come to know well and trust, is an important aspect that has to be planned, managed and coordinated. This is one reason why the development of residential 'key workers' as a means of establishing some continuity of care should be encouraged.

13. Another form of continuity is with the resident's former life. Wherever possible residents should not have had to move far from home; should be able to bring in their own furniture and personal possessions, to have the same trusted advisers, such as GPs or solicitors, and the same leisure opportunities. Links should be maintained with friends and relatives who should be able to support and give practical care to residents if the latter so wish.

Developing the Capacity for Change

14. Everyone should be thought of as having some capacity
for change and development, irrespective of increasing age and
infirmity, and residential staff need to be responsive and able to
adapt to any changes taking place in residents. Each new resident
means that an establishment has to change and become a different place to meet that individual's needs and staff have to be
capable of facilitating that change. One resident wrote about the
importance of being given opportunities for personal development, but she was concerned that cutbacks were reducing these
possibilities:

> And the extras that meant a lot to so many of the severely disabled.
> The art teacher who helped and gave so much pleasure to so many
> of the residents was made redundant last summer. There is talk of
> further staff cutbacks which doesn't create so relaxed an atmos-
> phere as would otherwise and did previously exist. The hours of
> occupational therapists, physiotherapists are fewer. And now talk
> of cutting back on the time of the teacher who helps the teens and
> twenties and even older residents discover and rediscover their
> reading and writing capacities seems likely to become a reality
> (P106)

15. Elderly people need variety of lifestyle, especially of food
and opportunities for participation and activity, all of which help
to retain their sense of individuality and appetite for life. One
resident depicts how this can be done in some very simple ways:

> . . . residents often have tea outside in the summer. Food is of good
> quality and well balanced and (the Warden) presents it in an
> attractive way, and also does some tasty home cooking. Residents
> are encouraged to help if they wish, which is good as it gives them
> a feeling of participation. Outings are arranged to . . . a seaside
> town, and they have been to the theatre, fetes and various other
> functions (P112)

This contrasts sharply with a resident's experience of another
home:

> I have not been happy (here). I feel I have had all my independence
> taken away from me. The staff are kind and do their best but I feel
> it is basic care that they offer. There are no proper facilities for (us)
> or sufficient trained staff. I do feel . . . it should be adapted to
> enable/encourage residents to use/develop their potential to the full
> (P122)

Clear Aims and a Common Philosophy

16. The service in a residential establishment can only be successful if it is informed by a set of clear aims and common values. The most senior member of staff will have great impact on those aims and values through his or her leadership position, and it is important that efforts are made to ensure commitment to those aims and values among staff. Although management and staff will take the lead in establishing aims and values, in doing so it will be important that they reflect the wishes and lifestyles of residents.

17. While scarcity of resources is undoubtedly an objective barrier to ideal practice, nevertheless this should not be made the excuse for lack of regard for the preservation of human dignity. Translating this principle into practice involves showing respect for the individual and, in the case of children, for their parents also. In personal matters, dignity includes arrangements for privacy at mealtimes if physical incapacity means that eating practices are likely to upset others; it might include choice in menus; the chance to choose when one eats and where. Dignity also depends on staff having a sympathetic attitude to requests for help in toileting, and on staff being available to assist in preventing incontinence; assessment of medication is of primary importance for the same reason. Dignity related to personal hygiene and appearance implies easy access to washing facilities when required, choice of bathing or showering and the necessary help for either, the availability of hairdressing, and alterations to clothing if there is weight change.

Barriers to Good Practice

18. We also need to recognise that there are often serious impediments to good practice. For example:

(i) *Lack of planning and organisation*
A lack of forethought and planning often results in insensitive and negligent practices. Not all planning issues are within the control of the staff, who may be handicapped by ill-conceived rotas, inadequate staffing establishments, poor building designs and lack of facilities. Complaints from correspondents often centred around:

poor diet 'I feel that diet must have a similar (to school children) effect on old people's mental and physical state—junk and convenience foods, little fresh vegetables and big helpings of food without consideration of vitamin levels...' (P97);

a poor environment '...the home is situated in the middle of a busy road and the traffic is awful. No pavement. She cannot get out as you step into the traffic' (P51);

poor design features 'Not enough room in the lounge—everyone with frames, wheelchairs etc like an obstacle course to get to the toilet and then only one toilet near the lounge for about 25 people' (H40);

failure to plan for individual needs 'They are supposed to do her washing etc but quite honestly it's a job to find any clothes. All were marked with her name so they have no excuses. To take her out you need to take dress, tights, cardigan.' (H72).

(ii) *Lack of leadership*
Some of the evidence, sadly, does reflect an absence of caring and committed attitudes, though these are a minority of submissions. There are a number of explanations—poor management, staff shortages, lack of effective delegation, and lack of training—that might account for any apparent lack of commitment by staff, but no-one could ignore the following:

There must be up to 30 residents and always at least 4 staff there. However, after their dinner at about 12.00 the staff are not seen until afternoon tea... Then the staff aren't seen again until the evening meal at 6.00. Anyone could have fallen, died, haemorrhaged, wet themselves and the staff wouldn't know (P169)
and
The staff appear to show little enthusiasm or interest in the welfare of their residents. There also appears to be serious lack of care in medical attention... There is also lack of attention generally. Nothing is organised for the interest and occupation of the residents. They are simply fed, bathed when necessary and put to bed. Between time they

are left to either wander around aimlessly or sit in the
lounge area. (H48)

(iii) *Fear of risk-taking*
There is fear of taking risks with people who are being
provided with some form of accommodation and services; this leads to responsibility for their own lives being
taken from them.

(iv) *Stigma*
Residential care continues to be widely seen as stigmatising in itself. Many residents are stigmatised, perhaps because they are dependent on state care or other
people's assistance, or because of their personal
infirmities or behaviour. People who can be readily identified as 'different' are often victims of the tendency to
lump people together in categories.

(v) *Lack of resources*
In many cases a lack of resources leads to inadequate
provision of services. For example, standards of care
cannot be maintained with inadequate staffing levels.

The Role of Management

19.   Expert management is essential for staff to be able to give
of their best and to ensure that high quality services are achieved.
Staff need clear leadership which combines an explicit philosophy
with maximum delegation, to enable them to work creatively and
confidently in the knowledge that they are appreciated and supported. In such a context all major decisions will be taken with the
staff so that they are fully aware of the reasons for them, and can
implement them with confidence. The management of a residential service involves some complex processes—such as encouraging self-determination, choice and independence, and
balancing the interest of the individual and those of the group—in
addition to providing basic necessities, like food and acceptable
standards of hygiene and cleanliness; satisfying patterns of daily
routines; and a comfortable environment in which people can live
together amicably.

20.   All staff must engage in these processes and be able to
take decisions collectively in accordance with a shared philosophy
of care, and in their residents' best interests. Inevitably, conflicts

of interest arise from time to time, and an important aspect of management is to be able to negotiate and resolve them. Another major management task is to ensure that staff have the necessary physical resources, training and support. Management needs to institute adequate procedures for consultation and for listening to staff difficulties in implementing policies; staff meetings and supervision are the main vehicles through which difficulties should be resolved and information passed on and discussed.

21.   Staff also have to be helped to work together as a team. This does not mean that everyone should be identical but that they should be complementary—different roles and personal approaches being valued and integrated into an effective working whole. In many establishments, effective team work can evolve without explicit intervention by the manager, but in some staff groups loyalty to colleagues can develop into a sub-culture, which opposes management, and works to the detriment of the residents. Authoritarian and confrontational management styles can aggravate such problems; managers need to be able both to offer professional leadership and to be regarded as integral members of the team. Delegation is another essential feature of effective management and of teamwork, so that staff can take on responsibilities which match their abilities.

22.   Many managers are responsible for the recruitment of staff, and therefore need to be trained to draw up job descriptions and specifications, to select staff who will be able to contribute to a particular philosophy and set of aims and will bring with them something of the diversity and richness of the community at large. Managers should always be involved in the interviewing and selection of their staff.

23.   Managers need to work closely with other professionals, the wider community and the relatives, friends and advocates of residents. They must develop skill in assessing the potential impact of newcomers on existing residents, and must be able to formulate contracts of care with prospective residents and their families.

24.   Many managers feel that they themselves are lacking support and supervision; but if they are to take on the professional support and development of their staff they too need someone to turn to for support and to whom to pass on the pressures of the job, be it their line manager or an external consultant.

The Role of 'External' Management

25. Residential establishments are often viewed differently from the 'inside' and from the 'outside' and tensions can arise, between agency management and the managers of the services themselves. There are many sources of such tensions. In some cases the 'external' managers have no direct experience of practice in residential settings and therefore find it hard to appreciate the problems. In other cases there is a continual battle for resources between individual establishments and their agency. In yet other cases the agency has unrealistic expectations of the establishments, which are seen as having a part to play within some overall plan, but whose internal life appears to be insufficiently understood. It is the view of a majority of our Committee that the immediate external managers of residential services should always have personal experience of work in such settings, and preferably in a variety of them. A minority however argued that such a requirement could on occasion stand in the way of appointing the most able person, particularly when radical change was desired.

26. We would urge all service-providing organisations to review their management practices in order to provide a framework within which positive practice can flourish and which encourages rather than stifles initiative. For example, it will be unacceptable for pension books to be held centrally at headquarters if residents are to retain control of their own money and pay their rent themselves. Similarly, the use of order books for the purchase of children's clothing and the supply of food in catering quantities, are both inconsistent with budgeting on a domestic scale, and are unhelpful too for people who are learning the skills of independent living.

CHAPTER EIGHT

Staffing Issues

1. It is vital that staff with the right personal qualities and skills are recruited and selected; that they are adequately paid, and have conditions of service and training opportunities which match the job. The fact that residential work is able to attract people of different ages, from various walks of life and ethnic backgrounds, possessing a rich assortment of personal qualities, skills, interests and experiences is its strongest asset, which needs to be built on. Also, as residential provision becomes more closely integrated into local services networks, we should expect staffing patterns to reflect the social and multi-cultural characteristics of neighbourhoods and communities.

Numbers of Staff

2. How many staff are there? The simple answer is that no-one really knows. This was brought to our attention by the Local Government Training Board, which for its most recent survey of manpower, training and professional qualifications (1986) has had great difficulty in obtaining accurate data on which to calculate staffing numbers. A similar problem confronted a workforce planning group, established in the wake of the LGTB survey to identify the elements of a comprehensive workforce planning and training strategy for the personal social services as a whole. (*Workforce Planning and Training Need. An Interim Report by Working Group on Workforce Planning in the Personal Social Services 1987.* Chair: Professor Adrian Webb. Copies of report available from CCETSW). Thus the staffing estimates in the following table are presented only to give an idea of the broad shape of the residential workforce. It can be seen that there are roughly similar numbers of direct service and domestic and other manual staff,

who form by far the largest proportion of the workforce. As most of the direct service staff are considered as manual workers i.e. as care assistants, we can also see just how far residential services depend on a vast army of low paid, untrained people; the majority of whom are women, many working part time. Insofar as it is the children's services that have been contracting, with the major expansion taking place in private sector, provision for the elderly, this position is unlikely to change substantially in the foreseeable future.

Numbers of Staff Working in Statutory, Private and Voluntary Sectors (Great Britain)

	Statutory	Private	Voluntary	Totals
Direct Service Staff (care assts,* child care workers etc)	62,900	27,000	20,000	109,900
Management and Supervisory	19,500	10,000	3.500	33,000
Domestic and Ancillary Staff	61,000	21,500	13,500	96,000
TOTALS:	143,400	58,500	37,000	238,900

(Sources: Working Group on Workforce Planning in the Personal Social Services 1987. Appendix Tables 1.3, 1.5 and 1.6)
* excluding Scotland

3.   Examination of workforce patterns demonstrates the need for a continuing forum for debate on these issues. Some are of concern to the Central Council for Education and Training in Social Work (CCETSW), some to employers or trade unions, but there is no overall body which is formally charged with workforce planning. A group representing the main interested parties could carry out this task, without which there is the continued risk of unintended and unmonitored consequences of decisions.

Principles for Setting Staff Requirements

4.   It is clearly important that there should be sufficient staff to carry out the tasks required of them in every establishment, but

it is extremely difficult to be prescriptive. If numbers are insufficient, residents' needs will not be met, and staff will often be driven by circumstances to adopt care methods which they know to be unsatisfactory. As a rule of thumb, it should be noted that to maintain one member of daytime staff on duty throughout the day requires a staffing establishment of approximately 3.5 full time equivalent staff, and for night staff the full time equivalent is 2.5. These figures are sometimes startling to people who do not appreciate the fact that services are provided round the clock, and that minimum cover has to be maintained. The Castle Priory Report (1969) has been widely adopted in relation to children's services, and the Social Services Liaison Group Report (1978)—reproduced in 'Staffing Ratios in Residential Establishments: a platform for the 1980s' (Residential Care Association, 1980)—has also been used extensively in the calculation of staffing for other establishments; but both these reports are now dated.

5. The sheer variety of residential services renders meaningless any simple methods of calculating staffing requirements. For example, at one end of the range, cluster developments may only need staff to drop in from time to time, while at the other, intensive units, such as those providing secure accommodation for children, require high staffing ratios around the clock. In between these extremes, most establishments require twenty-four hour staffing in varying numbers to match peaks and troughs in demand, and of varying types of skill and remit. Any guidelines need to take into account two main groups of factors:

—the first relates to the needs of the residents as individuals and of the establishment as a whole. This includes management, administration, personal care, social work, health care, leisure and educational activities. It includes not only what goes on inside the residential setting, but also external work with the local community and residents' families.

—the second relates to the needs of staff. In order to provide a certain level of service, account has to be taken of variables such as staff vacancies, illness, leave and days off, time spent on training, staff meetings and other agency responsibilities. These demands depend on conditions of service, and the levels of stress attached to the work.

Staffing Levels

6.   Staff recruitment is not only about filling vacant posts one by one, but is also about creating and blending together teams, who need to be able to work together to achieve common aims. Every team must be selected to match the tasks that are required of it and must contain a mixture of experience, personal resources, interests and skills. The basis for assessing staffing has to be the identification of residents' needs and the skills required to meet them; for example, properly trained and experienced staff working with behaviourally disordered children may work better as a small tight team while, if staff are untrained and inexperienced, a much larger number may be needed simply to ensure that they retain control of the situation. It should also be noted that a capable person being helped to independence may need just as much staffing support as a chronically dependent person. Thus calculations are complex, and there is an obvious danger of over-emphasising the practical tasks which are easier to quantify.

Organisational Factors

7.   An assessment of the services required by residents may indicate the range and volume of tasks that need to be carried out for them as individuals, but it does not take account of the management of the establishment, minimum cover requirements, training, and other functions such as the supervision of staff and students, which relate to the whole establishment. Consideration has to be given, therefore, to the way in which tasks are grouped for individual staff, and to the deployment of staff, for example through rotas. Standard rotas are imposed by some employers, but elsewhere those in charge of the establishment find their own solution in drawing up rotas which seem sensible. Considerably greater attention should be paid to ways in which staff may be deployed most effectively and senior staff training should prepare them for these responsibilities.

8.   In determining the number of staff required, consideration has to be given to the balance of full-time and part-time staff. Full-time staff provide greater consistency of care, while part-timers offer increased variety and flexibility, for example in providing additional hours standing in for sick colleagues. There are also

less obvious implications: for instance, as it is difficult to attract male part-timers, the exclusive use of part-time staff can lead to an all-female basic care staff.

9.   In developing methods for calculating staffing, account has to be taken of the system of external management. Local authorities work within nationally agreed conditions, which are designed to serve large numbers of other staff. Local authority establishments have a variety of external support systems, such as building maintenance, which supply services but which can take up a lot of staff time is negotiation. In the independent sector, these factors are unlikely to be present to anything like the same degree. We recommend that the DHSS should set up a working party, containing representatives of the main interested parties, to identify ways in which staffing requirements may best be calculated.

Recruitment and Selection

10.   We would expect employing agencies to develop and implement equal opportunities policies so that applicants are not discriminated against on grounds of race, colour, gender, sexual orientation and disabilities. In some situations positive action will be needed to recruit staff from ethnic minority communities, where they are under-represented on staffing establishments, and to enable them to move subsequently into more senior posts. It was evident, for example, in some of the children's establishments which we visited, that there were not enough black staff to act as appropriate role models for the children of Afro-Caribbean and mixed-race parentage who had been placed there. It is important when considering how to achieve an appropriate complement of staff to avoid creating the conditions in which institutional racism and racialism are allowed to flourish. Sensitive recruitment and selection policies are needed to overcome such problems and all agencies are recommended to formulate and apply them.

11.   When selecting staff it is important that the selectors themselves should include people with first-hand knowledge of residential work and of the qualities and skills it requires. To promote equal opportunities there should always be some ethnic minority representation on selection panels where posts are being filled for establishments with residents from these backgrounds.

It is important to have women represented on selection panels, particularly for senior posts, bearing in mind that these are at present largely filled by men.

12.   Considerably more work must be done to identify the attributes and skills which people possess and need to develop for their specific roles and tasks, for these personal qualities and skills rarely appear to be spelled out. Employers must be explicit about what they are looking for, and uppermost in their minds must be the basic values underlying the services they provide, the needs of the residents, and the composition of the existing staff team.

13.   A commonly held view of care work is that it is unskilled and consists of little more than domestic chores. It is seen as particularly suitable for women, consistent with their traditional roles in the home and as carers. A consequence is that the work is seen as less appropriate for men, and there are few male care assistants. Residential work, like other occupations in which women are numerically predominant, is low paid, with low status, and poor conditions of service. Add to this the lack of training, adequate planning and support for staff, and it becomes clear that residential work does not yield such high expectations as, for instance, field social work. We believe that changes in the status, conditions and training support for staff are necessary to redress these imbalances.

The Need for Better Staff Planning

14.   Many people employed to work in residential settings, particularly in direct service roles, are recruited without either previous experience or preparatory training. Several letters received by the Committee from residential workers included statements like 'I came into the work by accident.' A care assistant who has worked for six years in a local authority home for elderly people writes: 'I obtained the position from the job centre. I had no experience whatsoever of that particular type of work as I had always been in accounts.'

15.   It is fortunate that people are prepared to give up previous careers for one in which the rewards and satisfaction are so uncertain. However, we should not lose sight of the fact that getting hold of the right staff is something of a lottery and many

enter the work with their eyes shut only to be rudely awakened. Though some stay the course, many do not. This is only to be expected since they may receive little guidance or information about what they will be doing, or about the problems they are likely to encounter. Few are offered or taken through any form of systematic induction training on appointment. Reports of high rates of staff turnover and frequent absenteeism as a result of stress and sickness come as no surprise.

16.   As many who have submitted evidence have stated, there is a notable lack of structured opportunities to progress towards increased responsibilities and promotion. It is also difficult to move between different types of residential work and between residential work and day care or field social work, and between the statutory, voluntary and private sectors. Former residential workers who move into field posts on completion of their Certificate of Qualification in Social Work (CQSW) often tend to dissociate themselves in career terms from their previous experience. As part of every social worker's career pattern, there should be much more possibility of interchange between the different forms of social work; residential work should not be seen merely as a stepping stone for a career in field social work.

17.   It is true that people's motives for seeking jobs in residential settings vary. For some, residential work is undertaken from a strong sense of vocation or wish to develop a career in personal care; for others it is an opportunity to earn a living by performing socially useful work without their necessarily having any expectations of a career. For some it may be no more than a welcome source of part-time earnings. Many residential staff are clearly contented to work in caring roles without looking for promotion. For those wishing to develop careers, however, there are severe problems, including lack of qualifying training opportunities, the difficulty of moving from work in the specialist setting, and hierarchical structures which do not permit responsibilities to be gradually reduced towards the end of careers without loss to pension arrangements. The total impact of such factors is that many staff, particularly at senior levels, are trapped in high stress roles which lead to burn-out or unsatisfactory professional practice. Research into ways in which residential staff join or leave is needed to clarify the picture; together with measures such as conversion courses which will permit movement to other settings, and the introduction of pension arrangements permitting earlier retirement.

18. We accept that not everyone who obtains a post in a residential services setting is seeking or should be expected to follow a career in social work. We would, however, encourage policies whereby every person who seeks to pursue professional and career development should be given opportunities to do so. This would entail amongst other things ensuring that there are well-established systems for supervising and appraising progress, in addition to the provision of relevant training which we discuss in the following chapter.

Pay and Employment Conditions

19. More than most other jobs in social services, residential work has been equated with domestic and family duties, which themselves are poorly remunerated in this country, on the implicit assumption that parenting and the care of dependent relatives are unskilled and undemanding responsibilities. In the case of residential work, which is particularly geared to meet the needs of the most dependent, vulnerable and disturbed, it is especially inappropriate that the rewards should be pitched so low. In view of the high levels of skill and experience required to carry out the task, an equally high level of reward is warranted if staff are to be attracted, and not lost once recruited.

20. Wages are clearly much more variable in the private and voluntary sectors than in the local authority sector. In our view, pay for the same work rates should be broadly comparable across the three sectors. In local authorities residential staff, with the exception of a small band of senior staff in charge of large establishments, have been consistently less well paid than field work colleagues, while having to work unsocial hours, and a longer basic working week into the bargain. It is no surprise therefore that the value placed upon residential staff, implicit in these conditions, is reflected in their status in other respects, such as influence in decision-making or in priority for training.

Need for Unified Pay and Conditions in Local Authorities

21. A major issue in local authority pay systems is that the majority of tending tasks are carried out by staff paid as manual

workers—care assistants in residential settings and home helps in the domiciliary services—while their managers are paid as officers. (The corresponding posts in child care already have officer status.) This has always been divisive and dates back to the class structure of the workhouse. Although we have noted NUPE's reservations about the risk of financial detriment to their members, our evidence suggests there is widespread support for the abandonment of the division and for redefining all care posts as officers or a professional equivalent. We recommend accordingly. The evidence from the British Association of Social Workers (BASW) Project Group for Service Conditions, NALGO and many others—and also the Audit Commission's study on community care which addresses these issues in some depth—has convinced us of the need for a social services workforce unified in its conditions of service and salary structure. The potential benefits include enabling staff to transfer from one type of work to another, which would help employers to recruit and deploy resources to areas of greatest need, and enhance workers' career prospects. We further recommend that employers and trade unions should make a concerted effort to introduce integrated pay and conditions for all social services staff.

The Residents point of view

22. It is important that employment conditions should be designed to enable staff to meet residents' needs effectively. We have been given examples of changes in employment conditions which have had unintended consequences. For example it has been pointed out that realistic rent levels, introduced about five years ago in most local authorities, drove many staff out of being resident. While this gave a welcome break to some, it also changed the nature of the small group home, widening the gap between foster care and the shift-based approach now common in residential establishments.

23. National employment conditions should provide a firm but flexible framework to meet the variety of service needs. For example, a 39 hour week may be too long in high-stress establishments, while in those akin to a fostering model with independent residents, periods of supervision on call may suffice. Different

sets of arrangements need to be developed and negotiated separately according to the aims and methods of a particular establishment. If staff are to meet consumers' needs individually, they must be able to respond flexibly and inventively. Unfortunately, in determining conditions of service, those most affected—the residents—are quite powerless and the circumstances in which they live are, in the present system, initially negotiated by people who only have second-hand knowledge of the work. In our view there is a need for employers to examine how different staffing arrangements affect residents' lives, particularly the lives of children and young people in care. Moreover, we believe that residents should be involved in this process and their views taken into account.

Use of Staff Agencies

24. The use of agency staff and peripatetic staff are both ways of plugging gaps which should not be there. Some London establishments, for example, appear to survive on agency staffing, and this cannot be seen as acceptable practice, since consistency of care and staff identification with residents are inevitably undermined. Staffing establishments should be sufficient to absorb minor levels of absence, without the need to introduce additional outside staff. While staffing agencies may perform a valuable service in providing relief and temporary cover in times of crisis, they should not be used to cover up defects in recruitment and staff planning. The same applies to the recruitment and deployment of temporary foreign staff, young people seeking experience, staff employed on Manpower Services programmes, Youth Training Schemes, etc. If people from any of these categories are to be employed other than on an occasional basis, steps must be taken to integrate them within a coherent staffing framework, which involves consideration of appropriate induction, supervision and support, staff development and training programmes.

The Role of Trade Unions

25. It has been surprising that out of more than 200 submissions of evidence only 13 came from organisations specifically

representative of those either working in, or professionally concerned with, residential care; among these only six would be strictly be classed as trade unions.

26.   We have been particularly disappointed to receive comments from only one, NUPE, of the 3 unions which organise the Care Assistants currently graded in the local government service as manual workers—and that at the last moment. Noting that the ADSS, BASW and NALGO all gave strong support to the establishment of a single salary structure for all workers in residential care except those doing purely domestic tasks, the lack of response from GMBATU and TWGU to the Committee's requests, backed by the TUC, for their views is very much regretted. While there has been reason for disappointment at the apparent lack of interest among the trade unions concerned, NALGO's interest and detailed evidence have proved most helpful.

27.   The quality of residential care will always be dependent on the quality of staff, and staff to give of their best must be satisfied with their pay and conditions of employment. Much of what we recommend—for example, unified pay and conditions for all types of social work—may well prove to be dependent on the whole-hearted cooperation of professional associations and trade unions.

28.   Trade unions have an important role to play; we wish them success in seeking better levels of pay for their members in work which is often stressful and demanding and, in particular, in pressing for unified pay and conditions between residential and field social work. We believe the relevant trade unions are well placed, in conjunction with professional organisations like BASW and SCA, to insist on their members receiving the training they require before undertaking the delicate and skilled caring tasks expected of them. We would particularly hope to enlist their support in ensuring that none of their members is asked to undertake responsibility for an incontinent or confused elderly person without first receiving adequate instruction in the principles and practice of successful care.

29.   We feel bound, however, to express our misgivings about certain other aspects of trade union activity concerning residential care services. We have been distrubed to hear of instances in which trade union opposition has been mobilised to obstruct the closure of obsolete local authority residential establishments, and even the conversion of shared rooms to single occupancy. Whether the motive is to maintain the level of local authorities'

residential provision or, more narrowly, to resist the erosion of the job opportunities open to their own members, we can only reaffirm that consideration of the welfare and best interests of residents should always be paramount.

30. We would also expect trades unions to support agency initiatives to develop and apply equal opportunities policies that, amongs other aims, would counteract institutional racism. This would include encouraging rather than blocking strategies of positive action to ensure that more members of ethnic minorities are given promotional positions.

Recommendations

The DHSS should identify ways in which residential staffing requirements may best be calculated, and how staff may best be deployed.

The grading of care staff as manual workers should cease and their posts be redefined as officers or the professional equivalent.

Employers and trade unions should make a concerted effort to introduce integrated pay and employment conditions for all social services staff.

Every effort should be made to recruit staff from ethnic minority communities, where they are under-represented on staffing establishments, and to enable them to move subsequently into more senior posts.

CHAPTER NINE

Staff Support and Development

Stress in residential work

1. Our evidence, our visits and our own experience make
clear that providing the care required by people who live in residential establishments can be not only extremely rewarding but
also very stressful. Some of the letters we received from individual staff revealed how much they enjoyed their work which gave
them satisfaction in ways which few other jobs provide. Equally,
other letters and some of the formal evidence showed that
residential work is stressful and identified some of the major
causes. They fall into two broad categories, those arising from the
conditions in which the work is done, and those arising from the
nature of the work.

2. As we have noted in the previous chapter, unsatisfactory
conditions of service, low salaries and inadequate staffing
arrangements can all prevent care workers giving of their best.
The failure of management—whether the external manager or the
most senior person in the establishment—to provide staff with the
combination of support and freedom to act which they need, is
another factor. Some of the external causes of stress must be dealt
with by the agency, but even if these causes are removed the job
itself remains inherently stressful.

3. Stress arises from the nature of the people who are in residence and from the fact that the working situation is a residential
one (even if staff live out). Young people in residential care are
often deeply distressed and at times despairing; life has treated
them badly and they come into residence with all the emotional
scars of earlier experiences. Elderly people may enter residential
care in a state of shock, suffering from feelings of loss at having
had to abandon their accustomed way of life. People with a mental illness are often deeply distressed by their condition, anxious

and depressed. Working alongside people who are suffering from such painful feelings is bound to be difficult, especially since the work demands that staff relate to residents, and relating means feeling the pain of the other person.

4. Being with people who are emotionally distressed is always a strain, and staff in residential establishments are exposed to this strain for the whole of their working day. And this means being not with one person whose life is difficult, but with a group who may need help not only to live with themselves but to live with one another.

5. Staff in some residential establishments face daily the possibility of physical violence, and in almost all establishments staff will have to deal with people who are angry and who may vent that anger on them—whether or not they deserve it. Some jobs are physically demanding and unpleasant, such as heavy lifting, and the management of incontinence—practical duties which of themselves can give rise to stress.

6. Staff in residential establishments have not only to cope with residents' distress and disturbance, but also with the impact which this has on their own emotions. Dealing with other people's exposed feelings tends to stir up and expose similar feelings in ourselves so that underlying emotions of fear, sadness and anger are brought to the surface. Staff may become more vulnerable as a result of this, and of not knowing how to respond to the behaviour and emotions of others; they may fear the strong feelings aroused in themselves, be they of anger or love.

Coping with stress

7. We now turn to the kind of help which staff need in order to cope with these stresses, in whatever setting. For example, staff working with disturbed adolescents need to know that there will be an immediate response to a call for help or advice. Skilled senior staff will need to help them manage crises in a constructive manner and even to plan for them, rather than just allowing them to erupt. Managers must share with the staff who are in direct contact with adolescents the responsibility for disruptive and dangerous behaviour, assessing with them its causes and seeking to learn together. Violent and dangerous incidents will always occur in such settings but staff must always feel supported and

never blamed or abandoned at frightening times. Skilfully managed, such crises can result in increased cohesion and confidence amongst staff, and can give to adolescents a sense of safety from their own potential destructiveness and uncontrolled behaviour.

8.   Our evidence made clear that stress arose not just from interactions between residents and staff but also within the staff group. It is essential that management offers positive and constructive leadership and guidance. Mechanisms are needed to enable problems to be shared as they arise so that they are resolved and do not get out of proportion and become unmanageable. Thus we recommend that regular staff meetings are held in every establishment, as frequently as the pressure and complexity of the work require.

9.   Problems that may be present elsewhere become pressing in the residential setting and therefore a whole network of support is needed, including clear agency guidelines on risk-taking and residents' rights, and procedures for the care of residents with communicable diseases such as AIDS.

10.   Senior staff who should be expected to provide support are themselves working under considerable pressures, and may have been denied the training that would equip them to give effective supervision. We cannot state too strongly our belief in the importance of professional leadership from senior staff and managers. In most large establishments this will not be exercised by one person alone, but by the senior staff group who need to be able to work as a team and assume collective responsibility. We support the need for resources both to develop effective supervision programmes at all levels of residential practice and to train the appropriate people. We also consider that staff should have access to independent counsellors who can provide help and advice on a range of staff welfare issues.

11.   We are in sympathy with the aims of a campaign to promote better staff care recently launched by *Social Work Today*. As Jeff Hopkins wrote in the launch article (*Social Work Today*, Sept 14 1987, (p10):

> Staff are the most important and expensive resource in the personal social services. They are required to operate, as a matter of routine, in situations which are highly distressing for all those involved. . .Yet their employers largely abandon them to their own fates. More money is spent on painting the outside of the building than in maintaining the staff within it. The task facing the campaign is to turn that attitude around.

Staff development and training

12.   Training appears in the formal evidence almost twice as often as any other subject. Coming strongly through our evidence is a view that problems relating to training cannot be addressed and resolved in isolation from wider issues concerning conditions of service, salary structures, and the need for better staff planning, recruitment and selection. These need to be tackled comprehensively. Although there appears to be a consensus on training problems and issues—the current situation being regarded as wholly inadequate—there are contrasting and divergent views on the solutions needed. If there is agreement, it is that there is a need for improvements at all levels and for some assurance that in future people are appropriately trained and qualified to meet the different requirements of the range of jobs across the services. We would add that we see an obligation on individual staff members to take some responsibility for their own development.

13.   Many correspondents complain that insufficient resources are being devoted to training; others complain that the training given is inappropriate. A small minority have suggested that training is irrelevant. For example, a group of care assistants looking after elderly people cast doubt on the value of training 'because our job consists of mostly domestic tasks, you don't really need many qualifications'. This appears to be an instance where low expectations of the job have bred correspondingly low expectations about training.

14   Usually doubts about training focus less on the actual need than on organisation and methods. One commonly voiced concern is that too much attention is being paid to the pursuit of paper qualifications, implying that the training offered is insufficiently relevant. From discussions with former students and other sources it would seem that many courses for the Certificate of Qualification in Social Work (CQSW) have yet to develop programmes that meet the specific learning needs of prospective residential practitioners. This curriculum issue needs to be tackled with some urgency both in relation to the current CQSW and courses for the future Qualifying Diploma in Social Work (QDSW).

15.   Regrettably, because of the failure to improve the standing of residential work, a CQSW is seen as a passport out from low status and low paid work, involving unsocial hours. The remedy, surely, is to improve the conditions of service and

salaries in residential work. We note that the national training courses are interpreted very differently by individual local authorities and by employers in private and voluntary sectors. In the agencies which we visited, for example, the qualifications required on appointment for managers and other senior staff were different in each case. Although some employers seem to have raised their expectations in recent years for senior residential staff to be qualified, by way of CQSW or the Certificate in Social Service (CSS), we have not encountered an agency that has formulated a policy on the posts requiring qualified staff.

16.   It is evident that the wide spectrum of skills required for residential work is far from matched in current practice by either the conditions of service and salaries or the training made available. For example:

> Is it right that residential social workers, Grade 1, unqualified, are expected to run children's groups, offer bereavement and sexual counselling, practice high techniques in management control and act as a child's advocate in all situations they become involved in? (E169)

The answer is clearly no, and our impression is that such situations are fairly widespread. Moreover, we go further than this and argue that very similar abilities to those described for work with children are required for all kinds of residential work. The work of care assistants with elderly people, far from being only domestic (to refer back to an earlier point), includes abilities to work with groups and as a group member, to support residents in their experiences of separation, loss and grief; to offer sensitive supervision to those suffering from confusion or loss of memory, or subject to wandering; and to act as an advocate on behalf of residents with a complaint or grievance.

17.   These are not the only abilities required, but they provide a good indication of the levels at which skills should be developing if the services are to be of the highest possible quality. For any individual, these may well seem daunting requirements. Employers will need to identify staff with talents and propensities for work with people with particular needs, and to enhance these by a specialist component in their training.

Qualifying training

18. The facts speak for themselves. The 1986 survey by the Local Government Training Board states that, of residential and day care staff, only 7.5 per cent working with adults and 11.5 per cent working with children have a social work qualification; these percentages increase to 24 per cent and 34 per cent respectively, if non-social work qualification, e.g. in teaching or nursing are included. These figures compare with 67 per cent in field social work who have a social work qualification, and 71.5 per cent when other qualifications are included. We find these figures disappointing.

19. We are reporting at a time when proposals are being put forward by CCETSW for the reorganisation of qualifying training (Care for Tomorrow, October 1987) bringing together CSS and CQSW awards to form a new award—the QDSW. Their proposals aim at increasing the length of qualifying training for social work from 2 years to 3 years, stating the competencies required of qualifying social workers, and defining the role of the employers in basic training, in partnership with educational institutions. They also envisage a lower qualification, the Certificate in Social Care (CSC), which will be developed under the auspices of the National Council for Vocational Qualification (NCVQ). We welcome the general thrust of these proposals, which are of major importance for staff in the residential services. Two points, however, need making forcefully:

(i) all that we have said about the complexity of the work and the knowledge and skills required, makes it clear that people filling managerial and senior posts in residential work require a full social work qualification.

(ii) at all levels of the proposed training there will be an element of social work, and this means that no rigid distinction between the content of QDSW and CSC is possible. We therefore welcome the proposals that holders of the CSC should be able to progress to QDSW training and that holders of the Advanced Social Care Certificate be exempted from all or part of the first year of QDSW.

20. We recognise that it will not immediately be practicable for all senior posts becoming vacant to be filled by qualified staff.

We therefore recommend that it should be the policy of every employing authority and agency that within five years, every managerial and senior post should be so filled. For these posts the qualification should include a management element. If this is lacking, the qualification should be augmented by appropriate further training.

21. Some agencies accept nursing qualifications as relevant for residential care work e.g. with the elderly, but in doing so they ignore some fundamental differences between social work and nursing. We recommend that people with nursing or other professional backgrounds moving into residential service work should receive relevant 'conversion training' on an in-service basis, and those appointed to senior posts should be expected to undertake professional qualifying training in social work as early as possible.

22. We are well aware that whatever plans are made about training, there will remain an enormous backlog of staff, including senior staff, who have either not had the benefit of any training, or whose original background was not that of residential social work. These staff, many of whom do an excellent job and will continue to serve for years to come, must not be left behind, but they may well need to be helped through short courses to adjust to the developments we are recommending in this Report. We support the moves towards a validation system for all informal and formal training initiatives, which would ultimately lead to an award of equivalent standing to a social work qualification for experienced staff without qualifications. We appeal to all validating bodies—including the Industrial Lead Body for the Welfare Industry, CCETSW, ADSS, BASW and SCA—to give speedy effect to such a system.

Further and advanced training

23. Training does not end at qualifying level. We also seek to extend the opportunities for further and advanced training, which is indispensible for staff as they progress in their careers and enlarge their range of responsibilities and corresponding need for new skills. In particular, agencies should make efforts to ensure that staff from ethnic minorities are introduced from the outset to continuing staff development and training opportunities, which enable them to progress to senior positions.

Further and advanced training is also important for middle and senior staff who have responsibilities for planning and managing services at a strategic level. They need to have the expertise which in our view can best be achieved through practice in residential work plus training. Relatively few managers currently in post can claim to have the combination of experience of residential work, a relevant professional qualification and appropriate training in management of those services.

The goals

24.   We see the goals of an effective staff development and training policy as being:

(i) an ethos in which the needs and interests of the residents are paramount. This in turn requires the staff to be consistently seeking to change and adapt their own responses to the changing and varied needs of the residents. It further requires a commitment by staff members to learning as a continuous process; and an investment by employers of human, financial and material resources to create the means by which this learning can occur.

(ii) staff, working as individuals or as a team, being provided with a variety of opportunities to acquire the knowledge and skills relevant to their roles and range of tasks; to their needs as individuals, and to their future jobs and careers. In stating this we recognise that not every residential worker will be seeking a career in social work. But to ensure that the residents receive a good service, it is crucial that every staff member should be considered to have some training needs; to meet these, annual staff appraisals should include career planning for each individual.

(iii) staff whose responsibilities change or increase as a result of obtaining promotion, transfer or different job specifications, should also receive training matched to their changing roles and tasks. This applies particularly to people who move up from being basic grade practitioners to supervising other staff.

Training plans for every establishment

25.   We recommend, that every establishment—in statutory, voluntary and private sectors—should be required to draw up a staff training plan which should be subject to inspection procedures. The plan should be closely related to the aims and objectives of the establishment, and to its specific function and tasks. Although specific training plans will vary one from another there should be a common basis as follows:

(i) *Induction training*
    Every new member of staff should be given an appropriate induction programme. Also, where establishments are undergoing changes of functions, staff should receive some training in their new duties.

(ii) *Core training*
    Each establishment's training plan can be expected to contain some core elements, in which every member of staff will have some training. The core elements will need to be negotiated according to the purposes of the setting and needs of the residents, though it is expected that some common training criteria will be followed. Anti-racist and anti-sexist training should be integral.

(iii) *Team development*
    Because residential services work requires a high level of collaboration, careful attention should be paid to team development. This may need the services of an external consultant. All establishments should be expected to hold regular staff meetings and to seek ways of developing and improving their information and communication systems. Study days, when staff are given time to learn together, are an effective means of jointly working through problems and facing new situations.

(iv) *Regular appraisal of training needs*
    Every staff member should have regular opportunities to discuss and plan their training needs as part of a wider process of professional supervision. This process should begin on appointment and be followed through so that each person has a personal training plan. An establishment's training plan will emerge from the sum of individual plans and from the team training needs of the staff group as a whole.

Recommendations

All senior posts should be filled by staff with social work qualifications, and it should be the policy of every employer to fill such posts with qualified staff by 1993.

Every establishment should be required to draw up a staff training plan and this should be subject to inspection procedures.

People with non-social work qualification who move into residential work should receive conversion training, and those appointed to senior posts should be expected to undertake qualifying training in social work as early as possible.

Regular staff meetings should be held, and used to assist the development of staff as individuals and groups.

CHAPTER TEN

Some Particular Needs

Ways of Looking at Needs

1. The starting point of our deliberations was to look at the needs of different groups, as do the Research Reviews in Volume II of this Report. Traditionally residential services have been provided for a range of specific user groups, mostly identified by their disability or problem, so that individuals have only been able to receive a service if labelled and grouped with others in a similar predicament. We rapidly decided that problems which people face are often common to more than one group, and sometimes to all groups. Everyone needs care in childhood and most of us would find the journey through life impossible at times without companions through life impossible at times without companions and support. It is the legislation, systems and policies which, by treating people of different ages and with different disabilities in different ways, accentuate distinctions.

2. Because the Committee wish to emphasize above all the importance of the individual and their right of choice, we doubted the relevance of making extensive separate reference to particular user groups. Much of the preceding chapters can be seen to apply in equal measure to children, young people, adults, elderly and aged people. Most people, regardless of age or extent of disability, can communicate personal preference and choice, provided there is a will to listen to them and to understand what they have to say. Moreover, people wish to be seen as having strengths as well as weaknesses, aspirations and abilities as well as problems—and as individuals in a social context rather than as members of special disadvantaged groups.

3. Individual wishes may have to be tempered in the interests of proper nurturing, education, treatment or safety; for those with serious intellectual impairment, the extremely disturbed and

the elderly mentally ill, liberty itself may need to be limited. Some with extreme disabilities have a need for support throughout life, and for them its absence would mean that potential milestones of achievement might be delayed or remain for ever beyond reach.

4. A society that wants all its citizens to function as independently as possible for as long as possible has to be prepared to meet some special needs. Becoming and remaining a self-supporting citizen is a challenge to the most able; young people with physical or intellectual impairments have special developmental needs; pathways to recovery must be provided for those set back through illness, injury or addiction. For those with disabilities which have debarred them from ordinary learning experiences and for those who have not enjoyed the security, nurturing and modelling of family life, progression to independence can be painful and daunting. Those providing all such people with residential services need to have preparation for independent life as their prime objective. As faculties diminish risks increase. While those in full command of reason should not be denied the freedom to choose how they wish to live, those who have lost their self-help skills and awareness of what is around them must be protected from harm. We have to learn how to enable increasing numbers of elderly mentally ill people to relinquish their independence as gradually and painlessly as possible.

5. Although as a matter of principle, we do not wish to see people labelled in terms of their disabilities, nevertheless our Report would not do justice to the evidence received if we did not, at least briefly, present separately the main issues put to us by or on behalf of children, and of adults with particular problems. We have not included a section on those elderly people whose handicap is increasing physical frailty (as distinct from mental impairment) because we feel that their needs have been sufficiently discussed in previous chapters.

Children

6. Children's needs differ from those of other groups, because for them the whole purpose is satisfactory growth and development. In their case to separate issues of accommodation

from services and care is not really possible as it is with adults—
except perhaps for those young people who are at the threshold
of adult life. Thus whilst many of our recommendations apply
equally to children and adults, the circumstances producing the
need for children's services, the aims of intervention and many
of the ensuing issues warrant separate consideration.

7. Our comments on the role of residential children's
provision need to be read, as we have tried to stress throughout
this Report, in a context of evaluating services as a whole. We
start from the assumption that the broad thrust of social services
strategies will be to prevent family breakdown. We would hope
that compulsory admissions to care are made only as a last resort,
and admission is arranged on a voluntary basis, wherever
possible.

8. We share the concern expressed in some of our evidence
at the lack of any national child care strategy or overview. The
result is that there is no consistency in policies nor in levels of
provision and standards across the country. Further, there is a
pressing need to examine the relationships between the various
concerned services—health, education, juvenile justice and the
personal social services. Demands for residential care inevitably
partly reflect pressures on schools, courts, and the preventative
services concerned with children. In this context it is worth noting
that a large number of children are placed in boarding schools
because of emotional, behavioural or family problems; and that
others find their way into the penal system. The requirement
therefore is twofold: (i) a national strategy spearheaded by the
DHSS that takes such interconnections into account and (ii) local
strategies that reflect these same realities.

9. It is also important to note the shifts in policy during the
last decade or so which have resulted in many changes in services
for children. These have been partly due to recognition of the
detrimental effects of long term institutional care and, as a result,
alternative and in many cases more helpful forms of intervention
have become accepted practice. Thus the increased use made of
foster care has led to a marked reduction in the number of
residential establishments catering for children whose own
families cannot look after them. Financial as well as policy
considerations have contributed to this, although the financial
argument is now less strong, since properly supported foster care
has not proved to be a cheap alternative.

10. Unfortunately, admission of children to residential care is

too often the result of a crisis or a failure of planning; this has led to residential care becoming a residual resource instead of providing the necessary element of choice among a range of other services. For example, the increased use of fostering has resulted in a corresponding increase in the risk of foster breakdown, which recent evidence found to be disconcertingly high in some authorities. Many of the consequences of foster breakdowns have to be borne by residential services, which become used as a last resort without necessarily being organised to meet the tasks required of them. Many managers and field workers in social services departments are ambivalent towards residential services, with debilitating effects on residential staff and damage to their charges. Voluntary agencies are similarly caught up in this process as they cannot maintain group living accommodation for children and young people if the places they provide are not taken up by SSDs. All these developments have created a climate of uncertainty, damaging to the well-being of children in care.

Positive Role of Residential Care

11.   Our task has been, therefore, to identify the needs which residential children's provision can meet and the conditions required for it to discharge its various tasks effectively. We assert that residential services for children do have a positive role to play, so long as aims and objectives are clearly defined and the variety of provision results in an extension of choice. In this respect we have welcomed the evidence from the National Association of Young People in Care (E148) which is particularly well placed to provide a consumer voice. NAYPIC asserts that some young people prefer a children's home and choose not to be fostered; some young people find families, either their own or an alternative, difficult to cope with but can and do settle in a children's home; some young people simply need 'time out' of a family because of a crisis or difficulties coming to a head. NAYPIC summed up its evidence in one sentence—'We see residential care as playing an important part in an integrated community-based child care service, but at the same time we would like to see improvements made.'

12.   The recent DHSS White Paper *The Law on Child Care and Family Services* (Cm 62) points out that residential services for

children and young people should not necessarily be seen as a mark of failure either on the part of the family or of those working in support of them (para 21); and we welcome the proposal to change the law so that 'local authorities will no longer be under an obligation to diminish the need to receive children into care' (para 22). The emphasis on the 'positive aim of providing care away from the family home as a means of providing support to the family and preventing the risk of long term family break-down' is in line with the many pleas in the evidence sent to us for purposeful use of residential care.

13. Our evidence indicates that the main continuing need for residential child care service lies in the following directions:

(i) *Respite care*

Respite care, by providing periods of planned relief in residence, is of the greatest importance, enabling both natural and foster families to continue to care for their disturbed or handicapped members. This relief also needs to be available on an emergency basis to help natural and foster families to overcome crises without detracting from their ongoing responsibility.

(ii) *Preparation for permanent placement*

Residential centres are needed to prepare children for what are hoped to be lasting arrangements for them. It is evident that an increasing number of children who have experienced multiple breakdowns in previous living arrangements need a structured, caring, nurturing environment linked with a realistic plan for their future. This may be to prepare them for a return to their families or for foster care or adoption. Residential care may also be needed as a staged transition from hospital to family care and for children with severe disabilities requiring inte-grated education and care. (Barnardo's E149: p.4).

(iii) *Keeping families together*

Residential provision should be used to enable brothers and sisters to stay together. The importance of keeping families together is argued by Professor R A Parker in his chapter on children in Volume II: 'The whole question of sibling relationships warrants closer and more imaginative investigation. They provide a link with the past as well as with the future.' Evidence from young people shows that they clearly value being with their brothers and sisters and dislike being separated from them. Research has also indicated that it is important for links between children and their parents, and other relatives such as grand-parents, uncles and aunts to be maintained; and that this is often easier to achieve from a residential base than from a fostering placement. We therefore recommend that residential provision should be used to enable brothers and sisters to stay together, and that keeping them together should normally take precedence over a policy to foster every child.

(iv) *Care and control*

For a small minority of children identified as a risk to themselves or others, a certain amount of specialist provision will be required. Whilst we do not like the idea of secure provision being needed within a modern, progressive child-care system, it is preferable to having young people locked up in adult institutions, which is often the only alternative. We have been disturbed by the evidence summarised by Parker on the frequency with which youth custody and detention centres are used for young people, although we welcome the fact that their use now seems to be stabilising and even decreasing. When young people are admitted to secure accommodation it is imperative that their basic rights are protected; in this connection we would commend the draft regulations submitted by the Children's Legal Centre to the DHSS in 1984, which seem to us to provide sound legal safeguards and a code of good practice.

(v) *Therapeutic provision*

For socially and emotionally damaged children therapeutic provision has an important role to play. Some therapeutic communities, such as Peper Harow and the Cotswold Community, are acknowledged both nationally and inter-nationally to be centres of excellence. We would also commend the work of residential family homes such as the Frimhurst Family Centre, where children and their parents do not have to be separated and the training and counselling offered can be particularly relevant in cases of suspected but not proven abuse. Alternative forms of therapeutic provision, based on behavioural approaches, have also been found to be valuable.

Aims of Residential Provision

14. Respect for the individual, the philosophy underlying all our recommendations, applies equally to children and is well expressed in the evidence sent to us by the Children's Society (E147), who refer to their work as reflecting 'the basic Christian beliefs: that our actions should be guided by love and a sense of the importance of every human being; that differences between people enrich our lives; and that we are deprived and diminished when another person is devalued or oppressed.' To children and young people, who will often have suffered considerable hardship, privation and disruption to their lives, we owe opportunities to develop in conditions of security and stability, and skilled and informed assistance with any besetting problems. They also need to feel safe from previous experiences which have led to their admission to care, and to know that they will not be rejected when they act out their feelings.

15. Particular attention needs to be paid to the needs of young people from ethnic minority groups. Children of Afro-Caribbean or mixed-race parentage tend to be over-represented in the child care population, and often suffer further, while in care, because of insensitivity to and neglect of their specific needs, and lack of staff from their own ethnic background. NAYPIC has suggested that black children should be able to choose whether to be placed in a mixed-race or an all black setting, and be free to join the 'Black In-Care Group' if they so wish.

Admission to care

16. When decisions have to be taken about placement, it is important that the wishes of young people and their parents should be respected as required by law. This requires adequate information about the options and a discussion of their relative advantages and disadvantages, so that an informed choice can be made which has the support and agreement of all concerned. We are aware that there may be circumstances which make this difficult, and that lack of resources is often a serious constraint on choice. But these factors should not be allowed to override the underlying principle of developing and using resources in response to the expressed needs and preferences of potential

users, and of negotiating agreements where interests conflict. In this connection, the National Children's Bureau has noted that research in America has shown a markedly lower breakdown rate in placements to which children have given their consent beforehand.

17. The emphasis that we place on the right to be involved in the choice of placement implies the need for a wide variety of resources. We therefore view with some caution the policies which have resulted in local authorities closing all their children's establishments—as in Warwickshire, for example. It is of course important that unsatisfactory and inadequate provision should not be allowed to continue, and our thesis is predicated on the maintenance of a variety of provision which is of high quality. Nevertheless we firmly believe that there are circumstances in which group living will be the preferred choice and that the appropriate provision, which is not necessarily in the form of large establishments, needs to be made available and developed.

Ensuring Quality of Life

18. Children and young people in care are entitled to a number of basic provisions, which serve as a baseline of minimum standards. These include the need to have some personal space, lockers and cupboards which they can lock and retain possession of the key, access to telephones, uncensored correspondence, regular amounts of pocket-money and clothing allowances. Many organisations ensure that these basic provisions are identified and are met as of right, but it is important that they are made subject to regular review and inspection.

19. We continue to be astonished to hear that outmoded institutional practices are still perpetuated and may even be on the increase in some places, e.g. the bulk supply of household stores, the issuing of order forms to buy clothes etc. There seems to be no good reason for residential facilities having different financial arrangements from ordinary households. We cannot state too strongly that these need to be abolished where they exist. Young people being prepared for independent living, should be helped to learn to take full control of their finances and to learn from the consequences of mismanagement.

Education and Health Needs

20.   We endorse the views of the National Children's Bureau, amongst others, that considerably greater importance needs to be attached to the educational needs of children in care. Children's schooling is frequently disrupted as a result of changes in placement and their educational development is not always given the consideration that it merits, which as the Bureau states 'is particularly regrettable in view of the frequent reports from children who have left care that they feel they did not have adequate educational encouragement or opportunity'.

21.   No less regrettable is the frequent neglect of health care. While we would like to see the abolition of routine and largely meaningless medical examinations, children in residential care need a higher standard of medical services—preventive, developmental and curative. Individual health records are too often scant and incomplete, so residential staff should ensure that the record for each child or young person is, as far as possible, filled out and updated. Additionally there is a need for much closer cooperation between education, health and personal social services in regard to children for whom joint action is required; for example, those presenting difficulties at school and home, cases of suspected child abuse, and children placed in care because of school non-attendance.

Complaints Procedure

22.   We regard it as of great importance that every agency should have a formal complaints procedure, and that information about this should be made available to all children and their parents. The existence and use of such procedures could be written into a formal contract between the providing agency and parents and child, which would specify the respective rights, responsibilities and expectations of the parties involved. In this connection, we consider that children in care and their parents should always have access to an independent 'advocate' to whom they can take complaints or grievances, confident that their case will be heard and impartially investigated.

23.   For children who face the possibility of major changes in their lives, a system of guardian ad litem is already provided.

These guardians are, however, brought into play only by the courts and cannot, as the law stands at present, be invoked by children and their families. While we are aware of the problems currently being encountered in developing this service, we are confident that they will be surmounted; and we suggest that the possibility be explored of families and children themselves being able to ask for a guardian ad litem when they are unhappy with the provision being made for them.

Leaving Care

24.   There can be no doubt that the main objective for young people in care is for them eventually to achieve independence in the community. This requires careful preparation from an early period in care, so that they develop the necessary skills to cope with life on their own. What is missing for most young people in care is the interim period between childhood and adulthood, in which other young people can branch out with parental support, financial or otherwise, and where there is a continuing fall-back position when mistakes are made.

25.   Many other things are also required. In particular we would draw attention to the need for adequate accommodation to be made available for young people on leaving care. One example worthy of note is a Dr Barnardo's Sixteen Plus project within the London region, which provides a total package of resources to help youngsters acquire general life skills such as the ability to cook, clean and take care of everyday needs. The project also works at passing on to the youngsters more sophisticated skills that will enable them to deal with prospective employers, the DHSS and other agencies with the right combination of confidence and diplomacy. Another is the National Children's Homes project—The Bridges, Hatfield—which, from a residential base, offers help with finance, employment, education and housing to homeless and rootless young people.

26.   The other major area of need is for young people to receive some continuing support after leaving care to counteract the isolation which frequently prevents them from enjoying their independence. As happens in ordinary families, young people may feel the need to return from time to time to more sheltered forms of living. Regrettably the child care system does not always allow for this, and when it does it is often on a covert, almost illicit

basis, which suggests that the young person has somehow failed. We would like young people to have the opportunity to return to the caring establishment from time to time even though they may be over the statutory leaving age: Barnardo's has formally adopted this as part of its after-care policy. In this context we were disturbed to note from Parker's review a national decline both in the amount of accommodation available for older children in care, and in the use of section 72 of the Child Care Act 1980 which allows authorities to retain young people in care until they are 19 if they are considered unready at 18 to cope on their own. We therefore welcome the Government's proposal, in the context of the White Paper to strengthen the duties on local authorities: (i) to require them 'to advise and assist children and the young people for whom they are caring so as to promote their welfare when that care ends', and (ii) 'to extend the previous duty to advise and befriend all those who leave care after leaving school from 18 years up to the age of 21 years.' (Hansard 14 July 1987: Col 906).

27. We are however extremely concerned about the anticipated effect on these young people of the provisions of the Social Security Act when it comes into operation in April 1988. For unemployed young single people under 25, these provisions will mean a lower rate of income support with no provision in the Social Fund for grants or loans for deposits or rent in advance for accommodation. For young people in low-paid employment Housing Benefit will also be age-related. At the same time there are proposals to transfer the responsibility for meeting the housing element in the board and lodging charge from Income Support to Housing Benefit. This would leave heating, lighting and meals to be met from the income support personal allowances. Unless modified this will be likely to lead to board and lodging ceasing to be an option for unemployed or low-paid young people.

Adults who have Physical Handicaps

28. As a society, we lack sensitivity in the way we perceive adults who find themselves restricted in their functioning. This leads us to make responses more appropriate to the care and

nurture of children or to the care and treatment of illness. The commonly applied label 'disabled' emphasises disability at the expense of ability and, without discussion, assumes dependency. Which one of us would wish to be characterised by what we are unable to do? Which one of us is willing to accept unquestioningly the assumptions made by others about our needs and wishes? One of our respondents wrote from personal experience of physical disability: 'We find this whole enquiry deeply hurtful and frankly very annoying. Once again eminent persons are debating and deciding what will happen in our lives.' There can be little doubt that he spoke for many people with physical handicaps—and probably for users of all kinds of service. Had the Committee not already been committed to the principles of maximising consumer choice and independence, such a response would surely have been salutary.

29. Residential care certainly featured in our evidence as one of the recommended options for some people with physical handicaps, but always in the context of a flexible range of available services. The Special Needs Housing Advisory Service (E192) made the point that legislation encourages 'inward-looking, isolated homes that have to apply rigid categorisations of people in ways that are alien to ordinary living', whereas what would be of great benefit to users is a blurring of the distinction between community and residential services. This conclusion was in keeping with the limited research evidence available to us from Diana Leat's research review in Volume II, which suggests that very few, perhaps less than 5%, of adults with physical handicaps are in some form of residential care, and that many of these entered through force of circumstances rather than through positive choice. The relatively small numbers of people below pensionable age with physical handicaps make them liable to be overlooked, especially in times of economic stringency, and very local residential provision is rarely available. Voluntary organisations have been notably in the lead in providing services and accommodation, but there is still, as for other groups, a shortage of well-designed residential provision and consequently some people are left trapped in hospitals or homes for the elderly. Others find living at home difficult because of the shortage of domiciliary services. To remedy these shortcomings, much closer cooperation is needed between local authorities, health services and voluntary organisations and private provision.

30. The use of scarce residential resources for purposes of

assessment is rightly being called into question. In St Austell, Cornwall a multi-disciplinary team working with disabled people of all ages claims to have made admissions for rehabilitation and assessment almost redundant. A significant feature of this team approach has been the development of expertise and co-ordination in planning and providing services tailored to individual needs.

31.   Three areas of development are urgently required in relation to people with physical handicap: a cultural shift that would accord them the autonomy which is their right; services in accord with the actual—not supposed—needs of individuals and their families; and legislative enlightenment that would liberate resources rather than confining them to rigid modes of traditional provision. We cannot sufficiently emphasise that the essential for most people who have to overcome physical disability is simply cash—sufficient cash to enable them to organise their own lives in their own way. We are writing here of individuals who are adult and lucid, and as varied as the rest of us. For such people to be forced through lack of funds into institutional care which they neither need nor desire can only be seen as society's ultimate affront. We recognise that there are a number of alternative routes by which the necessary assistance could be channelled, and we urge the Government to ensure by one means or another that financial help reaches the individuals and families who need it.

People with Mental Handicap

32.   The support that everyone needs at some periods in life will be required by people with mental handicap in some measure throughout life, but generalised solutions are no more appropriate than they are for anyone else. The thinking that has begun to inform residential provision for the mentally handicapped is outlined in Dorothy Atkinson's research review in Volume II.

33.   Traditional attitudes to people with mental handicap are changing. Segregation and isolation are no longer the rule and institutional modes of provision are in process of decline. Care in the community is the preferred alternative and developments to make it a reality are being created—if too slowly. The challenge

to the hospitals has been to show that they have a vital role to play as resource centres of knowledge, learning and expertise. Nurses were among the first to recognise that people with mental handicaps should live like others in ordinary houses, whether on the hospital campus or elsewhere.

34. The process of change involves new dilemmas. Independent functioning is not the most likely outcome for those who have had a lifetime of protection, support and the kind of care which deprives the individual of ordinary life experiences. Parents who have become accustomed to coping and having to live with the constant imponderable of what will hapen when they are gone, now also have to wonder how their children will survive in the community.

35. The implications for the less able are that they will need to be able to cope in ordinary settings, and their ability to do so will depend largely upon the education, training and learning opportunities made available to them. A philosophy of education and training needs to permeate all service provision and be shared fully by parents, professionals and the public. At its simplest level this would be; that education and training should be designed with the clear aim that when the need arises young people with mental handicap will be able to live with minimum support in ordinary houses in the community. Without a clear statement of objective of this kind it is not possible to monitor what is being made available by service providers nor to measure their achievement. For people with mental handicap it is beyond question that care in the community can only become a reality with a massive contribution from the education service and particularly further education.

36. Supporting people with mental handicap in ordinary houses on a large scale within the community is uncharted territory. Finding and training workers who can live alongside without dominating, and who enable rather than direct, is a crucial challenge for service providers. The extent to which agencies succeed in meeting the demand will closely affect the spread and quality of community provision.

37. The limitations deriving from intellectual impairments cannot be argued away, but at the same time every person of whatever degree of impairment must be seen as an individual. The temptation to impose solutions because what is wanted is not immediately or clearly articulated needs to be resisted, and the assumption that the wishes of parents and children of adult age

are synonymous should be questioned. To protect the rights of the individual, there is a need for an independent advocate who has the ability to listen to and understand all viewpoints and put forward acceptable alternatives, taking into account the availability of resources.

38. In a period of change it is tempting to abandon all that has gone before. People with mental handicaps are, however, among the most vulnerable in society and could be put at great risk unless the alternatives are proven and apt. Rather than losing faith in what they are doing, providers of traditional services should be encouraged to demonstrate their capacity to respond to new objectives in helping people with mental handicap to take an ordinary and constructive place within the community.

Adults who are mentally ill

39. There was a lengthy period during which mentally ill people were kept in large isolated mental hospitals, partly to insulate them from the adverse responses of others, partly to protect others from the behaviour of some mentally ill people. Institutional solutions have recently been challenged as a result of a series of well-documented scandals and in reaction against excessive medical control; they are now thought to reinforce the stigmatisation and damaging isolation of mentally ill people. Nevertheless, services for mentally ill people still have to provide for people who may be prone to extremes of emotional response or unusual behaviour.

40. One of the traditional services for mentally ill people has been the provision of 'asylum'—a place away from the stresses of daily existence—to promote the recovery of emotional and intellectual stability. The availability of asylum (not necessarily in a hospital) is also an important relief for relatives and carers whose life may be disturbed by bizarre and difficult behaviour, although it is important to recognise that such relief should not be enforced unthinkingly, contrary to the freedoms of mentally ill people.

41. Mental illness often arises from an accumulation of events and circumstances; and crisis intervention endeavours to step into the spiral of problems at a point when people may still be able to mobilise energy and skills to get themselves on to a better

footing. Some crisis intervention services use residential care for respite or skill development. One example is the well-documented Coventry service where a number of residential places are offered for brief periods at the 24-hour centre with staff support and training available. Better public services (housing, health, child care and police) may well prevent some of these problems accumulating and save the long-term costs of care and treatment.

42. Throughout our evidence, there is widespread support for the closure of the large mental hospitals, with reservations among those most affected by closure about the availability of adequate alternatives, and the adequacy of the mechanisms designed to ensure coordination between the health and social services. There are widely mixed views about existing residential establishments, and a good deal of support for a broader range of residential services and for more care provision in ordinary housing. New forms of residential provision ranging from hospital-hostels to supported housing seem to be preferred by their residents to living in hospital. It seems that well-supported multi-disciplinary teams, backed by day-care facilities and a range of supported accommodation, can maintain in the community most of those who would previously have been in a psychiatric hospital. It is important to note that many mentally ill people are in need of more than accommodation, treatment for their condition, and care. They are active adults and residential services need to be linked with leisure, occupation and work opportunities within the community. In many cases, going out from a residential base into ordinary community facilities will be the best option and can provide a way to build up relationships with people not affected by illness. In the present and foreseeable employment situation many more special work opportunities need to be created for mentally ill people.

43. Closure of the hospitals leaves an existing population of mainly middle-aged and elderly mentally disabled people to be provided for, plus people newly affected by disabling forms of mental illness. The variety of conditions involved in the blanket term 'mental illness' requires individual planning for each person among a range of respite, short-term, long-term, and asylum provisions. The variation in condition of any one person requires not only monitoring but the possibility of movement between flexible services, all of which need continuing medical and health service involvement. Community developments, if they are to

succeed, must involve the public and be seen to offer protection to the one who is ill, their families and the larger community who might be caused disturbance and anxiety by unusual and occasionally frightening behaviour. There is widespread anxiety about the level of funding available to support community care, the lack of bridging finance to maintain hospital services while community ones are built up, and the level of social security funding which will be available to the mentally ill. No one knows what proportion of discharged psychiatric patients have become homeless, or to what extent more restrictive hospital admission policies may have diverted some of them to prison. The low level of existing services requires strong investment to provide and maintain an appropriate range and intensity of service and to ensure support from carers and public.

44. The significance of the voluntary sector contribution in the field of mental health is widely recognised and valued. Consistent with our view that all sectors have a role in residential provision, we would like to see the development of good quality private sector facilities in this field also. But the need for active rehabilitation, and the changeable nature of many of the conditions concerned, call for close interaction with specialist health and social services. Furthermore, the residential care allowance for this group of residents is not much enhanced compared with that for elderly people, and may not be adequate except for residents who only need minimal long-term care and support.

45. The ambience and regimes of homes for mentally ill people should get as far away as possible from the institutional model. Thus, extreme fire precautions and night time bell pulls are hardly necessary for recovering mentally ill people who are physically fit. We believe that registration authorities could exercise greater flexibility in balancing the risks against the rehabilitation needs of residents.

46. Over and above the requirements of good practice common to all residential care, some points need special emphasis in relation to people with mental illness. For instance, whilst there must always be clarity and purpose about the principles on which a residential home or housing scheme is organised, there is equal need for it to be adaptive enough to accommodate the changing therapeutic and rehabilitation needs of each individual. Consistent treatment and careful observation of behaviour and mood change demand continuity of staffing and programme. Care staff, whilst offering protection to those inside

and outside the establishment, have to be on their guard against the dependency of residents. Where relationships and understanding are disturbed it is crucial that contacts with ordinary life—family, friends, and the larger community—are maintained and strengthened. Choice is an important factor, both as a counter to the institutionalisation of hospital and also to help residents retain or regain contact with reality and experience the consequences of their own decisions.

People with Alcohol and Drug Problems

47.   Abuse of alcohol and various drugs presents particular problems for residential services, partly because of the nature of the conditions and partly because of the history of services attempting to deal with them. Individuals with alcohol and drug problems present difficulties because their problems straddle—or fall between—housing, health and social services.

48.   There is often a moral ambivalence towards people with problems of alcohol and drug abuse. This leads to their receiving variable priority in both charitable and government funding and in political attention and concern. Both problems are to an extent related to offending and criminality. Abuse of alcohol and various drugs is financially expensive for the individual, and theft and debt are common. Intoxification with mood-altering substances may lead to individuals offending. Habitual use of alcohol and drugs often leads to the affected individuals cutting themselves off from family and friends and establishing a new lifestyle centred around their dependence which is alien to other people. These problems are common among single homeless people, and many young drug takers lead a fairly nomadic existence in groups in informal accommodation.

49.   There is no consensus as to the best methods of help for these people, partly because the debate about the nature of the problem continues. Some people tend to regard these individuals as ill and would emphasise a medical or health service response. Some would see the solution as requiring the sufferers to make a personal commitment to fight their way out of their problem. Others suggest that alcohol or drug abuse is a result of underlying social and personal problems which need resolution or treatment. This latter view is often strongly resisted by those who argue that

solving underlying problems is inappropriate and that the alcohol and drug abuse are the central problems to be resolved. The consequence of this view is that in order to prevent deviance back into the drug or alcohol abuse some specialist regimes are rigidly controlling and repressive and would not accept an exploratory treatment-oriented approach which does not impose such discipline. These regimes are often based on behavioural approaches with residents passing through a hierarchical series of stages.

50.   Residential services are needed to fulfil a variety of purposes. Broadly speaking they have to cater for three main groups; drug and alcohol abusers who continue to abuse their preferred substances; individuals who are attempting to grapple with their drug and alcohol problems; ex-users who remain vulnerable to relapse.

51.   People in the first group are most likely to have a nomadic existence, lack family ties and be unemployed. In addition they often have major health problems and because of their lifestyle may have difficulty in obtaining primary health care. At street level there are hostels which simply provide basic accommodation for homeless people. There is need also at street level for quickly available accommodation which may be alcohol and drug free or permit controlled use while people are weaned away from their current lifestyles. Hostels allowing use of drugs and alcohol even in a controlled fashion will present special problems to the staff working there. The advantage of special facilities for this group is that they provide the opportunity for acknowledging the problem and seeking some kind of help.

52.   Individuals in the second group will have recognised that they have problems and made some kind of commitment to changing their way of life. Accommodation, and where that accommodation is situated, is of vital importance to these people as they will be under considerable pressure to return to previous habits. Some individuals will at this stage enter health service provision—for example, specialist addiction units, or rehabilitation centres with varying ideologies. In addition drug or alcohol free hostels may be needed for some time while detoxification and re-stabilisation is achieved.

53.   For the third group, i.e. ex-users, a range of supervised accommodation may well be appropriate. This would include bedsitters and flats as well as less rigidly run hostels, all with the aim of re-integrating the individual into the wider community.

Elderly Mentally Ill People

54. The term 'confusion' is used to describe elderly mentally ill people and because it is used so widely it has become meaningless in the context of accurate diagnosis. Elderly mentally ill people fall into two main groups, those suffering from organic illness and those suffering from functional illness.

55. Organic states refer to those where there is some structural brain change, for example the various forms of dementia, brain tumour, and head injury. Dementia implies a deterioration, usually irreversible, of all intellectual states. Delirium due to physical illness can, if untreated, progress to dementia, so proper psychiatric assessment is essential.

56. Functional illnesses include depressions, personality disorder, anxieties and phobias. Elderly people suffering from functional illness, like their younger contemporaries, can usually be successfully treated in the community and do not need residential care unless their condition is particularly long-lasting and severe. Sometimes, because their concentration is so poor, they cannot grasp facts and appear to have memory loss and are then erroneously described as demented. This, again, highlights the need for proper psychiatric assessment in mentally ill old people.

57. The growing numbers of elderly people with dementia present the medical and social services with their greatest problem. Proper provision must be made for all sufferers in this group. About 5% of people over 65 are afflicted with this condition, a proportion that rises to about 20% for people aged over 80. The whole of the elderly population is increasing, and in particular the numbers over 80 will increase by 25% by the end of the century. We were disappointed with the lack of formal evidence received; the only substantial representation came from the Alzheimer's Disease Society (E57) who argue that most sufferers will at some stage of their illness need residential care, either for respite or long term.

58. People suffering from dementia can be looked after in a community setting with proper provision until quite a late stage before they need residential care. Those suffering from additional physical infirmities or who are living alone will need residential services earlier. Memory loss is very disabling and soon puts the individual at risk. Adequate staffing levels and trained and motivated staff teams are never more needed than in residential

services for elderly people with dementia. The evidence of several enquiries and personal letters to the Committee underline the fact that where standards are not acceptable, residents are caught in a downward spiral of increasing confusion and disorientation. Unfortunately it must be said that people with dementia will eventually deteriorate because of the condition itself.

59.   The issue of segregation or integration of elderly mentally ill people within ordinary residential establishments continues to be a contentious one. Those who favour separate facilities argue that they provide a safe, planned environment in which containment need not be overt, and that other elderly residents are not stigmatised by association. The other view is that people with moderate dementia do quite well in ordinary residential settings, provided that there are no major problems with aggression or wandering, and if they are reasonably able to cope with daily living, they should not represent a problem to other residents. Individual functioning is best maintained when residents are stimulated, and methods such as reality orientation and reminiscence techniques have proved effective. However substantial the degree of dependency, services should support the rights of the individual and protect their dignity and freedom of choice.

60.   A compromise which has evolved is that of residential accommodation with special units staffed at a higher level, although to some extent the issues have been overtaken by events. In recent years residential care has been offered to ever more dependent elderly people, and it is now known that a growing proportion of residents in ordinary establishments are suffering from mental illness. The success of community care policies in maintaining people in their own homes for as long as possible inevitably reinforces this trend. Whether residents are dependent due to mental illness after admission, or present as highly dependent prior to admission, can have a critical effect on levels of tolerance of confused and anti-social behaviour. The phases of assessment, allocation and admission become important check points for successful placements.

61.   The proportion of people in residential establishments with severe dementia is increasing and problems arise because they need a greater degree of care and supervision. There is a case for providing nursing home facilities with joint care and health staff, probably in association with existing residential care facilities. Eventually residents will need an even greater degree of care which, in the future, could be provided in community

hospitals, or hospital sections within general resource centres with which residential and nursing homes would have established links. To make such provision possible there needs to be greater liaison between local authority and health personnel.

Recommendations

Residential services should be among the options available to children and their parents, and should be developed to offer: respite care; preparation for long-term placements or for independent living; a staged transition from hospital to family care; integrated education and care; a means of keeping siblings together; integrated therapy and care.

The needs of children and young people from ethnic minority groups should receive particular attention.

Bulk buying of provisions, order forms for purchase of clothes and other institutional practices should be abolished.

Greater importance should be attached to the educational and health needs of children in care.

Adequate accommodation should be made available to young people on leaving care.

Information about the agency's complaints procedure should be made available to children and parents, and access to an 'advocate' should be available to children in all forms of residential care.

The Government should ensure that adults with physical disabilities receive sufficient financial help to enable them to purchase the services they require.

Education and training for young people with mental handicap should aim at enabling them to live with minimum support in ordinary housing.

Investment is needed to extend the range of services in the community for people with or recovering from mental illness.

Residential services should be developed for a variety of purposes for people with alcohol and drug problems.

Proper provision must be made for all elderly mentally infirm people. This will entail closer cooperation between health and social services. Nursing home facilities should be developed in association with existing residential establishments.

Principles

People who move into a residential establishment should do so by positive choice. A distinction should be made between need for accommodation and need for services. No one should be required to change their permanent accommodation in order to receive services which could be made available to them in their own homes.

Living in a residential establishment should be a positive experience ensuring a better quality of life than the resident could enjoy in any other setting.

Local authorities should make efforts, as a matter of urgency, to meet the special needs of people from ethnic minority communities for residential and other services.

Every person who moves into a residential establishment retains their rights as a citizen. Measures need to be taken to ensure that individuals can exercise their rights. Safeguards should be applied when rights are curtailed.

People who move into a residential establishment should continue to have access to the full range of community support services.

Residents should have access to leisure, educational and other facilities offered by the local community and the right to invite and receive relatives and friends as they choose.

Residential staff are the major resource and should be valued as such. The importance of their contribution needs to be recognised and enhanced.

Recommendations

Positive Choice

1. Local authorities should take the lead in the strategic planning of accommodation and support services. (*Chap.6.10*)

2. A statutory duty should be placed on local authorities to propose a reasonable package of services, enabling a person to remain in their own home if that is their choice and it is reasonable for them to do so. (*Chap.3.22*)

3. Statutory and voluntary agencies should use every means available to contact informal carers in their area, so as to find out what services they may need. (*Chap.5.9*)

4. Further study should be given to a system of Community Care Allowances, which would enable people with special needs to procure care services of their choice. (*Chap.3.24*)

5. Anyone for whom residential provision might be an option should have available to them the skills of a nominated social worker, whose primary responsibility would be to act as their agent; a nominated social worker should always be appointed where a prospective user has no relative and is deemed unable to exercise effective choice. (*Chap.3.6*)

6. Local authorities should develop systems of delegated budgeting whereby nominated social workers exercise direct control over financial resources. (*Chap.3.16*)

7. The public library service in each locality should coordinate, and periodically update, comprehensive information on the range of services available. (*Chap.3.2*)

[115]

Rights of the Individual

8. Every adult person entering a residential establishment with a view to an extended stay should be entitled to a trial period during which nothing would be done to dispossess them of their previous accommodation. At the end of the trial period, acceptance of the terms and conditions of the residential establishment should constitute a contract binding on both sides. (*Chap.4.14*)

9. All people in residential establishments capable of arranging their own affairs should be entitled to retain their pension or allowance book, and to pay from it the agreed sum for accommodation and services. Residents should be eligible for Housing Benefit in the assessment of their accommodation commitment. (*Chap.4.15*)

10. No one should be required to share a bedroom with another person as a condition of residence. (*Chap.4.12*)

11. In new residential homes as from 1990, and in existing homes as from 1995 there should be only two double rooms to every ten rooms. (*Chap.4.12*)

12. Each person in a residential establishment should be entitled to a personal key for their own room. (*Chap.4.9*)

13. There should be a statutory review every six months for those residents who are unable to exercise effective choice or give effective consent. (*Chap.3.17*)

14. Each local authority should have a clear and well-publicised complaints procedure, and comparable measures should be taken by private and voluntary agencies. (*Chap.3.20*)

15. People who require assistance in presenting their complaints should have the services of an advocate or personal representative who is entirely independent of those providing the service. (*Chap.3.21*)

16. Information about the agency's complaints procedure should be made available to children and parents. Children in all forms of residential care should have access to an independent advocate. Consideration should be given to extending the system of guardian ad litem to enable families and children to request a guardian ad litem to safeguard children's interests. (*Chap.10.22,23*)

17. The differing levels of capital disregard and of personal allowance in the local authority, voluntary and private sectors should be brought into line at the higher levels. (*Chap.4.16*)

Particular needs

18. Residential services for children should be among the options available to children and their parents, and should be developed to offer: respite care; a staged transition from hospital to family care; integrated education and care; a means of keeping siblings together. (*Chap.10.13*)

19. Greater importance should be attached to the educational and health needs of children in care. (*Chap.10.20,21*)

20. The needs of children and young people from ethnic minority groups should receive particular attention. (*Chap.10.15*)

21. Adequate accommodation should be made available to young people on leaving care. (*Chap.10.25*)

22. The Government should ensure that adults with physical disabilities receive sufficient financial help to enable them to purchase the services they require. (*Chap.10.31*)

23. Education and training for young people with mental handicap should aim at enabling them to live with minimum support in ordinary housing. (*Chap.10.35*)

24. The provision of supportive accommodation to enable people with disabilities to leave the parental home needs to be expanded. (*Chap.5.13*)

25. Investment is needed to extend the range of services in the community for people with or recovering from mental illness. (*Chap.10.43*)

26. Residential services should be developed for a variety of purposes for people with alcohol and drug problems. (*Chap.10.50*)

27. Proper provision must be made for elderly mentally infirm people. This will entail closer cooperation between health and social services. Nursing home type facilities should be developed in association with existing residential establishments. (*Chap.10.61*)

Setting and Maintaining Standards

28. Local authority, voluntary and private residential establishments should be subject to the same system of registration and inspection. (*Chap.6.17*)

29. The Department of Health and Social Security should draw up national guidelines for the registration and inspection of residential establishments, and should give equal attention to standards of accommodation, quality of life and the qualifications of management and staff. (*Chap.6.17*)

30. Serious consideration should be given to a unified registration and inspection system for residential and nursing homes, to facilitate continuity of care. (*Chap.6.25*)

31. To ensure independence and impartiality, no agency should undertake the inspection of its own residential establishments. (*Chap.6.17*)

32. As an adjunct to inspections consideration should be given to appointing panels of independent assessors from all three sectors. (*Chap.6.19*)

33. Local authorities, voluntary organisations and the representatives of private proprietors should promote systems of self-evaluation and performance review in all residential establishments; no new establishment should be registered which is not prepared to introduce such a system. (*Chap.6.20*)

34. Small establishments caring for three or fewer people should be subject to preliminary vetting and to periodic visits; but when one proprietor operates more than one such home in the same neighbourhood providing for a total of four or more residents, then the full requirements of the Registered Homes Act should apply. (*Chap.6.22*)

35. Residential establishments operating under Royal Charter should be brought within the scope of the Registered Homes Act. (*Chap.6.23*)

36. Communities, religious or secular, which continue to provide a home for members who have become old or infirm, should not be deemed to be within the scope of the Registered Homes Act. (*Chap.6.24*)

Staffing and Training

37. The grading of care staff as manual workers should cease and their posts should be redefined as officer or the profesional equivalent. (*Chap.8.21*)

38. Employers and trade unions should make a concerted effort to introduce integrated pay and employment conditions for all social services staff. (*Chap.8.21*)

39. All senior posts should be filled by staff with social work qualifications, and it should be the policy of every employing authority to fill such posts with qualified staff by 1993. (*Chap.9.20*)

40. There should be a match between the ethnic composition of the people in a residential establishment and the staff group. Advice on special needs should be sought from representatives of the relevant ethnic communities. (*Chap.5.15*)

41. Every effort should be made to recruit staff from ethnic minority communities where they are under-represented on staffing establishments, and to enable them to move subsequently into more senior posts. (*Chap.8.10*)

42. Every establishment should be required to draw up a staff training plan and this should be subject to registration and inspection procedures. (*Chap.9.25*)

43. People with non-social work qualifications who move into residential work should receive conversion training, and those appointed to senior posts should be expected to undertake qualifying training in social work as soon as possible. (*Chap.9.21*)

44. The role of wardens in sheltered housing should be strengthened, and they should receive formal training; local authorities should consider whether wardens should be employed in Social Services rather than Housing Departments. (*Chap.2.17*)

45. The DHSS should identify ways in which residential staffing requirements may best be calculated and how staff may best be deployed. (*Chap.8.9*)

Appendix I

Guide to the Evidence

ELMA SINCLAIR

APPENDIX I

Introductory Note

At their first meeting on the 13th May 1986 the Committee decided to invite written evidence 'from concerned organisations and from individuals who are engaged in providing residential care or who have contacts of any kind with residential care services'. A set of guidelines was drawn up outlining some of the main topics of interest and copies of this were sent to some 150 organisations and individuals.

Initially, the closing date for submission of evidence was set at September 30th but many organisations had difficulty in completing their evidence within the time allowed. By the end of November, however, the Committee had received 180 submissions, many of substantial length, and a further 30 were received in the course of the following months.

Concurrently with this quest for formal evidence, members of the Committee expressed keen interest in hearing from members of the public about their own impressions of residential care, and from people employed as residential care staff about their work experience. In July 1986 the Chairman wrote to the editors of ten periodicals with a special interest in the residential field, enclosing a message which they were asked to publish in a form in which it could be cut out and displayed on a home's notice board.

A welcome response to this initiative came from Thames Television, who offered time on their *Help* programme on 10th November to a member of the Committee to appeal directly to elderly people in residential homes and their relatives to write in about their experiences. Over 80 replies were received as a result of the programme, and a further 130 came in over a longer period in response to the message printed in the professional journals.

While every submission and every letter was copied to the Committee members as soon as it was received, and exercised a major influence on their discussions, it soon became plain that it would be helpful to be able to identify, and refer easily to, evidence on particular issues. With this in view, the Committee commissioned a Guide to the Formal Evidence and when this was delivered they found it so useful that they decided to add a similar summary of the personal correspondence.

Together these constitute an archive of considerable interest, as much for the directness and immediacy of the experiences and feelings depicted in the correspondence, as for the wide range of issues discussed in the formal evidence. The Committee were fortunate in obtaining the services of Mrs Elma Sinclair, who had herself worked in residential care and brought a wealth of personal experience and insight to the preparation of both summaries, which are reproduced in full in this Appendix to their Report.

Guide to the evidence

(ii)   The Formal Evidence

(i)
The Personal Evidence

Introduction

In one of Conan Doyle's stories, the silence of the dog which did not bark in the night was immediately perceived by Sherlock Holmes to be of the greatest significance. The story has an obvious application to the personal evidence to the Committee, a striking feature of which is the silence of the mentally ill, the mentally handicapped and children. Given the importance accorded in the formal evidence to the wishes and rights of consumers and the variety of methods by which the Committee has sought to encourage the submission of personal views, this inability of three of the five major consumer groups to make their voices heard must itself be a cause for concern.

In relation to the mentally ill, the silence in the personal evidence is total. The 214 pieces of evidence provide 321 separate views of residential homes (some correspondents describe experience of two or more very different homes; some evidence includes contributions from several staff or residents). Of these not one is from the mentally ill themselves, from their relatives, friends or the staff who care for them. This is particularly unfortunate as it is in relation to this group that the greatest anxiety is expressed in the formal evidence. Only three personal views of care for the mentally handicapped are offered—one by parents and two by staff. One young adult provides his assessment of his childhood in care, and 21 child care staff also contribute, but they are concerned more with issues of staff ratios, training, wages and conditions than with the child's eye view. Paradoxically, it is to the formal evidence that we must turn for direct contributions from the recovering mentally ill (through the Richmond Fellowship and Wandsworth SSD) and children brought up in care (through NAYPIC). The evidence summarised here is therefore overwhelmingly concerned with the care of the elderly (273 views), but also considers briefly the care of young physically handicapped adults (23 views).

The particular value of the personal evidence lies in the immediacy with which it conveys experiences and feelings. This summary therefore

[129]

uses as far as possible the correspondents' own words, which are altered only to prevent identification. Through the eys of residents (105 views), relatives, friends and visitors (100 views) and staff (116 views), it examines in turn good, bad and mixed experiences of residential care. Issues considered important only by staff are dealt with separately. Finally we look at the measures which correspondents suggest could encourage good practice and prevent bad.

Where a correspondent specifies whether a home is run privately ('private'—125 views), by the local authority ('SSD'—57 views), by a voluntary society ('vol'—51 views), or by the NHS ('NHS'—5 views) this is indicated, but in many cases (83 views) this information was not given.

'H' numbers distinguish responses to the *Help* programme from other personal evidence ('P').

The Good

The overall picture of residential care presented by the evidence is heartening since 3 out of 5 judgments provided by residents, relatives, friends and visitors are positive compared with 1 in 5 which are negative and 1 in 5 which include both good and bad features. (Staff were excluded from these calculations as they are not consumers. If the opinions of residents alone are considered, the verdict is even more favourable, just under 70 per cent being positive.

These figures are not necessarily 'statistically representative', since those living in good homes are more likely to have had access to the media, from which they would have learnt of the Committee's existence, or to have been informed by the staff that their views had been requested. The incontinent and confused elderly said by their relatives to have been tied to their chairs all day are unlikely to have been provided with pen and paper to record their opinions of residential care. Nevertheless, the extent and warmth of the happiness found by so many elderly people in residential homes of all types is vividly conveyed in their letters and provides the essential background against which the misery of others must be viewed.

This perspective was obviously lacking to most of the correspondents, who are aware of the low reputation of the residential sector. Many of those who are happy with the care received assume that they have been 'fortunate' enough to discover something almost unique, certainly 'the very best in town'.

> My experience was utter amazement. The staff were angels, and the home was well organised. The food was very good, and the care and attention was first class, this was Home from Home. (H23, resident, SSD)

We were so fortunate to find such a lovely place where she can be so comfortable and happy (H25, relative, private).

It's a council home for the elderly and I cannot praise it high enough...The staff really seem to care for all the old folks and I feel we were very lucky to get my mother into such a good home (H32, relative, SSD).

So conscious are some correspondents of the gloomy reputation of residential care and so impotent do they feel to change it that they are fearful of the outcome of the Review.

I love living here. I have made a lot of new friends and old friends, and I ask you now please, do not let our home be destroyed. I am very happy and I would like to keep on being very happy at this House (P93, resident, vol.)

I would not wish her to return to hospital—particularly to a geriatric ward—and this would seem to be her fate if this House discontinues as a nursing home...My husband and I wish to recommend very strongly that this Nursing Home should continue (P73, relative, private).

More correspondents, however, feel that the Committee will believe in their happiness if only they can be persuaded to come and see for themselves.

So much is being said about bad homes—I felt I must write and tell you all about this one...It is a huge building holding about 103 people—some are medical and others just residents...It is one of the finest homes in the county but you must see it to believe my word—does that sound to you like an invitation? I really would like you to come and see for yourself. I am 83 years and have been here ever since it opened two years ago and am still as happy as when I was in my own home...Do visit us if you can. You will be amazed (H19, resident).

As in the above quotation, they emphasise that this happiness is to be found even in large institutions and among the very elderly—

This is a home of 40 residents...It is a very happy home and every resident is encouraged to keep their independence...The average age is 91, we shall have three 100 years old birthdays next year. We have a residents' Committee and do our own magazine, am sending you a copy of the two previous editions...The home is open at all times for a visit. If you would like to do this please contact Matron (H34, resident)—

and in homes from all sectors—

We have a lovely Christmas party...If you would like to come you can come with a friend, let me know...So why don't you come and see for yourself what a lovely good home it is? (H38, resident, private).

I have been here 15 years, and they have been very happy ones...I wish you could see our dining room laid for meals, it is really beautiful...the Matron and I would be delighted to see you (P11, resident, vol.).

A number of residents are at pains to make clear that what they are describing is not mere acceptance, but a positive happiness, which in some cases is greater than they knew before admission and in a few cases greater than at any previous time in their lives.

> I hope I stay here until I go on my last move. A more loving, caring Matron and her staff cannot be matched. Thanks to her efforts and the Red Cross, I am now sleeping on a bed for the first time in four years. I am suffering severe arthritis and am a Parkinson's Disease advanced case. . .I have never been so happy since I lost my husband, nearly forty years ago (H20, resident).

> At the time I could only manage a week's stay. I was so happy having company around me, and also the staff are very kind. When I went back home, I wrote a letter to Mrs Thatcher, I told her about being alone and asked if she could help me, my letter was passed on to the DHSS. . .I cannot tell you my joy as the letter informed me that they would help me. . .I am very happy that through prayers, these problems have all been taken care of (P94, resident, private).

Relatives express similar thoughts:

> We can be completely relaxed and confident that she is happier and far more content than she has been for the previous three years living on her own (H25, relative, private).

> My dear mother died there two months ago after spending the three happiest years of her life there (H30, relative, private).

These quotations illustrate that some correspondents were able to find happiness in residential care irrespective of their own physical condition, the age of other residents, the size of the home or the sector it came from. In the letters from the elderly and their relatives, very little attention is paid to these matters and expressions of happiness seem to come with similar frequency from homes of all sizes and sectors in both urban and rural settings.

What does seem to be important is recognition of each person's individuality, dignity and worth and it is this which is the underlying concern of most correspondents. In the letters, this recognition is seen taking many forms. For example, the provision of choice wherever possible can maintain a resident's sense of freedom and being in control. Good physical care and facilities enable dignity to be retained. The encouragement of visitors and activities gives recognition to a resident's continuing relationships and abilities. Companionship with other residents and warm relationships with staff confirm personal worth. We look next in more detail at the ways in which good homes maintain choice, dignity and a sense of personal worth for their residents through the different aspects of residential life.

Admission

Several correspondents make clear the importance of the admission process to their favourable experience of residential care, emphasising that they feel that the decision to enter was their own.

> As far as I am concerned it has been a big success...At first I was against the idea but was persuaded to go and visit one of the homes. I was quite impressed and said I would try it for four weeks to see how I liked it. After two weeks I was settled down and quite at home and expect to spend the rest of my days here (P114, resident, SSD).

> Having made this decision of my own free will with no influence from my family made it easier to accept the change, which cannot be denied, though difficult at first has proved very successful for me and my children (H71, resident).

> As far as it is possible for a newly-widowed man to be happy, then I am happy here...and contentment has come because I chose to come here' (P16, resident, SSD).

Physical and Medical Care

However, even the most unpropitious admission sometimes leads to a happy stay.

> I and Mrs Fyson have been here about two years. I was directed here by my Doctor after a stroke to my left side and she was turned from her home and had nowhere to go. We have made very good friends and are very happy here. We enjoy the freedom and care and advice (P14, resident).

The companionship and freedom from anxiety which reconciled these ladies to their new home perform the same function for many others. Some have found solace after a recent bereavement:

> I came here after being a widow for nine months and it was the best thing I have done since being a widow (in two words a great success) (H67, resident, vol.).

> Being a widow I wanted companionship...This is a real home to all the ladies living here...We are cared for and loved by the staff as if we were their own family (P40, resident, private).

Others have found relief not only from isolation but also from helplessness:

> After living in a sheltered flat and getting no help or kindness and unable to help myself properly...I decided to try for a Rest Home (I am 78 years). I am pleased I did as I am having good meals at regular times, also baths, I could not get in on my own for years, clean bedding and clothes, medical attention when needed which I do from time to time. I could fill a page as the owners of this home are kindness itself (H18, resident, private).

While many value security in such day to day matters ('Homely atmosphere, no worry, regular meals, warmth', H71, resident), others place even greater weight on the knowledge that skilled medical attention is always close at hand and facilities are available to counteract disability.

> I am surprised at the statements made by the people who spoke [in *Help* programme], especially the men who said they would prefer to stay in their own homes or flats...I have amputation of my right leg also I have paralysis of the left arm. I spend most of my time in a battery-operated wheelchair, also I am a diabetic on tablets. I am very happy here, there are five doctors in attendance...I have a pleasant room to myself with washing and toilet facilities, with night and day nurses (H26, resident, vol.)

> We have very good care. If we are not well during the night we only have to pull an emergency bell and someone comes immediately and we have a nurse who is wonderful. Also we have a lift in case you can't climb stairs and a minibus to take us out so we are not cut off (H43, resident).

Security over the provision of good food, physical care and medical attention frees these elderly people to appreciate those qualities of life which bring positive enjoyment and it is at this point that we begin to examine the features which distinguish the good regimes from the merely adequate.

Activities
It is clearly important to our correspondents that residents should be enabled to continue in a variety of roles—host or hostess to daily visitors, to whom they may also be grandparent, parent, sister, brother or friend; customer at local shops; member of local clubs and churches; confidante and friend to other residents; perhaps helper, committee member or organiser of an activity within the home. Several correspondents give a picture of a life rich in such activities and relationships.

> I have my own room and attend the Disabled Centre 3 days a week where I am very busy with different activities...The home itself is a very happy and nice place to live and we are all very good friends and are treated by the Officers who run the home with great respect and humility...There are no restrictions on visitors coming to see you as they are welcome at any time and I can say I have lots of friends as well as my two daughters and four grandchildren who never fail to see me every week...To write about all that I do and all the things that happen here would take many, many pages to tell (P90, resident).

A lounge where social activities are not limited by the wish of others to concentrate on television can contribute to companionship and shared interests within the home.

Friendliness and care of matron and staff. 3 comfortable lounges with tele-vision. 1 Quiet Lounge, no smoking, no TV, but with record player, radio cassette, where you can talk, knit, read, write letters or entertain visitors who are welcome at any time (H71, resident).

The most fortunate are still able to feel part of the activities of their local community.

It has been a tremendously successful stay for almost 3 years...The Rest Home fits into village life and plays its part, so the residents still feel part of a caring community with a happy loving home where relatives are always welcome (H58, relative, private).

Special occasions can provide an opportunity to draw together the different strands of residents' lives in a celebration shared with friends old and new.

We have a lovely Christmas party when Mr Jones sends invitations to our relatives and friends. We have an excellent cook who provides all the food and that's plenty (H38, resident, private).

On October 31st they did a Hallowe'en Cheese and Wine evening, all the staff returned in the evening and dressed as witches, and the dining area was transformed into a real Hallowe'en night. The food as always was beautifully laid out, and there is always a very good attendance by all relations concerned. Nothing is too much trouble for any member of the staff (H54, relative).

The availability of a variety of activities, roles and settings appears to both accompany and contribute to an 'atmosphere of freedom and friendliness' (P124, resident, private), 'the friendly atmosphere and the freedom of being able to behave as you would do in your own home, helping in any way possible' (H82, resident, private).

Many factors are mentioned as contributing to such a quality of life, ranging from possession of a minibus for outings and the accessibility of shops and clubs to the provision of tea-making facilities for entertain-ing visitors. More important than any of these, however, is the relation-ship between residents and staff.

Relationships between Residents and Staff

In the eyes of many correspondents the most significant thing about a home is that it should have 'the whole atmosphere...of a loving caring family' (P107, relative, private). Some state specifically that this was what they looked for when selecting a home:

I chose it because of a homely atmosphere and a genuine feeling of caring (H41, relative, private).

The importance of the head of home in the creation of such an atmosphere is recognised by many, including a niece who was 'mainly attracted to the pleasant homely smiling person who was the proprietress' (P56, private). This relative's judgment was proved sound, as was that of the resident who writes:

> There is generally a good atmosphere which strikes the newcomer immediately, an atmosphere engendered by the happy personality of the matron (P16, SSD).

The letters show that where there is encouragement from the officer-in-charge, staff and residents are able to enjoy each others' company and value each other as individuals.

> The owner and staff said they had more fun and laughs since Mother was there than they ever had. They all, staff and residents, loved her and to put it cruelly 'spoiled her rotten' and she thrived on it, Bless her...Every night whoever was on duty went into Mother and kissed her goodnight. They said they were proud to have known her and it was a privilege to have her there (H30, relative, private).

> He had a room of his own...that he liked to spend a lot of time in...The staff used to visit and talk a lot with him in his room, they were young so he loved it...When he was ill, they held his hand and talked in the night, he told me himself. I felt he was as happy as he could have been anywhere (P45, relative).

Such relationships appear to be as important to the satisfaction of staff as to the happiness of residents.

> What do I enjoy most about the job? I enjoy the residents. They are delightful and give me much pleasure (P101, staff, private).

Mutual esteem is expressed in a variety of ways including, as already seen, physical contact.

> Our daughter is always excited to come home for weekends, but also excited to go back again after the visit. She is always welcomed with hugs from the staff (P80, relative, vol., mentally handicapped).

> A cuddle and a kiss eases many problems, especially at bed-time—a little love goes a long way (P64, staff).

Another indication of being valued is the use of Christian names.

> I could not receive better treatment anywhere. Every one is so friendly and helpful and we all call each other by our Christian names (H58, resident, private).

Birthday celebrations, like Christian names, are mentioned frequently. Both are powerful symbols of our personal identity and this may give their recognition special significance.

> We the residents are on first name terms with everyone in the home...When anyone has a birthday we are given a party and presents (P12, resident, private).

On her 100th birthday she was treated like the Queen Mother...One of the residents...happened to say Mother said she liked venison, so all of them had venison for lunch that day...and a most wonderful tea all home made by the owner and staff. As each resident has a birthday, they all have a lovely tea, and beautiful birthday cake (H30, relative, private).

The final signs of respect and caring come as death approaches. The importance of staff sensitivity at this time is acknowledged by a relative who writes:

Perhaps the final comfort was the recognition that my Mother had only a few hours to live so that I was summoned to be with her as she died (P49, private).

An Example of Good Care
Finally, a 96-year-old lady provides a description of her home which can fill in with daily detail this outline of a happy life in residential care.

'*Situation*—good district with trees and gardens.

Accommodation. I have a pleasant, comfortable room—large window so can watch passers and traffic. Good toilet arrangements. Bed can be folded up during the day if desired. Also a colour TV. There is a pleasant comfortable lounge with armchairs and TV and radio. Dining room well furnished, view of garden. The lounge also has a view of the garden. Tables very well appointed. Bathroom—very modern with all latest equipment for disabled persons. Those on 2nd floor have a lift, so do not need to use the stairs. Each room has an Intercom.

Meals. Breakfast served in bed. Tea. Cereal, toast with butter, and jam or marmalade. 11 am Coffee and biscuits. 1 pm Lunch. Always a choice of both 1st and 2nd courses. I am a vegetarian and am very well catered for, as is a lady who is a diabetic. Sweet courses very good (followed by coffee), 3.30 pm Tea and cake. 6 pm Soup and something on toast or sandwiches. Bowl of fruit—choice of apples, bananas, oranges, pears. Cup of tea. Hot drink at 9 pm.

Outings etc. A mini bus equipped for disabled takes us for a ride about once a month when the weather is good, and visits to theatres etc are arranged. We had a lovely party at Christmas and again at Easter. A birthday is celebrated with a cake and singing *Happy Birthday to you*...Two gentlemen also visit, one plays guitar and sings—the other shows slides of local interest.

Extras. A hairdresser pays weekly visits, and a chiropodist about once a month. There is a Bingo session one afternoon in the week—sweets for prizes. Every Friday afternoon a lady comes to take a class in exercises for those who wish. Every Sat. pm the proprietor takes four of us in his car for a drive by the sea and countryside. All the rooms and corridors are well heated with radiators. Each room has equipment for making tea and coffee for visitors who are always welcomed. There is also a telephone for residents. I have my own in my room—very convenient! Several doctors visit—each their own patients, and many of the staff are SRNs. All the members of the staff are most kind and helpful, also smiling and cheerful and make us feel that nothing is too much trouble... Four residents who are in the Nursing Home dept. are brought in wheel chairs to join us in the lounge whenever possible, and are also taken out in a wheelchair. I can still take my stick and go for a walk, either to some good shops quite near or the other way to admire the gardens' (P127, resident, private).

This lady concludes her letter, 'I wish all "Homes" were as good as this one', a wish which must surely be echoed by all who read the letters we consider next.

In Summary
Correspondents appear to be happy in situations where:

Admission has been the resident's own choice.
There is good food, warmth, physical and medical care and provision for disability.
Furnishings and facilities are satisfactory in both public and private areas.
Services such as chiropody and hairdressing are available.
Visitors are always welcome and there are facilities for their entertainment.
There is provision for a variety of activities and outings.
Birthdays and special occasions are celebrated.
The resident is free to come and go or choose what to do at any time.
Relationships are such as to allow the use of Christian names and reassuring physical contact.
Conversation and companionship are encouraged both between residents and between residents and staff.

The Bad

Evidence of so much real happiness in old people's homes of all sectors has a three-fold importance. First, it restores a balanced view of residential care for the elderly. Without this balance, a resource which can bring contentment to many may be undervalued because of the emotional impact of the unhappiness of others. Secondly, the evidence has shown that even correspondents who are happy with their own situation are likely to believe that good Homes are rare and difficult to find. Such a conviction makes those who are trapped in appalling situations reluctant to contemplate moving because they think that there is nothing better to be found. The personal evidence enables the Committee to combat this particular form of hopelessness. Thirdly, it is clear that many people are happy in residential care, and the factors that make them so are relatively consistent and definable and some of them are neither impossible nor expensive to reproduce. Homes in which the majority of residents are unhappy are therefore inexcusable rather than inevitable. This knowledge that constructive solutions can be found perhaps makes more bearable an examination of the causes of the misery revealed by the correspondents in this section.

Cruelty and Ill-treatment

Of the 105 judgments made by residents themselves, 16 were totally negative. Relatives and others were equally critical in 23 out of 100 views. The numbers are not large but at least half a dozen letters from staff are of a similar nature and the depth of the inhumanity revealed is extremely disturbing.

There are allegations of deliberate cruelty:

Another old lady, now 98 yrs, has been tipped out of her wheelchair onto her face on two occasions by a female officer who seems to have a mean streak (P21, resident, SSD).

I witnessed a member of staff (female) on several occasions squeezing residents' breasts as a joke. On other occasions I saw a blind and disabled woman being teased with her chair being tipped back to frighten her (H5, staff, SSD).

One male resident was doubly incontinent on his bedroom floor. The care assistant gathered it up in white tissue and wiped it across the resident's face. When she related the story in the office at report time there was laughter all round (H17, staff, SSD).

More common are stories of neglect of a degree which amounts to ill treatment.

She was left in great pain and distress, her night bell was tied up so she could not reach it, her legs were tied together. It was not until I asked the Matron to have a look at my mother's foot was anything done. Three days later my mother had her foot amputated (H14, relative, SSD).

The younger aunt fell at the home some 3 weeks prior to her death—help was not called that same day despite me subsequently being told that she was screaming in pain on being moved. The following day...following the doctor's visit she was taken to hospital where it was discovered that she had a fracture to the neck of her femur. She never left hospital (P78, relative, private).

> She would be locked in her room with no heating, no curtains, just venetian blinds, a light bulb with no shade, no carpeting and was just generally neglected (P55, staff, private).

> She was locked in a chair to stop her lying on her bed. I never forget how she cried (P51, relative, private).

The homes in which such misery is found appear to share an atmosphere which is the opposite of that found in good homes—an atmosphere in which residents are deprived of choice and freedom and in which there is no mutual respect or affection between residents and staff. Denial of dignity, independence and worth takes the place of their recognition and can similarly be traced through all aspects of residential life.

Admission
Just as in good care the process of enhancing residents' feeling of self-worth and control over circumstances begins at admission, so it is apparently at admission that recognition and control are first removed from the less fortunate.

> It is such a sad story of two sisters. One had an accident...and was in hospital for some time, so her home was put in the other one's room, she had a large bedroom. She °the second sister$ was knocked down by a car and ended up in hospital and the house was sold and both of them wondering where it's all gone to, who gave permission...A lady from the League of Friends and Social Services were doing for them, I guess they thought neither of them would be fit enough to look after themselves again but one of them has more stairs to climb than she had in her own home (P51, relative, private).

> It happens that an old person will be told that they are going to spend a couple of weeks in 'care' while their supporters have a rest and holiday. They suspect that they will not be fetched home and almost unbelievably this happens. The feeling of total abandonment is overwhelming. The only people who could have helped have rejected them and there is no one else to whom to turn...They wonder who has got and been given cherished possessions and the whole collections of their lifetimes. They find themselves denuded of the personality that had developed and accrued largely because of their position in the community in which they may have spent their whole life (P102, resident, private).

> I was eventually asked by my sister if I would like to try a residential home for 3 weeks to give her a break. Once in the home my sister refused to allow me back home and I have been here for the past twelve months (P122, resident, SSD).

Physical and Medical Care
For these residents, admission brings no freedom from anxiety or sense of being cared for. Their awakening is to a regime where facilities are

primitive and their needs and wishes have not been considered.

> My mother was upstairs—shared a bedroom with three others...Morning call was at 5.30 am with a cup of tea—not allowed to dress until told. A bowl of water by the bedside so no privacy for washing. One toilet (in the bathroom) to share with 6 upstairs residents and staff. Commode by the bedside and folk expected to use these (no privacy) (H35, relative).

The more unfortunate can find themselves in danger of losing every aspect of their previous identity, from personal dignity to choice of companions.

> Toiletting often occurs with 2 or 3 people being toiletted at the same time with the door wide open. Most of the residents were not allowed to go to their rooms during the day. The majority of residents have to share rooms, 3 or 4 to a bedroom...in other words for many of the residents there is no time when they are on their own (H5, staff, SSD).

> We have no room to invite visitors in and I have to share with a very unpleasant resident and I get very little rest at nights because they have to come and change her and the bed sometimes 2 and 3 times during the night and sit next to her in the lounge all day with a terrible smell (H12, resident, private).

Some relatives are particularly concerned about lack of care over clothing, which is perhaps to them the most obvious sign of the attack on a loved one's identity (poor furnishings, crockery and cutlery arouse similar feelings in others).

> The clothing is communal. I have stood my husband up and his trousers would fall round his ankles being much too big or too small so couldn't be done up. I might add I took lots of clothes for my husband but they just went missing including new trousers (H6, relative, NHS).

> They are supposed to do her washing, but quite honestly it's a job to find any clothes. All were marked with her name so they have no excuse. To take her out you need to take dress, tights, cardigans (H72, relative).

For residents, however, insufficient food is a greater cause of concern.

> We do not get enough to eat...If we are five minutes late we have to go without...the dishes the food is brought up in are too small and there is not enough to go round...when we ask for a little more so that we all have enough, we get told there isn't any more (H55, resident).

There are complaints not only about inadequate quantity but also about quality, and of insufficient time allowed for old people to eat it, of food removed uneaten from those incapable of feeding themselves, and of a pudding being refused to those who have made a mess with the first course.

We have already seen that medical care is sometimes neglectful, but in addition to such serious cases, there are several complaints about painkillers being refused or delayed, and about anxiety caused by lack of control over or information about drugs.

> One large red pill—for what? I asked for paracetamols—painkillers—two weeks ago, this was on a Friday afternoon—they said there would be no more until Monday...In any case who ordered the large red one this morning? There has been no doctor (P59, resident).

These residents do not even go to bed with the same sense of security as those in more caring homes.

> There was only one person on duty at night to look after 11 people. Some, as my aunt who was blind, needed help with the toilet, the result was they called for help, but it was sometimes a long time before help was given (H11, relative, private).

> Very rarely is there more than one staff on and she has cooking and everything to do. Nights the one who is on duty goes to bed. When I asked her about my sister falling down the stairs which is propped open with a house brick, I was told they lock the door. So what would happen to anyone downstairs or up if there was a fire? (H72, relative).

The last quotation is made more horrifying by the fact that it relates to a home with 12 residents, including several elderly mentally infirm, which was in the process of being extended to take four more.

Activities

Not surprisingly, homes where there is so little concern for residents' physical well being appear to make little effort to encourage choice, increase activity or broaden horizons by arranging outings. Even the most minor power of decision over normal daily activities may be removed.

> The residents have almost no control over their daily lives at all. When they get up, when they go to bed, the food they eat, when they go to the toilet, whether or not they watch TV or listen to music...are decided by the staff (H5, staff, SSD).

Shortage of staff is sometimes suggested as a reason for the regimes which treat residents more as goods to be processed than as human beings to be enabled or friends whose company can be enjoyed.

> I observed the rapid and brusque processing of residents through the daily routine of waking, washing and toiletting. This was achieved with the minimum of ceremony or verbal contact. (One 91-year-old had the blankets stripped from her and had been bodily heaved onto a nearby lavatory in the space of about 10 seconds 'because she could be stroppy'). This process was obviously partly in adherence to a strict timetable...One resident's excreta-covered catheter and urine bag were roughly washed down with the owner's face flannel' (P99, staff, private).

'The shortage of staff was so bad that the confused had to sit in one position all day long, apart from meals and toiletting. The television would be on all day and if they moved they were told to sit down. Very often they would sit in soiled underwear because nobody had time to check them' (P63, staff).

It might be expected that where staff are too busy to spend time with residents, visitors would be especially welcome, but the opposite seems to be the case in these homes.

Once up everyone sits in their chair, all meals put before them, and very little 'elbow room'. There is nowhere to walk at all...Visitors are not made to feel welcome—there are no chairs for visitors—no outings, no form of any entertainment or conversation with the staff' (H35, relative).

A relative describes those she has talked to as 'going mad with the feeling of being left out of this life' (H10), a sentiment echoed by a resident in another home.

The sheer boredom causes real hardship...There is a constant feeling that 'there is a great big world out there and I should be part of it', but residents are cut off completely from everything (P102, resident, private).

Lack of care for residents' emotional and intellectual needs is sometimes reflected in poor facilities, which contribute to the assault on a previous identity.

I have no chair or table in my bedroom so have to do my writing sitting on my bed (H12, resident).

In particular, lack of a lift (lifts are mentioned with surprising frequency) means both physical pain and curtailment of activities.

There is no lift which means Mum has to be carried downstairs by 2 nurses which hurts her (H63, relative, private).

There is no lift and this restricts movement both within the home and in taking mother out in a wheelchair. She has to be manhandled up and down stairs. The common room is on the Ground Floor and she doesn't often get down to mix with others (H81, relative, private).

However there are a number of examples of lavish surroudings leading to admissions which were later regretted. The following quotation refers to a home which was charging roughly double the amount most correspondents appeared to be paying:

The next place I tried...was the worst possible place because of the attitude of the so-called Matron who was hardly ever there but who had to be referred to by telephone for a decision. There was a different sister three times a day—all different nearly every day—all with different rules. The patients were nearly all suffering from dementia and were on liquid diets and treated very badly by the staff—even the lowest grade kitchen workers. Even though it was known I was fairly normal I was locked in and at times not allowed to telephone my daughter. There was a lounge with a television which never worked... The furnishings were very good in fact a bit too good with opulent lighting etc. I have learnt that it is the caring attitude of the person-in-charge which is most important (H42, resident, private).

Relationships between Residents and Staff

The lesson which this lady says she has learnt after experience of three homes is the same as that which emerges from the evidence of those who are happy in good homes. The attitude of the officer-in-charge establishes the pattern of interaction for the home and individual junior members of staff are powerless to change it. At its worst, this can lead to what is almost a conspiracy of cruelty:

I was told by a member of staff that she has witnessed a member of staff hitting a resident, and she tried to make a formal complaint. She was ostracised by the rest of the team, told she was exaggerating or lying and finally dissuaded from making the report by her 'superiors' (H5, staff, SSD).

A female resident splashed a care assistant when she was being bathed. So the resident, in her 90s, was ducked under the water. She told the story at report time to the amusement of most of the staff. The care assistant was not reprimanded (H17, staff, SSD).

More often it leads to staff reactions which undermine residents' adult status and so make unlikely any feelings of mutual esteem.

They keep you waiting
Then suggest
That your request
Is most unreasonable.
We don't let our old ladies
Have kettles in their rooms,
They might have accidents.
We can't allow you to have
A tray upon your knee.
Who says they can't allow?
What sort of way is that to speak
To grown up people in their 'home'?
(P102, resident, private).

In such establishments, staff and residents are unlikely to seek each other out for companionship or the enjoyment of shared interests and activities.

Between times they are left to either wander around aimlessly or sit in a lounge area day in and day out without anyone showing the slightest interest (H48, relative).

At worst, a relationship which we have seen can offer respect, friendship and affection is turned into one differing little from that of gaoler and prisoner:

The people who live here must NOT have ANY money unless the Mrs gives it to one she does not like one to have any...I wanted to try to get a different home but how can I, the Mrs said we have to give a month's notice. Who would keep a room open for 1 month without payment and Mrs knows we have no money to pay, she looks out for that (H56, resident, private).

Guilt of Relatives

The final horrors of bad residential care are reserved for the relatives and begin when they are not informed of impending death.

The final indignity when my Mother was dying at this home was that I wasn't even informed so I could be with her. At least in hospital when a loved one is dying one is informed (H7, relative, private).

I was so shaken I went to the Matron and asked if something could be done—she came in, gave him an injection, and within 15 minutes he was dead! She had not even phoned any of us telling us that Father had pneumonia or that he was ill (H52, relative, private).

Relatives who had previously felt 'helpless and appalled by the conditions' (H48) are propelled by the old person's death into a situation where there is no longer any practical way of relieving their sense of guilt.

All this has been a nightmare to me these past years. My poor Mum's last months worse than anything I could have seen (H7, private).

I cannot describe the conditions my Father had to endure for the past 10 months of his life...It was only in retrospect that I see all that he suffered unnecessarily. If only I hadn't been so ill myself it would never have happened and of course I thought he would live to see the excellent home in Surrey (H52, private).

Grief and Anger

This is perhaps the point at which we should stop to take note of some words of caution from the proprietor of a private home:

Recognition that the label 'elderly' does not necessarily confer nobility on a character would be a major step in the right direction. The elderly are just like you and me—simply older. They suffer from the same foibles but with greater frailty and from the same fears but with greater justification. Like you and me, they can be aggravating, self opinionated, grudging, obstinate and afraid of death and dying (P92, private).

A subjective interpretation of the unhappy letters sent to the Committee would suggest that while most come from people in homes where 'care' in every sense is almost unknown, a few are from residents in homes of a reasonable standard who are unlikely to find happiness anywhere. The reasons for this can be as many as the people concerned.

Some individuals may be natural 'loners' who are unable to adapt to a physical condition which forces on them contact with others. Probably more are unable to recover from bereavement, rejection, or loss of home and identity. Yet others are engaged in a fierce struggle against all that accompanies the inevitable approach of physical deterioration and death. Dylan Thomas spoke most memorably on their behalf in his poem on his father's death:

> Do not go gentle into that good night,
> Old age should burn and rave at close of day;
> Rage, rage against the dying of the light.

Underlying the personal evidence can be heard a faint echo of this, a plea that the old should be allowed their anger and misery, not forced into a mould of clean and smiling content.

> Until that time they have had some autonomy, responsibility and freedom of choice. Often this has evolved into querulous bullying and selfishness and become unbearable to guardians and helpers, but still the old person should be included in discussions and ultimate decisions over matters that concern them (P102, resident, private).

A final word of understanding and acceptance comes from an untrained care assistant:

> Some residents in rest or nursing homes would grumble wherever they are. Most of them have been fiercely independent all their life and can become irritated and resentful because they have to depend on other people for help...It's down to the people who look after these elderly residents to understand their grievances and grumbles (P64, staff).

In Summary
Correspondents appear to be unhappy with homes where:

Cruelty, ill treatment or neglect are overlooked by those in charge.
Admission has not resulted from a resident's own considered decision.
Regimes are designed for the convenience of an inadequate staff rather than to maintain the choice and comfort of residents.
Activities and outings are few or non-existent.
Visitors are not made welcome.
Food, furnishings and facilities are poor.
There is no respect for residents' dignity, individual personality or ability.
Conversation, shared enjoyment and affection are not valued or encouraged.

The Mixed

Most letters provide views of care which are 'all good' or 'all bad'. The features they describe might be expected to arouse general approval or general disapproval; the homes have good features or bad features but not both; the correspondent is completely in favour or completely against. In some letters, of course, the issues are more complex. The homes have good and bad points, or a relative sees bad points in a home which the resident enjoys. In this section, we are concerned with three particular kinds of mixed reactions:

(a) those of residents whose attitude to residential care is more positive than their actual experience of it;

(b) those of residents who are negative about the idea of residential care but whose experiences leads to a more positive attitude;

(c) those to features that are viewed in differing ways—described by some negatively and some positively.

The Ideal and the Actual
Some correspondents have positive views about what can be achieved by residential care but are frustrated because their current experience of it falls short of this potential. Physically handicapped correspondents form the majority of this group and their evidence as a whole can most appropriately be considered here.

The evidence from the physically handicapped is encouraging because even those who are most unhappy about their current situation have obviously thought long and hard about it and are prepared to fight to improve it.

> I have always objected to the restrictions placed on my lifestyle and environ-ment, not always because of the nature of my disability, but usually by so called 'professional' people who say they 'know what's best' for me... I find it very important to be able to speak for myself, and have people listen to me and treat me with respect (P87, resident, SSD).

This correspondent sees the answer as lying in 'Consumer/User participation' in the planning, running and assessment of services. Another points out that, 'The residential staff have to do exactly what is expected of them... The individual is not at fault, it's the system' (P125). This will change, it is suggested, when care in a home is seen as 'a joint resident/staff responsibility, otherwise the place is, or will become, an institution...the confidence of a shared responsibility will alleviate most errors' (P93, resident).

A physically handicapped young man waiting to move into residential care describes how he would like to see these principles working out in practice.

> It would be essential that each person's flat is their own to do with as they see fit, to decorate in any way they choose and to have any visitors at any time they choose. The staff must have absolutely no say in this whatsoever. The emphasis of the entire establishment should be of the staff depending on the residents for their jobs and not the residents depending on the staff for anything other than 'hired muscle'. I would even go so far as to say that it should be the residents who determine policy and that they should have a say in the selection of staff' (P103, prospective resident).

A few correspondents have been fortunate enough to move into situations where such conditions already exist and their experience justifies the expectations of others who are still struggling for them.

> 'Where I was before I didn't feel that I was a human being...all my responsibilities were taken away from me. I even went to the loo when they told me to... Where I am living now I control my own life and no one tells me what to do. One of the main things that makes the difference is the philosophy of facilitation, which means the staff are our arms and legs. It means I can control my own life (P104, resident).

Those who have moved into such care from the parental home, those transferred from large institutions and those who have struggled and failed in the community have all found a new freedom and self-confidence.

> I feel more independent being on my own. The care workers give me my independence but are there when I need help (P117, resident).

For some physically handicapped residents (as for the only correspondent who had been brought up in care) such a combination of independence and security may be important as a 'halfway house' on the path to greater autonomy.

> I moved into this building having previously tried and failed to live on my own in a totally autonomous complex... When I am older and maturer I may move out of here into a flat which could be loosely defined as 'A PLACE OF MY OWN' (P93, resident, vol).

Another resident saw himself achieving autonomy while still living in the same house:

> I believe it to be an ideal solution to my problems with regard to independent living... In my position I believe that within 5 years I should be able to pay my own rent and live financially independent of the state. I think this is only possible to achieve because I have moved here (P93, resident, vol).

Such letters justify the call for a different kind of residential care by those at present living under more restrictive and unimaginative regimes.

Realism and Acceptance

While many of the physically handicapped appear to have the physical and intellectual energy to set about changing their situation, for the elderly and their relatives faced with a type of care they would not have chosen, acceptance sometimes appears the only route to contentment. A 90-year-old sums up this position: 'I hated giving up my home but realised I couldn't go on. I've adapted' (H65, resident, private). As we have already seen, the companionship of other residents or the warmth of staff can sometimes make the sense of loss endurable.

> I did not really want to come, but I could no longer be left in my own home alone. My sight isn't very good, I don't read or watch TV and I spent many, many hours each day by myself. . .I would like to live back in my bungalow with Matron to stay with me! (H57, resident, private).

Realistic expectations obviously make it more likely that a resident will appreciate what advantages there are:

> I knew there would be snags and probably things I wouldn't like. . .I can't emphasise how happy and content I am. Mind you that doesn't apply to all, but most of the patients are old and helpless and need a lot of care and attention and get so impatient and think they are left out, but the staff are doing their best and really work hard (P65, resident, private).

A similar realism on the part of staff allows sadness to be expressed and overcome.

> Understandably the residents are sometimes hard to please because ideally they would rather be at home or with family. I feel though that generally all our residents and staff are able to get to know each other well and are happy here (H57, staff, private).

> Most of our residents seem quite happy. When new ones come in they take time to adjust, usually the worst day is when they are told their home has been sold. Occasionally they moan about the food but you can't please all of the people all of the time (P77, staff).

Some relatives, particularly of sufferers from Alzheimer's Disease, have had to recognise that complete happiness is no longer possible. It is one of these who sums up a position which may well be more common in residential care than our evidence indicates.

> Of course the care is not perfect—nor was the care that I provided. And in the real world it won't be. . .Is she happy? Often not. But then she wasn't at home in recent years, and she was far, far worse in hospital. And me? I sleep at night now—after 20 years of getting up' (P17, relative, private).

Mixed Attitudes

This summary has so far concentrated on widespread attitudes which could have been illustrated from a number of letters. There are, however, some features of residential life on which it is important that minority as well as majority voices should be heard, since the wide difference of attitude towards them suggests a need for a variety of provision.

It is not surprising to find that some residents like to be able to look out at passers-by in a busy street, while for others a lovely view consists of open countryside, trees or a flower garden. And it might also be expected that while some residents long for 'a more substantial meal', relatives and a nutritionist will worry that too much stodgy food will lead to obesity and lack of mobility. It is, however, more surprising to find deeply felt disagreement over the desirability or otherwise of single rooms. It will already be clear from some of the quotations relating to bad regimes that lack of privacy or an incompatible room-mate can contribute to real unhappiness. However, a different point of view is also represented in the correspondence. In one home a lady writes, 'I enjoy sharing the room at night because we can talk together. I am not lonely any more' (H57) and a gentleman who obviously feels excluded from such companionship complains, 'I have a private room but I don't like being on my own very much.' Two Nursing Home proprietors make similar points:

> The local council has ruled that 75 per cent of all rooms must be single rooms, but confused residents need company. To be left alone for even short periods distresses them (H31, staff, private).

> Many ladies, having lost husbands, prefer to share a room. One lady, almost blind, shares with one who, without her hearing aid, is very deaf. These two people complement each other superbly, each becoming more independent than she could ever be in a room alone. I could tell you more such symbiotic stories (P26, staff, private).

The possibility of such mutually supportive relationships even leads to some criticism of high staffing ratios on the grounds that they make it difficult for the more active and alert residents to play a useful role by helping the less able. On the other hand, low staffing ratios which might be thought desirable in units preparing teenagers for independence are reported to leave some children feeling that they have received too little support at this time.

Such features cannot, therefore, be seen as good or bad in themselves but only as evidence of the need for as wide a choice as possible at every level, from choosing a pudding course or window outlook, to deciding on a single or shared room or a type of residential care.

It is at this last level that the correspondence shows how crucial are the differences of attitude which can make the same facilities ideal for one person and unbearable for another. Two of the more unhappy ladies who wrote to the Committee might each have been content in the other's situation. One writes poignantly of her loneliness and isolation in sheltered housing:

> Unless a permanent Warden can soon be found, I shall be stuck in this small room until the autumn, facing the large Common from which never a sound comes day or night. Ever since I have been here, I have longed to hear a car pass—or anything which will prove that I am not alone...I am tired of looking at the silent common from my silent room (P116, resident).

It will be remembered that one of the correspondents quoted earlier had found companionship and care in a good home after moving from a similar situation.

The other correspondent writes:

> Although I would dearly love to live as independently as possible, perhaps in a warden controlled property, I think I will be in residential care for the rest of my life (P122, resident, SSD).

The Staff Viewpoint

In the preceding sections, a number of quotations have demonstrated the concern and understanding for residents shown in many letters from staff. However, staff see good treatment of residents as being connected with better status, training and conditions of work for those who look after them and are therefore concerned with some issues of which residents and relatives are only marginally aware. Much of what they write about inspection, registration, wages and conditions, staffing levels, training and qualifications echoes what is treated in more detail in the formal evidence, so we examine here only any new light which is shed on these matters. On status, morale and job satisfaction, however, they provide some insights as vivid as those given by residents into their own lives and here once again we must rely on quotations to convey the full impact of these letters.

Staff from all sectors have suggestions as to how inspection can be improved and these will be dealt with in the final section of this summary. As might be expected, registration is the concern mainly of private home proprietors, frustrated that the exact measurements of a room appear to be of more concern to registration officers than the quality of care.

Wages and Conditions

Low wages, again predictably, are a major cause of concern, but here there is particular emphasis on what is felt to be the unfairness of rates for care staff in special schools, and on the effects of low pay in the private sector. Wages of £2 to £2.50 per hour were thought likely to attract only unskilled part-timers, uninterested in training; to lead to a shortage of applicants and therefore the appointment of unsuitable staff; and to result in high staff turnover and reluctance to work at weekends. Several correspondents regard the unsocial hours as one of the most unpleasant aspects of their work and some of those who have worked in small private homes for some time are frustrated by the lack of career opportunities. Small homes in any sector are thought to be more likely to require a large proportion of unsocial hours.

Staffing

In the private sector, there are complaints about 'matrons' who own more than one home and are rarely present when needed; and also evidence of abysmally low staffing levels, with at least one example of a new, untrained assistant being left in sole charge at night. Perhaps the most surprising thing to emerge about staffing levels is the extremes to which they vary. In the child care field, for example, there is one desperate letter from a care worker in a maladjusted school where on some evenings there was only one member of staff present to every 14 boys, and the current ratio of five houseparents to 38 boys was about to be reduced to three because of the difficulty of recruiting staff. In contrast, a local authority establishment for children in long-term care with an annexe for those preparing for independence had a current ratio of 7 children to 10.5 residential social workers, a cook, 2 domestics and a part-time handyman. They still saw their major need as being for more staff, preferably a typist and an accountant, to allow them to spend more time with the children. Whatever the situation, the reason given for needing more staff is the desire to have more time for direct contact with residents.

Training

The personal evidence places the same emphasis on training, and for the same reasons, as the formal evidence, but it does add a vivid sense of the difficulty and frustration suffered by those attempting to go on courses.

> I have had to apply and on many occasions been turned down...These courses are few and over-subscribed and so training can take a great deal of time...training must be given a much higher priority but with the lack of money within Council budgets I don't hold out much hope (P94, SSD).

I applied to go on the CSS, was interviewed and accepted for the course. However, since then I have been offered a place two years running but have not been able to go as Divisional Office will not send two members of Management at the same time. I have applied to go on Social Care Courses but Divisional Office say there is insufficient funds to pay for me to go (P110, SSD).

The other overwhelming impression about training given by this evidence is how few correspondents have received it. Of the 116 staff who wrote in, only 13 appear to have been trained to CSS level or higher, and of these, seven were working in child care. About the same number have come from other professions such as nursing or teaching, and around 30 have either attended short courses or received 'in-house' training. Approximately half, however, have received no training at all.

It should be added that a couple of those who have received training comment that they learnt as much from a good head of home as from their training. It is also true that some of the most perceptive comments about the feelings of residents come from untrained staff, and perhaps the last word on training can be given to one of these:

Training is extremely important, especially for young people, but they must have within themselves a nature that is caring and courteous, to be able to relate to a person's integrity, not just humour them...The dignity of the person is what matters most' (P60).

Status and Morale

Both the personal and the formal evidence suggest that training will improve the status and morale of residential workers. If this is so, it is indeed important, for morale is certainly low among these correspondents.

Unless the Review itself actually does produce something in the not too distant future...the disillusionment experienced by many in residential work can only get worse...How much lower can morale sink while everyone waits? (P89, SSD).

The feelings expressed cover a wide range, from being under-valued—

Residential workers feel like '2nd Class Citizens' and do not feel that they are properly consulted or treated as professional colleagues (P18, vol)—

and underfunded—

I find that the homes are running on a dedicated few who give all they can, but do become very disillusioned and bitter. We all know and can give the better care that is needed but do need money and support from Government' (P94, SSD)—

to being actively persecuted—

> The average working 'life' of a carer is estimated to be no more than five or six years, before stress takes an inevitable toll. Apart from foolhardiness, to pursue the occupation beyond that period calls not only for resilience in withstanding the pressures of the work itself but also for the donning of armadillo scaling to resist the mistrust and lack of understanding from the community at large—and the capacity to suffer the constant slings and arrows of outraged self appointed vigilantes (P92, private).

> We deserve something more than to constantly suffer the barrage of criticism currently being hurled at us (P71, private).

Morale reaches its lowest where such lack of appreciation by the outside world is compounded by staff tensions and resident unhappiness.

> Staff morale is very low there, with continuous moaning, bitching and bickering. People take a great deal of sick leave...a lot of resentment between the officers and care assistants...Resident morale is very low (H5, SSD).

Satisfactions

So why, we may ask, does anyone choose to work in residential care? The answer given by these correspondents is quite clear. They love the work—enough to compensate for the poor pay, unsocial hours, low status and public criticism. The correspondent above who estimated the 'life' of a care worker as five or six years was himself still doing the work after 26 years! There is remarkable unanimity about the satisfactions which the work offers and which seem to be the same for trained and untrained workers and in homes for the elderly, children and the physically and mentally handicapped. Most are encapsulated in a letter from a previous field worker:

> 'It is difficult to give reasons for my decision to move from field to residential work. Obviously one must be job satisfaction—on a personal level I enjoy being involved with people, field work only provides limited involvement, and residential work provides opportunities to be involved with the 'whole' person...I enjoy all areas of work from cooking the dinner to caring for the young people's physical and emotional needs...The relationship between members of staff is important—the relationship between residential workers tends to be different to that between fieldwork colleagues. In a residential setting staff must work well together (P18, vol).

First and most important of the satisfactions then is the relationship with the residents. Small wonder that in homes where residents are treated with contempt, staff also seem to be unhappy. Recognition and encouragement of the resident's abilities is an element of the relationship which brings particular satisfaction.

The most rewarding part of my job is working on self-help and behaviour modification programmes with the children and also getting parents involved...There is a great sense of achievement for everybody involved when a child does something new for the first time (P7, vol).

An untrained worker with the physically handicapped who is very clear that care staff 'are only there to give help and support when needed...never to tell anybody what to do and when to do it' enjoys best the times 'when you help them to achieve things that they thought it was impossible to achieve' (P118, vol).

Even for those working with the elderly, there is the 'satisfaction of seeing the change in a person who has been at risk in the community responding to the warmth and good food, so in some cases making confusion and forgetfulness less' (P110, SSD). This worker, however, also expresses the satisfaction of being able to bring comfort at bad times:

To spend time with a frightened lonely old person when they are ill and be able to give them reassurance that no matter what happens they will not be on their own is one of the most rewarding things you can do (P110).

This is a satisfaction mentioned by several correspondents, including child care workers:

One of the nicest things about the job is being in the fortunate position of helping a child to realize that people do want them—and help them over their initial period of feeling totally isolated and rejected (H80).

The variety of the job is also a popular feature.

I...enjoy leaving work having resolved a crisis, relieved the anxiety of a client, and got the petty cash to balance (P81, SSD).

I enjoy the demands made upon me by the present post, the administrative work, attempting to operate effectively. Improving the quality of life and promoting aspects such as self-determination, choice etc—I also enjoy the responsibility that goes with a large complex (P89, SSD).

Where all these aspects of the work are right, there is then the additional satisfaction of playing a part in the teamwork which 'is essential to harmony and happiness within the home' (P85, private).

Improvements

We considered first those letters which describe the features of good residential care, second those describing practices which cause unhappiness, third those which raise more complex issues and fourthly the issues of special concern to staff. Finally we turn to the practical measures by which correspondents suggest the Committee can support good residential care and improve the bad.

First among such measures is publicity for good residential care, the motive which has led many correspondents to write:

> Adverse publicity of private homes causes relatives who have no other option a great deal of concern, unhappiness and guilt...There are good ones to be found and this comforting thought should be more widely recognized (H25, relative, private).

> I felt it might help someone to know about the home my Father-in-law was in. I know it is very difficult for families to decide what they can do for the best. I have been in the same situation...I think they are very good places if chosen well. The home my Father-in-law was at was marvellous, the staff treated him as good if not better than I could have done myself (P45, relative).

> I'm sure that there are many lonely people [who] would be happy in the right kind of care if we could destroy the idea that every home means isolation in some workhouse (P44, staff).

Correspondents hope that more widespread knowledge of the good standards of care which can be found may make people less likely to enter an unsatisfactory home in the first place and also counteract the hopelessness that makes others reluctant to move—

> After all if it was possible to move somewhere else what chance is [there] that it would be any better? (P102, resident, private)—

and afraid to complain—

> I wanted to complain to the Matron but one has to be careful as my Mother has to go on living there (H10, relative).

> I know and we all say we should complain but it's where they have you, if we do where would she go? (H72, relative).

Complaints, Inspection and Registration

A satisfactory complaints procedure would be welcomed by correspondents. Those who have attempted to complain, whether to officers-in-charge, social services departments, health authorities or MPs, have had no apparent impact. The correspondence suggests that what is required is a simple, well-publicised system, which will deal with the resident's fear of retribution but which will not contribute to the staff's feeling of being subjected to constant criticism by 'self appointed vigilantes'.

There is an underlying feeling that complaints might be less necessary if there were more efficient monitoring of homes and tighter restrictions on who is allowed to run them. Probably the most frequent requests to the Committee are those for improvements to the system of inspection and registration, and in particular for quality of care to be regarded as of more importance than quality of buildings.

> Caring and listening can be more valuable than having so many square feet when eating in the dining room. A family atmosphere is very important (P47, staff, vol).

It is also thought important that visits should be unannounced and that inspectors should spend some time talking to residents without staff present. Inspectors should remain in an establishment long enough to assess the atmosphere and the quality of interaction between staff and residents. When a home changes hands it should be inspected again. Minimum qualifications for heads of homes are suggested as a condition of registration.

One correspondent suggests that Community Health Councils or a similar body might provide the most impartial inspectorate since they will be less likely to be influenced by the necessity to find places for those in need of care. There is also a suggestion that the issue of merit stars or rosettes (as to hotels) might encourage a desire for excellence in the private sector.

To safeguard the interests of unhappy individuals it is suggested that social workers should have periodic contacts with residents. It is also thought that residents who have no relatives or friends might benefit from visitors arranged by voluntary societies.

Importance of Finance

It is not only safeguards against bad practice which correspondents wish to see, but also encouragement for the good and for this, it is pointed out repeatedly, money is necessary. The quotations from staff letters have already made clear that the major obstacle to staff training is lack of money—not only money to pay course fees but also money to pay for relief staff or increase the establishment to allow for secondment. More money is also necessary if the activities available to residents are to be improved. Instead the opposite appears to be happening. A physically handicapped resident writes of cuts in the hours of occupational therapy, physiotherapy and art and literacy teaching. It is against this background that we must read pleas that local authorities should provide adult education, occupational therapy and physiotherapy in private homes and that all homes should receive better social, library, chiropodist, ambulance and medical services.

Communications

Better communications at all levels will, however, make few financial demands. Correspondents believe that if more information were available to prospective residents fewer bad decisions would be made and the admission process might be less stressful. A list of all homes in each area with basic information about them would be welcomed. Within social services departments, it is thought that communication could be improved not only by more line managers with residential experience but also more respect being given to the views of residential workers, who should make a point of expressing their requirements and grievances clearly in writing. Within the homes good changeover procedures are thought to bring efficiency, and intercoms and staff always within earshot to give peace of mind to the residents. It is suggested that staff also need help within call at time of crisis so 'there should be an ''out of hours'' support group available to support all small units in a particular community and these should be given priority if future community-based development is to go ahead' (P18, staff).

Elderly Mentally Infirm

The personal evidence appears to favour separate provision for the elderly mentally infirm. Their presence is a cause of unhappiness to alert residents who find themselves confined by locked doors intended to control wanderers or seated with a companion incapable of conversation. Relatives of the confused seem to prefer the specialist care of those specially trained for this work.

> The home where my mother is caters only for psychiatric clients, mostly over active dements. The patterns of care are geared to this group, the staff are recruited for their skills in this area of work—or their ability to learn those skills...The staff have a commitment and a real personal concern for each resident (P17, relative, private).

A community psychiatric nurse worried about the wrong approach of untrained staff to violence and incontinence suggests that the answer is either 'smaller EPHs with better trained staff or accommodation purely for the Elderly Mentally Ill with trained nursing staff' (P70).

Importance of Choice

Finally, the solitary representative of children brought up in care repeats the message given by NAYPIC in the formal evidence. Following a stable childhood in the same children's home with the same officer-in-charge until the age of 9, he had then experienced four unsuccessful attempts at fostering. He tells the Committee:

> I feel that residential care is an essential resource for social services...I resent the fact that people feel residential care is not good for people...I feel that choice of where you live once your family has broken down is important, many people are forced into fostering without any other options being explored...Please don't get me wrong, for many young people foster care is quite appropriate and better than residential care but what about those for which this isn't the case? (P128, ex-resident).

It is perhaps the best summary of the correspondence—for those whose families cannot look after them, choice is important, and for some, residential care will be the first choice.

In Conclusion

The majority of correspondents have been motivated to write by enthusiasm for good residential homes or indignation at bad. It may be expected that the number who have 'mixed' opinions are greater than their representation in this sample suggests, since those with less extreme experiences will have had less incentive to write. For information about the proportions of happy, unhappy, satisfied or resigned old people in residential care we must therefore turn to the research evidence. The personal evidence does, however, have its own importance. What correspondents wrote about was not guided or limited by researchers' questions or social work theories. It therefore reflects which matters concern residents and carers most deeply.

In these letters, the elderly who are happy in residential care value most the companionship and affection found in 'a loving family atmosphere' (which perhaps compensates for the family they have lost). The young physically handicapped adults, however, place their emphasis on care as a means to greater independence from family or institution. That these two groups value such different aspects of residential care emphasises again the seriousness of the lack of any direct evidence about what is important to children, the mentally handicapped and the mentally ill.

The correspondents who are unhappy in residential care can be divided into three groups: those who are unhappy in homes where no one could reasonably be expected to be happy; those who might be happier with a different form of care; and those who are likely to be unhappy anywhere. Correspondents hope that the Committee will improve conditions for the first group by instituting a system of inspection and registration which will pay greater attention to quality of care and atmosphere, and make impossible the ill-treatment and neglect experienced by some correspondents. For the second group, it is suggested that availability of a wider variety of types of care (eg sheltered housing) together with better admission procedures would bring a greater chance of happiness.

Throughout the correspondence there is evidence that three factors are essential to the happiness in good homes and that their absence leads to unhappiness in bad. These are the provision of choice at every level of residential life from type of care to daily routine; respect for residents' dignity as shown in appropriate physical care and recognition of their abilities; and enhancement of residents' feeling of self-worth through support for old relationships and the establishment of new ones. The correspondence demonstrates well-defined and practical ways in which these factors can be incorporated in the daily routines of residential life but above all it emphasises the degree to which they depend upon the staff and in particular the head of home. If staff are to reach the required standard, they will, it seems, require better status, better training and better pay.

The task which the personal evidence presents to the Committee is then to devise measures which will provide sufficient monitoring to prevent bad homes, sufficient choice to prevent inappropriate care, and above all, the conditions in which staff and residents can work together to create 'an atmosphere of freedom and friendliness', 'a fun-loving place with lots of love in it'.

(ii)
The Formal Evidence

Introduction

The predominant concerns of those who have given formal evidence to the Wagner Committee are neatly summarised by the Association of Directors of Social Services in four paragraphs on the second page of their evidence (E137), where they refer to

> an increasing need for organisational coherence which sets residential care in the context of a spectrum of care networked according to the needs of individual clients. . .the feelings of being 'dumped on' so prevalent amongst residential social workers. . .the need for more and better trained staff; buildings which maximise flexibility and capital funding which permits modifications and adaptations. . .widespread acceptance of the concept that small is beautiful, that local is best and that normalisation is the aim. . .the tension between respecting the rights, needs and privacy of the individual and yet providing residential care for quite large groups of people.'

One has only to add concern over the inequities of DHSS funding for residents and the application of the Registration of Homes Act 1984 to cover most of the major themes discussed. This summary indicates majority views on such principal issues, but attempts also to cover the entire range of concerns and ensure a hearing for the minority worry or the dissentient voice. The result is closer to an expanded index than to a normal summary.

On some of the subjects mentioned above, the great majority of contributors had something to say and to list every reference would be superfluous. The method adopted, therefore, has been to give for each topic a brief summary of the majority view, to illustrate this by quotation where possible, and then to give references to sufficient mentions of the subject to indicate the range of opinion among contributors. Where there is lengthier examination of the issue and the evidence was considered important to the Committee's consideration of a subject, the reference is in italic.

[161]

It has been impossible to use any consistent system of references, since the evidence itself ranges from simple page numbers to elaborate sections, sub-sections and sub-sub-sections. Moreover, some pieces of evidence consist of a number of separate documents. Each reference is therefore identified on an *ad hoc* basis in whatever way seems most likely to enable it to be found. For those who wish to follow up these references, a complete set of the evidence received is held in the library of the National Institute for Social Work.

Philosophies of Residential Care

The guillotine was 'innovatory' and provided 'good practice' in performing its function. The morality of the function is therefore not questioned by either of those words (E147, p5,B).

The value base of most existing residential care services is unclear and. . .we would urge that it be clarified by the Review—then at least the real reasons for current developments may be tested (E147, p4,A).

Using your categories has been a stimulating exercise but sometimes they have squeezed me into terms and categories I would not have chosen to use. Looking back I find no or little mention of vocation, faith and charity which are perhaps the heart of the matter (E38, p11).

This summary is, of choice, organised around the Committee's guidelines and categories, but to meet the above points it begins with the wider issues of philosophy, theory, definition and the distinction between the real and the ideal.

Philosophy and values
Very few pieces of evidence deal in any depth with the philosophy or value system underlying practice. Those which attempt to examine it fall roughly into three categories: a) those based on the value of Christian love, b) those based on the therapeutic value of communal living, and c) those based on recognition of the rights of the individual.

(a) *Christian love.* The Children's Society (E147) provides in Appendix A a full statement of its philosophy 'that our actions should be guided by love for and a sense of the importance of every human being', and presents its evidence in the light of this. The Children's Family Trust also bases its evidence on 'our overriding belief in the power of love, and the intrinsic worth and infinite potential of each child in our care' (E81, p11, 8). A similar belief pervades the evidence of Keith White of Mill Grove (E38).

(b) *The therapeutic value of communal living.* The Richmond Fellowship 'asserts the value of living communally with other human beings' (E75,

2.8) and claims that 'good residential care can only be found where the fact of living together is actually used to further the potential of residents' (*ibid*, 2.11). How this may be done is explored in more detail by the Camphill Community (E93), the Cotswold Community (E49) and Medvale (E144), and on a personal level by Nigel Bailey (E200) and the respondents to Wandsworth ssd's questionnaire (E184, App C).

(c) *The rights of the individual.* The vast majority of contributors follow the Campaign for People with Mental Handicap (CMH) in making the rights of the individual the value base from which residential care is viewed (E100, p1). The National Federation of Housing Associations states, 'The philosophy of management must therefore encourage people to live as they wish, to be as independent as possible and to ensure that people do not have to revolutionise their lifestyle once they enter a scheme' (E153, 5.2).

Theory

It might appear that this emphasis on the rights of the individual is incompatible with the importance given to relationships in the former two categories. However, respect for each individual is seen as a necessary part of such relationships, so in practice the gulf is not always wide. The Children's Society (E147, Appendix A), the Richmond Fellowship (E75, 6.3–5) and CMH (*passim*) would all support certain practical policies which could also be found under the umbrella of 'normalisation', the theory which, despite occasional challenges, dominates the evidence. The theory is discussed in most detail by the National Council for Voluntary Organisations in E90, Section 2, 2.3, but its influence can be perceived in most contributions and references to it abound.

Except in relation to therapeutic communities and normalisation, there is very little discussion of the theoretical basis of residential social work. The Association of Therapeutic Communities (E188) suggests that the reason for the current unsatisfactory state of residential care is that it 'is not sufficiently founded in "theories of institutional functioning"' (p2). Masud Hoghughi (E131) offers an examination of the rationale of social work as a whole and Jeff Hopkins (E84) an analysis of the positives of residential care (alongside which might be read CMH's analysis of its negative aspects, E100, p2). The Social Care Association gives detailed consideration to the language of social work, an exercise justified by the Richmond Fellowship resident who wrote:

> The very term 'residential care' has a stigma attached to it and implies some form of primitive restraint. We urge most strongly therefore that new terminology be developed which better reflects the dignity and individuality of human beings bearing in mind that everyone [in this house] is here of his or her own free will (E75, 2.2).

For this and other reasons CMH suggests that the concept of 'residential care' should be 'discarded and replaced by the dual concepts of "housing" and "support services" ' (E100, p3).

Definitions

The term 'residential care' might also be thought unsatisfactory because of its vagueness.

> There are difficulties of definition as to what is and what is not residential care under current legislation which the Wagner Committee ought to address (E153, p8,7.2).

Keith White supports the Barclay definition that residential care

> embraces any type of living situation distinct from a person's own home (from fostering to Part 3 accommodation). Obviously this will include boarding schools, hospitals and hotels (E38, p3,A).

Essex SSD, however, excludes fostering and individual adult placements (E88, 2.5). The Residential Services Advisory Group thinks it 'should be defined as care outside the family' (E68, p1). The National Federation of Housing Associations suggests,

> Residential care is the provision of both housing and care, including board, by one organisation (or, in the case of the voluntary sector by two organisations working in partnership) (E153, p3, 2.3).

Only the Association of County Councils looks in any detail at whether the new forms of accommodation designed to encourage independent living can properly be called 'residential care' (E67, 2.5–7). It decides that 'a broad and flexible definition of residential care is necessary'. The broadest definition in the evidence is perhaps that given by the Voluntary Society for Handicapped Children:

> If such a [residential] service is equated with a 'home making service' (which may provide specific and additional services in situ), then the parental or another family home may be included at one end of the spectrum, with housing association or unstaffed housing at the other (E186, p2,4).

The great majority of the contributors make no attempt to define their subject.

Real or ideal?

> It would help if the Working Group could distinguish between the potential of residential care in essence, and the practical realities at present (E38, p3).

It is a fault in the formal evidence that lack of clarity applies not only to the definition of residential care, but also to the distinction between reality and the ideal. Few contributors are as frank and clear as Strathclyde SSD:

It is not difficult to make a statement that the current pattern of residential care for people who are mentally handicapped requires to be reviewed with urgency, imagination and vigour. It is more difficult to effect change (E118, Mentally Handicapped, 7.1).

Often it is unclear whether a piece of evidence is describing current practice or summarising the pattern which is thought desirable. Notable exceptions are Essex SSD (E88), which analyses current problems at some length before discussing aims and objectives; and Devon SSD (E115) which follows a detailed blueprint for good care with almost equally detailed research findings on the hard reality. Whether intentionally or not, Cambridge SSD (E76) makes a similar point with three Appendices, the first a plan for standards of care drawn up in 1981, and the other two, recent papers revealing the current state of progress.

The Nature of Residential Care

Why do we need residential care?
There are instances when residential care will be the preferred resource, given the circumstances of the client(s) at the time. A residential centre can provide much needed asylum and a degree of personal space; there is the opportunity for residents to form helping and supportive relationships with each other; and the availability of staff, either on duty or on call, offers security and proof of caring (E185, 2).

Even though we are carrying out a fairly major relocation programme we do still see the need for our on-site services to be retained. Some of our residents have expressed a wish to stay, having lived here for many years. Others are highly dependent and need nursing care. . .We also find that we need to provide a temporary retreat 'occasionally' for some people who find it difficult to cope with community life (E25, pp1–2).

The statement by VOPSS that '[Residential care] should be provided because it meets the needs of this individual, not because it is available, safe or the cheapest option' (E170, p2) expresses the general feeling of the evidence. The needs it is seen as meeting are illustrated above and may be grouped under four headings:

(a) *The provision of choice*
Residential care is also needed in order to give families the choice whether or not to care at home. Because most families do go to great length to continue caring, it is too easily assumed that all wish—or ought—to do so, and no consideration seems to be given to the adverse effects on all concerned, including the sufferer, if people are forced into caring (E62, p1). (See also E4, A(b)).

There should, therefore, always be the possibility available for people to choose to go into residential care when they feel that they are in need of greater companionship, care and social contact than they are able to achieve within their own home (E53, A(i)).

The right of choice is the reason most often given. Further examples are found in E39, p1; E41, PtIII, p1; E51, p2; E52, a(iv); E55, 1(2); E60, E67, 2.14; E72, 4; E97, p1,A; E112, 19; E120. p1,A; E142, 7; E169, p1; E176, 5; E177, 2.1 & 3.

(b) *The provision of specialist resources*
The special communication system required by deaf-blind people means that there are very strong arguments for having some residential accommodation separately provided for deaf-blind people. . .The prevailing philosophy has tended to be that different groups of disabled people should be catered for lumped together. This is termed 'integration'; for a deaf-blind person based in a unit for mentally handicapped people, it should more appropriately be termed isolation (E3, 1 & 3(ii)).

I know there are probably thousands of children who are severely disturbed and in need of specialist help. Whether or not they get it seems to depend on the attitude of their particular local authority (E49, letter).

See also E41, III, p1; E97, G4; E98, p3; E99, p2; E112, 39 & 40; E199, p1.

(c) *Shortage of domiciliary resources for the foreseeable future*
Properly orchestrated assistance to a continuing life in the person's own home is rare (E32, A(i)).
See also E45, p1; E86, PtI, A; E97, p1,A; E106, 5; E158, p7; E199, p1. (See also 'Finance: impact of finance'.)

(d) *The provision of various types of short-term care*
Examples can be found in E32, G(i); E52 a(i) & (ii) and under separate headings in the next section.

What kind of residential care?
Several local authorities and a few voluntary societies listed the types of residential care they thought necessary to meet the above requirements: E44, A(7); E66, A,1.2; E67, 2.13; E80, 1; E88, 2, 6–7; E95 p1; E118, II Elderly, A,7; E137, p2; E175, pp2–3.
    There is a substantial amount of agreement in these lists which include the following kinds of care:

(a) *Long-term.* In five of the above lists and, obviously, mentioned frequently elsewhere (eg E105, 1.4(b)). Discussed more fully in E175, pp9–11, 1.9.

(b) *Respite.* In all but one of the lists and frequently mentioned elsewhere (eg E6, p1; E118, II Elderly, B5; E177, 1.5 & 2.6).

(c) *Assessment*. Included in six of the lists, and discussed in E175, p3, 1.6. Some evidence questions the need for assessment, particularly for children, to take place in a residential setting (eg E148, 4,(iii); E191, p17; E203, p4; E210, H(b)).

(d) *Rehabilitation*. Also included in six lists and mentioned frequently elsewhere in a variety of connections. Discussed in E175, pp5–9, 1.8; E184, 24.

(e) *Therapeutic or treatment units*. See E49; E66, A, 2.3; E68, p4; E175, pp5–9, 1.8. See also 'Children'.

(f) *Training*. Included in four lists.

(g) *Convalescence*. Included in two lists but seldom mentioned elsewhere.

(h) *Crisis or emergency*. Included in only two of the lists but mentioned elsewhere and discussed in E175, pp3–5, 1.7.

(i) *Shared Care* and *Flexible Care* are also mentioned (eg E33, A, 4 & 5; E148, 4(v); E175, pp11–12, 1.10.

Residential care for whom?

Lists of those for whom residential care may be appropriate are given in E21; E29, p2; E56 A; E111, II, 23; E137, p3 and most evidence deals with at least one or two categories. The following groups of clients are mentioned:

(a) Those who are completely physically, mentally or psychologically infirm and without relatives who are able and willing to care.

(b) Those who need external discipline or stimulation.

(c) Young people who are homeless or unwilling to live in a family.

(d) Those who choose residential care, particularly for reasons of loneliness or insecurity.

(e) Those who need to live in a group as part of therapy.

(f) Those who require specialist treatment or assessment.

(g) Those who need temporary care in a crisis.

(h) Those who need to learn new social behaviour.

(i) Those who cannot tolerate close family relationships.

(k) Those who cannot manage on their own (eg 'tramps and drunks').

Oldham ssD felt those with severe behavioural problems caused by brain damage, senile dementia or chronic mental illness should be cared for in their own homes rather than residential care (E29, p2).

Aims and objectives

No residential care should be functioning without clear aims and objectives which enable an identification of the people whom it is best able to serve (E149, p4, A(ii)).

Residential care must always be a planned and positive experience for its particular client group and have clearly articulated aims and objectives to ensure a positive experience for the individual (E26, 2A).

Clear aims and objectives are thought essential to good management, evaluation, staff morale and cohesion, admission policies and care planning for individual residents, although it is acknowledged that 'a single unit may have very different aims for each resident' (E38, p3).

The objectives of the residential care should be the achievement and maintenance of the individual's maximum independence and choice (E32, A(2)).

The objective of residential care should be to enable people to live, as near as possible, a normal domestic life within their own communities whether this be within an institution or result in a return to their own home (E96, p2,A).

The goal should be to provide a package of care which is relevant and beneficial to the client at that particular point in time (E113, 4).

Residential care. . .should seek to help each person to achieve their fullest capacity with pride and joy (a profoundly deaf, 88-year-old resident with failing sight and mobility, and diabetes, E41, II, p2).

Between them, these aims sum up those expressed or implicit in the rest of the formal evidence. Their influence will be seen on almost all the remaining subjects we shall consider.

The Roles, Quantity and Quality of Statutory, Voluntary and Private Sectors

It is appropriate that residential care should be offered by various agencies, allowing the client and his/her family to choose the most suitable style, locality and amenities. After all the life styles of clients cover the whole spectrum of society and this should be reflected within the choice of residential care (E106, 7.2).

The statutory sector

There is emphasis throughout the evidence on the need for a more positive image for residential care as a specialist resource rather than a 'last resort'. Nevertheless, a surprising number of contributors still see statutory care as 'a place of last resort' (E4, A(c)) for those with the most difficulties (E67, 2, 8–9), from the most deprived backgrounds (E32, A(3)), to be used 'when all alternatives fail' (E135, Elderly, p1).

More, however, would share the view that

> Public authorities are in a unique and advantageous position in being able to offer residential care as part of a range of services. . .They can provide care which is expensive in unit cost terms e.g. short stay and respite care or which offers focussed interventions eg assessment, rehabilitation or treatment. . .Locally based staff can provide access to a network of services (E137, p4).

Only the statutory sector is seen as potentially reliable nationwide.

> There should be statutory placements available on demand, as a separate sector so that quality and availability are standardized through the country as of right (E154, p5).

There is frequent criticism of the fact that some local authorities have chosen not to make such provision, especially for children. The statutory sector is urged to

> rebuild its crumbling residential provision in order that the balance of supremacy can be held with them and consequently made more accountable (E83, p5).

It is pointed out that 'The private market is subject to market forces and is therefore far too unreliable' (E105, AppII, p15; also E66, 4.3) and that the statutory and voluntary sectors must take the responsibility for 'ensuring a more reliable source of housing for the future' (E105, App.II, p15). (See also E88, 8.6; E178, 2.5.6).

The quality of the statutory sector is generally considered better than that of the private sector in respect of staffing, but poorer in respect of furnishing and decoration, a view vividly illustrated in E86, I, p3.

The voluntary sector

> Small voluntary agencies have a role in developing models of good practice for wider use (E13, A).

> The non-statutory organisation has a vital role to play in the provision of personalised care as an agent for and in partnership with the statutory sector. It tends to be able to respond to individual and group needs in a more immediate and innovative manner (E26, p2,A).

The voluntary sector is generally seen as innovative (E41, III, p2; E81, III, 6; E129, p4; E149, p2; E153, 4.3) and a source of specialist provision (E3, 3; E80, 2; E129, p1; E141, 4, 1–2; E154, p3A). It fills gaps in statutory provision (E7, I, 2.24; E41, III, p2; E107, p2) and is important for ethnic minorities and those with religious beliefs (E38, p10, G3; E132, B, 5). It is able to put together packages of funding from different sources, cross professional and sector boundaries and involve community interest (E75, 3.6). It is anxious that the Committee should make a clear distinction between the voluntary and the private sectors (E75, 3.6).

The quality of care in the voluntary sector is considered good by most who mention it, but there are some worries expressed that it may be deteriorating recently through lack of funds. Children's homes particularly have been affected by uncertainty about the level of places to be taken up by local authorities with rapidly changing policies (E9, p1; E149, p1; E160, p2).

The private sector
Oldham and District Registered Residential Homes Association describes the role of the private sector as

> To provide a) freedom of individual choice relating to personal need and care within a chosen accommodation environment and b) to supplement inadequate availability of Part III Local Authority accommodation and services (E117, 1).

Shropshire Association of Registered Residential Homes writes:

> We see our role in the private sector supplying a more varied and wider choice, less institutionalization and more homely atmosphere often [in] closer proximity to their own homes (E45, A).

Much local authority evidence would support this view, regarding partnership with the private sector as necessary if sufficient care is to be provided for the increasing number of frail elderly (E16, passim; E162, p26) and placing the private sector alongside the voluntary as 'well to the fore in anticipating current and future service needs' (E76, 1.6). Norfolk SSD sees 'a core of professionalism at the heart' of the private sector (E16, 5.1), benefits of size and homeliness, and availability of a local service.

Others point to the degree of variation in the quality of the private sector (E97 p1, A).

> My experience. . . is that there are some very good homes indeed (much better than Part III), that the majority are of a good adequate standard, and a few (certainly less than 5 per cent) cause us quite serious concern (E71, F(2)).

However, the Health Visitors Association is only one of a considerable number who are 'concerned that a proportion of private sector provision is unscrupulously motivated by profit without due regard to the standards of care for the elderly' (E77, p1). The British Legion fears that some private homes 'provide less than the necessary care and many which provide adequate care charge what our experience suggests are exorbitant fees' (E5, G(2)). Similar reservations about standards of care and cost are expressed in E34, B; E42; E86, I, P3; E99, pp4 & 15.

By coincidence, the cases for and against private care each find their most detailed and vehement expression in the two final pieces of evidence, E211 in favour and E212 against. The British Federation of Care Home Proprietors include in E211 their Code of Practice for their members.

There are indications that whereas at present the 'customer/proprietor relationship' avoids institutionalisation (E159, 3.1), the big companies are beginning to move into private care, and while they have the financial resources to provide multi-level care in large complexes, this may have serious consequences for statutory control of policy (E106, 17.1 & p7) and force small, homely owner/manager homes out of business (E137, p4). The dangers involved in the movement of big business into care of the elderly are examined in most detail in E212, Section 6.

The increase in private facilities for all types of clients foreseen by Essex SSD (E88, 9.3) and Oldham RRHA (E117, 21(c)) is viewed with concern by many contributors, particularly in relation to children, the mentally handicapped and the mentally ill (E29, p3(b); E67, 8.18; E103, p3; E149, p6, A(iii); E186, p17,2). The Children's Legal Centre draws attention to 'the recent development of what amount to private "lock-ups" ' and the fact that at present private children's homes 'remain entirely unregulated' (E116, p3). MIND (E151) devotes the first part of its evidence to the lack of rehabilitation in some private and voluntary homes for the mentally ill. BASW points to the need for social work support in the private sector (E175, p20, 4.5.5; see also E186, pp7–8,(iii)).

Quantity

Concern over the expansion of the private sector relates not only to future growth in the child care and mental health fields, but also to past and future development of care for the elderly (E119, 11.4–5). BASW writes of the recent explosion of private homes:

> There was no available manpower for the back-up services required, no consultation, no planning, and thus little cooperation as these homes sprang into being (E175, p20, 4.52).

Some of the evidence from medical bodies complains of the problems this creates for GPs (eg E65), and the private sector itself feels that the number of homes in any area should be related to the needs of the population (E36, p1). DHSS payments to the private sector are thought to have diverted resources which would have been better spent on domiciliary services (E90, p27), and to have 'skewed the development of the personal social services' (E175, p20, 4.5.2).

The insufficiency of statutory provision is thought by some to be one cause of this explosion (E96, p6, F; E103, p2) and there is anxiety that in future private care should develop only as part of a plan involving all three sectors (E96, p2, A). It is, however, acknowledged that the extent of need for places is difficult to assess for a variety of reasons (E71, B, 1; E101, 1; E177, 3.2), including the 'needs v choice' dilemma dealt with under 'Evaluation'.

Nevertheless, the majority view is undoubtedly that more residential provision will be required over the next 20 years (E175, p42, 2; E33, B15; E77, p3).

Children As indicated earlier, there is especial concern about the run-down of residential provision for children.

> The unfortunate coincidence of an over-statement of the advantages of sub-stitute families with a financial motivation to close homes. . .limits the choice for children and young people, and makes it very much less likely that local authorities are fulfilling their paramount duty to safeguard and promote the welfare of the child. There is a great danger that if the residen-tial sector of the child care system is reduced much further it will become an increasingly stigmatising sector for 'hard to place' young people (E116, p1).

Similar fears are expressed in E38, p5; E81, VIII, 2; E83, p1; E141, 2.4.5 & 6; E148, p1; E154, p2; E160, p1; E169, pp1–2; E176, 6. NCH has observed a rise in requests for residential care for children aged 5 to 11 (E141, 5.5 & 6) which is confirmed elsewhere.

For other client groups also the following evidence considers pro-vision inadequate:

Elderly E32, B1; E40; E46; E57, 1(a), 2(a); E88, 3, 10(ii); E96, p3 B; E158.

Mental Handicap E17, G(2); E25, p2; E118, Mentally Handicapped, 2.1.

Mental Illness E76, 1.5; E105, 1.1 & 4, 6.1; E184, App B, pp3–4.

Mental Handicap and Mental Illness E152, 2.6.2–3

Physically Handicapped E37, 5–7, 10–17, 21; E89, p1

Gaps in Provision
There are said to be gaps in the following types of provision: respite care; pre-care or transfer from hospital; after-care for the profoundly handicapped; specialised provision for some groups of handicapped children; young single homeless and teenagers leaving care; families with problems; under-18 mothers and babies; ethnic minorities leaving long-stay hospitals; frail or confused elderly; 50-65 year old physically

handicapped or mentally ill; female, young, black or gay problem-drinkers; minimal support group homes and high dependency residential care for those with mental health problems.

Networks of Care

There is. . .a priority need to develop local cohesive planned policies for the placing of:
(i) Homes in relation to community need;
(ii) Patients in relation to individual need (E12, B1).

It is essential that some method be found of ensuring that resources which interlock in a complex manner are developed in a rational and co-ordinated way. . .the alternative would seem to be the likelihood of less than optimum use of public money at the best and the mis-use of it at worst. Perhaps even more importantly it will mean that many people in need of services will not receive them, while those less in need do (E52, p6).

Everyone is agreed on the necessity of cooperation and coordination, which is the second most popular subject for contributors' Recommendations. However, many also recognise the 'inherently stubborn problems' (E175, p14, 2.7).

The problems caused by lack of such cooperation are examined in E56, pp3–4; E112, 11–12; E118, Elderly, A, 12–13; E123, p1, A; E149, p7, A(iv); E167, p9, 2–3.

Ideas suggested to remedy the situation include a 'lead' authority to coordinate ('Health' E105, 2.3; 'Social Services' E75, 3.5 & 3.7), identified liaison workers (E124, 2.1), a community care forum (E105, App II, p16) and Child and Family Service Centres (E103, p4, 4).

Cooperation and coordination between sectors

There is a basis for partnership based on an agreed philosophy of care. The local authority will bring skills, contacts and some finance; private proprietors will offer homeliness, flexibility and local services. The advantages would be better care for residents, and an economic way for comprehensive services to be developed (E16, 4 (2)).

Inter-agency cooperation is one of many themes to which everyone is committed but when difficulties arise, it is invariably the fault of the other party (E149, p6, A(iv)).

Further thoughts on the subject can be found in E5, H(2); E16; E33, A8–11; E44, A10; E50, B(4); E67, 2.16–19; E75, 3.5 & 3.7; E80, 2; E81, II, 5 E88, 2.12–2.15, 2.17; E189, p2. Four of these refer to what is described by Christian Concern for the Mentally Handicapped as 'the inherent desire to control so often manifested by local authorities, which leads charities to respond cautiously to their approaches' (E17, A(4)).

Cooperation and coordination between departments

> Evidence of the emergence of a strategic, formalised and workable framework in which Social Work, Education, Housing and Health Authorities can jointly plan their respective contributions proves to be elusive. Such a framework is crucial to the success of not only a prudent residential care policy, but also to a community care strategy (E66, 1.3).

The vast majority of contributors subscribe to the importance of such a framework, but, presumably because of its elusiveness, few have anything specific to say about how it might be achieved. A selection of those advocating coordination can be found in E6, p3(2); E44, A12; E66, 1.3; E71, A4; E77, p2; E88, 1.4, 2.15–17, 19–20; E90, pp27–28; E99, p3; E101, 2–5 & E; E105, App I, p9; E149, p7, A(iv); E167, p9 2–3; E175, pp14–15, 2.7–9; E192, 21; E196, 39–46.

There is some evidence that cooperation is better at the level of workers and clients than further up the hierarchies (E75, 4.2–4; E175, p13, 2.5). To show what is possible, BASW offers the cheering example of the provision made for mentally handicapped children under the leadership of the National Development Group (E175, p11, 1.10).

Cooperation and coordination within social services departments

> There is a strong case for more inter-disciplinary exchanges between the different staff groups if we are to promote closer integration and a stronger sense of common purpose and shared identity (E113, 5).

Cooperation within a social services department is clearly affected by the gulf which residential workers currently feel separates them from their field work colleagues. Measures to reduce this gulf such as those quoted above are discussed under 'Training' and 'Wages and Conditions' (qv). In this section we deal with matters of organisation.

It is clear that social workers themselves are thinking about this problem (E64, G(ii)), and some departments are already making attempts to deal with it (E69, p2; E88, 2.18; E188, Elderly, D1; Mentally Handicapped, 1.7). These have involved reorganising their departments on an area basis and moving towards the local networks of care which most contributors appear to consider desirable practice. It is hoped that such measures will cause residential care 'to be defined as part of a lateral spectrum rather than. . .at the bottom of a vertical scale of services' (E44, A5).

Local networks

Among those who express support for the neighbourhood 'network' concept are E35, 1–4; E44, A(11); E51, p1; E57, 1(e); E62; E67, 2.2–3; E80, 4; E88, 2.21–26; E112, 28–33; E119, 2.2–3; E175, 3.1–2; E180, 61.4–5; E186, p5(iv). Residential establishments are often envisaged as playing a central part in these networks as 'the main focus of social work services. . .including assessment, home care, fieldwork and residential care' (E121, p2).

> Residential services should be managed from as central a point as possible and where possible, having regard to the needs of residents for dignity and privacy, they should become resource centres for both their client group and the local community. Its administrative management must essentially be linked wherever possible to the network of neighbourhood services (E66, A, 3.2).

The residential unit is seen as a resource centre in E44, A9; E47, p2; E67, 2.2, 2.15; E71, A.5; E95, I, p7; E112, 30; E119, 8.1–2; E124, 2.2; E184, App A, p3; E191, 1(a) & (d). Although all would doubtless support the rights of residents, there are no more provisos like that in E66 above, concerning 'dignity and privacy'. In E135, for example, suggestions to ensure 'more comfort and privacy for the child', are followed by one that the establishment should be 'used for play groups, drop in centres and some types of day care'; and in a different section it is envisaged that a hostel for the mentally handicapped 'should become a multi-purpose facility offering a wide range of functions' including a creche, short term care, shared care and long term care, rehabilitation, assessments, training of staff, a meeting place for local voluntary groups, an office for the mental handicap team and a 24 hour emergency service.

'Normalisation' and resident's rights do not, however, lack defenders:

> Those social services departments which are structured on a 'patch' basis sometimes use the residential homes as the focus of services in each patch. In many ways, this overcomes the isolation, but another danger is created, that of the residents' 'home' becoming an office with all the interruptions of telephones, callers and crisis admissions (E175, p15, 3.1; see also p31, 2.8; E100, p4, 3 E209, p2).

> It is sometimes tempting to use such ground or buildings for some purpose which will benefit other disabled people. . .Care should be taken to pre-serve the privacy which is a treasured part of daily living (E59, Handbook I, p23).

It is possibly such reservations which lead some contributors (E53, p1, A; E86, I, p2, A; E133, Unit 3, A(v)) to believe that residential care should remain a separate sector. Warwickshire, for reasons not speci-fied, has recently re-organised into separate departments its residential, field and domiciliary services which were previously coordinated under Area Offices (E7, II, p35).

There are indications in the evidence of how these conflicts may be resolved.

> The design of the building plays a crucial role in the balance of the privacy of residents and the utilisation of the resources for elderly people in the community at large (E118, Elderly, A15).

Obviously the complexes and 'core and cluster' systems discussed under 'Management and Organisation' (qv) will make it easier to both safeguard the privacy of the resident's home and provide facilities on site.

Links with the community
An alternative method of avoiding isolation of the residential unit and maintaining links in the community is suggested by the reference of the WRVS to the enjoyment residents find in going out to a Day Centre (E53, p1). That there may be double benefits to this arrangement is suggested by the comment from Doncaster SSD that

> the mix of permanent residents with day care clients can often be uneasy and in conflict, giving difficulties not only for residents but also for staff whose opportunity to provide personal care becomes even more limited by work pressures (E162, p23). See also E180, 61.9; E208, Report, Chapt 10, pp13–15.

Doncaster's suggested solution is 'the specific designation of one or more homes to undertake short term and day care work'. This would also deal with another problem mentioned several times in connection with using homes as community resources—the unsettling effect on long-term residents of constant comings and goings for respite care (E97, p4, G3, H3; E100, p4, 3; E180, Letter & 61.7). The suggestion that residential care staff might provide domiciliary support for elderly and handicapped people living in the immediate neighbourhood (E150, p5 G(iv)) indicates another way in which the residential unit may be linked into the community by movement outwards rather than inwards.

There is, not surprisingly, emphasis throughout the evidence on the importance of residents maintaining or establishing community links by going out from the establishment. This is seen as particularly important in the case of the physically handicapped and those recovering from mental illness (E75, 6.2–6.6), but there is also recognition of the need for those elderly people who are able to do so to continue to go shopping, visit the pub, attend church worship and visit friends. Children and young people are seen as developing links with the neighbourhood in the natural course of events (E149, p7, A(v); E38, pp4–5).

Shared care in which parents, relatives or other carers come into the home to help the staff in the care of residents also provides natural links (E57, 1(e); E112, 16; E119, 9.7; E175, p11, 1.10; E191, p3). The importance of maintaining contact with families, problems which arise over visiting and ways in which these can be overcome are discussed in E180, 61.11; E186, p9, 1–3; E187, p2; E193, p1. The role of volunteers in helping to establish relationships with the community is examined in depth in *E108*, and also less fully in E59, Handbook I, p46; E79, p2; E149, pp7–8 and E194, p2. There is a general feeling that voluntary societies can most easily involve members of the public and private homes are likely to have most difficulty in attracting volunteers.

L'Arche (E13A) believes that 'Capacity for working together comes from long term service and trust in one locality; "administration of a network" would be no replacement'. A similar belief underlies the doubt expressed in E4, A(e) about the effect of rapid staff turnover and contract hours on links with the community. Some reservations among child care staff about contacts in the community are said to stem from anxiety about sexual abuse and assaults on children (E149, p7, A(v)). Finally, there are several reminders that the central task of residential staff is to create a good atmosphere in the home and they should never become so involved with community activities that this is neglected.

Evaluation

The Review may have to tackle the difficult issue about what is the criteria for success in social work. The definition of success is different depending on different value systems (E11, p2). (See also E88, 3.2)

Measuring effectiveness is much more than collecting statistics and more research needs to be done nationally about the appropriate ways of evaluating the effectiveness of residential care (E51, p2). (See also E67, 3.8)

There is general recognition of the difficulty of evaluation of residential care, which is seen as arising from a variety of factors including the need of a value system, 'the paucity of a sound data-base' (E137, p6), and the desirability of obtaining the views of the users (E66, B2).

The Voluntary Council for Handicapped Children, which provides the fullest discussion of the importance of evaluation and methods of carrying it out (*E186, pp19–25*) emphasises its positive contribution:

Inspections are often about 'minimum standards'. Evaluation in its truest sense of the word is about *maximising* quality of life (p23, 4).

An essential ingredient in evaluation is 'catching the staff doing something right' and encouraging good practice (p21,5).

Others who attempt to outline how it may be done would mainly agree with Berkshire SSD that, 'Evaluation . . . should be primarily focussed on the achievement of specific and pre-determined objectives and assess the quality of life experienced by residents' (E120, p2). Their suggestions can be found in E67, 3.1; 3.6–12; E88, 3.1–6; E91, p1; E120, p2. The use of PASS (Program Analysis of Service Systems) is suggested as an evaluation tool (E147, p5). The Richmond Fellowship urges the need for special funding to give voluntary societies the resources to do adequate evaluation.

Keith White suggests that evaluation 'involves reflection long after the event' (E38, p6) and BASW appears to agree (E175, p25, 3.2). BASW also suggests that 'market forces' in the form of consumer choice may eventually evaluate and influence standards of care (E175, p26, 5.1).

Are costs of placement justified by results? Could resources be used more effectively?

The Association considers the question of justifying the costs of placements by results to be wholly improper . . . the only real measure of 'results' in providing a home for individuals is individual contentment (E175, p24, 3.1). (See also E88, 3.5)

To attempt to assess financial justification for such placements seems impossible, we are dealing with human dignity and quality of life (E154, p5).

Sadly the main criteria . . . is value for money . . . But so many of the pros and cons of care in a particular establishment may have more to do with factors which cannot be recorded on a balance sheet (E17, B2).

The need for evaluating the effectiveness of risk taking in relation to results is at least as important as the current preoccupation with evaluating cost in relation to results (E51, p2).

Contributors appear to be as concerned with attacking the morality of the questions on cost effectiveness as with answering them. Those who do consider them give most attention to the difficulty of providing an answer. Firstly, there is the problem of making fair comparisons between residential and community care costs (E157, 3.3). BASW suggests that the hidden costs of boarding out may be as much as four times the cost of the actual boarding out payment (E175, p25, 3.3). Then there is the fact that unit costs for residential homes are rising because smaller units are caring for more highly dependent residents, but because more are being supported at home, the unit costs of the service as a whole are dropping (E92, 4). And would it be fairer if measurements were based on caseloads (allowing for after-care and support in the community) instead of bed occupancy? (E68, p2).

A wholly different dilemma is that of 'need versus choice' in the disposal of expensive resources (E66, A4.1). To whom is it more appropriate to give residential care—those who obviously 'need' it through frailty and lack of community support but who do not really want it (and who might have remained in their own homes given sufficient domiciliary support, see E32, B2), or those who are less dependent but who long for residential care because of their fear or loneliness (E118, Elderly, A8; E150, A, p2; E119, 10)? Which is the more effective use of resources? The difference between efficiency and effectiveness is pointed out. It might be more efficient to use beds for a high proportion of frequent respite care to delay long-term admission but is it effective if it leads to old people feeling disorientated (E66, B4)?

There is also the question of what constitutes 'resources'. 'Careers are a resource' (E57, 2(b)) is a point made several times, and the same is asserted for volunteers, but, 'Residential staff are often unwilling and inexperienced in sharing with volunteers' (*ibid*).

Having made all these points, few contributors, apart from Essex SSD (E88, 3.7–9), answer the questions in any detail.

Monitoring

> The present range of standards of care . . . covers the whole spectrum from excellent to 'downright grotty'. There is therefore an urgent need to strengthen the present monitoring structures in all areas (E12, B3).

> Evaluating and monitoring systems would be much improved if those considering standards could be resident for some days and take part in the life of the homes and the needs of the tenants (E41, II, p3).

The evidence is far more specific about monitoring. Methods of monitoring are given in E88, 3.15; E100, 7; E111, 36–38; E131, pp17–18; E181 and E204, pp13–14; in E26, B(i) & (ii) and E75, 7.3 & 18.1–9 for the voluntary sector; and for the private sector suggestions are made in E12, B3–B9. The necessity and difficulty of better monitoring for the private sector are emphasised in E12, above, and in E29, p6. The Health Visitors Association agrees but wants universal standards for all sectors, and lists some of the bad conditions regularly reported by its members (E77, pp1–2). These points are echoed in many responses to the questions on Registration (qv). It is suggested in E100, 7 that the private sector might be happier if the 'stick' of monitoring and inspection were accompanied by the 'carrot' of training and advice. The Shropshire Association of Registered Residential Rest Homes, however, thinks it would be better if local associations were able to self-monitor private homes (E45 (B)). Help the Aged suggests that a committee similar to a board of school governors, consisting of residents, management and independent appointees might become part of the monitoring process (E163, Annex p2).

It is thought important to monitor both the establishment as a whole and individual cases and to involve outsiders (E129, p2); to seek the views of residents (E116, p4; E118, Elderly, A16; E170, p6; E183, 4.9(iv); E186, p25, (viii)); and to pay particular attention to the quality of staff (E33, 31).

The staff of one children's home write, 'We also wonder how much monitoring is done after a child leaves care' (E133, B, p7).

Innovation and good practice

> There is a need to publicise more effectively the areas of good practice . . .
> and evaluate these at the same time as evaluating failure (E51, p2). (See also
> E83, B.1)

The Committee is not given as many examples of innovation or good
practice as might have been expected. The NCVO looks in detail at a
number of examples of good practice in both residential and domiciliary
care (*E90, pp15–19*). Other specific examples suggested are the
Abbeyfield Society (E34), Camphill Communities, the Children's Family
Trust and St Christopher's Hospice (E38), John Groom's Dolphin Court
(E89), the Motor and Cycle Trade Benefit Society complex (E99) and the
establishments described in Appendices H–K of E88 and Appendices III,
IV and V of E105.

Less specific examples of good practice are 'core and cluster' for the
mentally handicapped (E44), resource centres linked to establishments
for the elderly (E44) and mentally handicapped (E51), multi-disciplinary
assessment panels for the elderly (E51), a coordinated, integrated fieldwork and residential support service for child care (E51), a Local Child
Care Planning Group (E56) and provision of units particularly for
dementia sufferers (E66).

Two examples of the last category are described in the evidence—
group homes provided by Age Concern, Chorley (E102) and Burrows
House by Servite Homes (E104). There are also interesting descriptions
of the day centre attached to new accommodation for the physically
handicapped at Fernan Street, Glasgow (E118, Physically Handicapped,
11–13), of shared housing provided by Wandsworth Association for
Mental Health (E63), and new designs for accommodation for the
Leonard Cheshire Foundation in the folder by Keith Cook, 'Planning for
Freedom', accompanying E59.

The Residential Experience

> For some groups, the experience of something better may be difficult to con-
> ceptualise; for others there is an innate reluctance to complain (E88, 4.1).

Essex SSD is one of the contributors to the formal evidence who try to
explain the lack of client views in their contribution, a lack which is
indeed surprising in view of the general insistence throughout the evidence on the importance of client wishes and choice. In the formal
evidence, the client's experience is conveyed first-hand only in the contributions of three physically handicapped residents (E15, E182, E206),
one elderly lady (E41, II), the members of NAYPIC (E39 and E148), two
current care workers who were themselves brought up in care (E203 and
E206) and a group of residents and staff in a hostel for recovering men-

tally ill (E184, App C). E86 is one of the few pieces of formal evidence which describe how residential staff experience their daily life. The voices of relatives and friends are not heard at all. To understand the depths of unhappiness of clients in bad homes and the contentment of those in good ones, the satisfactions and frustrations of staff, and the anxiety, guilt or relief of relatives, one must read the personal evidence. This section deals mainly with the residential experience as viewed by administrators.

Admission
Apart from general criticism of the inadequacy of domiciliary services, there is little in the evidence about the circumstances which lead to admission. They are considered in any detail only in an account of a survey in Norfolk (E16, 3(2)) which showed a serious lack of that careful planning and assessment which most contributors assert to be so important a feature of the admission process. (See also E90, 4.7; E115, 4.2.1 & 2; E204, pp6–7). The possibility of conflict over admission between client and carer is dealt with in E119, 10.2 and the Committee is asked its opinion on the necessity of an appeals procedure against the local authority decision. The importance of ensuring that children, the elderly, the mentally handicapped and the mentally ill either speak for themselves or have an advocate to speak for them is emphasised in E44, 25. Another point made or implied several times in the evidence, particularly with regard to disturbed children, is that admission should not be 'delayed beyond the point where a positive contribution or maybe positive care is possible' (E119, 3.1). A 'last resort' policy may adversely affect rehabilitation, choice and cost (E162, p24, 6(c)).

Intake criteria and admission procedures (often, it may be suspected, ideal rather than actual) are described and discussed in E19, C, 1 & 2; E51, p3; *E59, Handbook I, pp33–36*; E76, pp4–5, 1.1–2.3; E95, I, p3; E103, 5(iv); E111, 41–4; *E115, 4.1 & 2*; E123, pp2–4; *E129, p2 and Appendix and admission forms*; E160, p3. As mentioned above, there is emphasis on the importance of adequate assessment (eg E35, 6; E90, 4.7; E119, 10.1). Good information about the client's life prior to admission is also seen as important but currently not always adequate or reliable (E13, D; E50, C5; E99, p8).

Most contributors recognise the importance of the admission procedure and experience, and many show sensitivity to the feelings and anxieties of the new resident (E38, p7; E39, p1; E56, p6; E81, V, 2, 3; E95, I, p4; E135, Elderly, p7; E150, p1A; E197, 3; E209, p2).

> There is nothing worse than a new resident finding someone else's clothes hung up, or in one case I know of, finding a set of false teeth in the bedside locker. Even residents who appear to have settled well into a home may in fact be grieving for their old home, old friends, even missing the trains that thundered past each night (E27, p4).

Several contributors mention the advisability of a trial period (E53, p2; E75, 8.6; E76, p4, 1.2 & 3; E99, p6) and others the importance of not giving up a tenancy too soon (E27, p5; E53, p2; E76, p4, 1.3).

Daily life

The evidence about daily life in residential care is sparse. Some picture of life in homes for the elderly can be gleaned from E4, C(a) & (c); E76, III, 2.1; E86, I, C; E135, Elderly, pp3–5 ('Many elderly people like routine and for the confused it can be a blessing in keeping them in touch with reality'). A day in the life of a tetraplegic is described in vivid detail by Steve Comerford in *E15*, and the reality of caring for the handicapped is conveyed by E86, III, p7. Residents from the Richmond Fellowship give some details of their experience in E75, 9. In E179, an architect describes how daily activities can be encouraged or discouraged by building design.

There is considerable concern in the personal evidence about the lack of activities for elderly and handicapped residents and this is confirmed by the evidence of Age Concern (E85; see also E204, letter and pp8–11). Examples of the kind of activities and participation to be found in the better Homes for the elderly are given in E4, B(d), C(c); E40, C and E53, pp2–3 and for the mentally handicapped in E26, p1.

For the physically handicapped it is declared that 'The maximisation of independent living should be a goal for everyone even if that maximum is merely to straighten one's own bedcovers' (E118, Physically Handicapped, 15), but how far this is from the general reality can be seen from E15. The importance of intellectual stimulus, education and physiotherapy is emphasised for this group and others, but acknowledged to be insufficiently provided (E123, p3; E33, A(ii); E85). Leicestershire library service points out that the effectiveness of their contribution depends upon the interest and encouragement of staff (E74). Books and educational toys are said to be notably lacking in children's homes and family centres (E191, p8).

The availability of all services, not only educational ones, to residents is thought to be poor. 'Residential care should not exclude people from other services' (E52, p2), but it seems that residents get less than their fair share of adult education, physiotherapy, chiropody, district nursing, occupational therapy and transport (E32, H, 1.1; E96, F, p6; E99, p5; E99, V, p15; E103, 2, p1; E106, 13.6; E112, 10; E124, 3.1; E184, 19; E187, p3).

Stress

Any setting in which a group of people from varying backgrounds live together is bound to be a breeding ground for everyday friction . . . this is called human nature (E94, I, p2).

Stress on residents receives very little attention in the formal evidence, and stress on staff a great deal—a balance which is redressed by the personal evidence. The personal evidence does however confirm the accuracy of the stresses noted in the formal evidence.

The causes of stress on residents which are mentioned include being unable to get away from people who are not liked (E4, C(d); E94, II, p3; E99, p6); (for the elderly) being upset by personal habits of other residents (E4, C(d)), anxiety caused by confused, wandering residents (E94, II, p3), unhappiness at unkindness over incontinence (E99, p6); (for children) having to adjust to changing adults as a result of the shift system (E23, 16(7)). Lists of stresses for the elderly are given in E99, p7 and for children in E133, Unit III, p4. Attention should, perhaps, be drawn to the absence of any detailed evidence of the stresses faced by the mentally handicapped, or indeed, of their experience of residential life in general.

A final word on stress comes from Cecil Houses (E4):

> It is as well, however, not to lay too much stress on the problems of living in residential care, as one could very well produce a long catalogue of problems and stresses caused by people living in their own accommodation in such stressful situations as high rise flats, areas of social unrest, violence and muggings and so on (E4, C(d)).

Leaving care

> From every residential treatment setting there ought to be an effective programme of 'termination work' (E19, C3).

> There was scarcely any mention of participation or method of departure. This absence of comment is regrettably most likely a point worthy of note, especially for elderly clients (E23, 13(1)).

It is a strange feature of the formal evidence that, despite the emphasis on training for independence, there is very little discussion of leaving care for the physically or mentally handicapped or the mentally ill (but see E75, 10; E129, App 10a; E186, p5). Stranger still is the almost complete lack of comment on death, the means by which the majority of the elderly will leave care and surely a major feature of life in homes for the elderly. This is acknowledged by Doncaster SSD with recognition that care staff need time 'to counsel and comfort the sick and dying' (E162, p17, 6) and by the RNID in their description of staff preparation for dealing with death (E129, App 10a). Apart from this, it is dealt with only by Devon SSD, who treat at length such matters as the rights of the dying to know or not to know of their condition, to see friends, relatives or ministers of religion of their choosing, and finally to leave the home with dignity and respect rather than being hustled down the back stairs in a bag so that other residents do not see. It also deals with how the other residents should be told and their right to pay their last respects to a friend after death and be helped to attend the funeral (E115, 5.24–34).

Children All other major concern about leaving care centres on children, who often face 'a termination that is by default, in contrast to the normally careful admission to care' (*E78*, p1).

> How do you teach a youngster not to be lonely? Because staff and their managers recognise their own failure in effectively helping them make such a crucial transition, such a problem does not become identified, ie does not exist! (E83, C2). (See also E39, p1).

Barnardo's believe that the preparation for leaving must start from day one that the child is in care (E149, p11; see also E203, p5) but the evidence deals mainly with the periods immediately before and after leaving. Setting the leaving date, sharing anxieties, hopes and fears are dealt with in E160, p8; the need for budgets in cash for homes preparing children for independence in E118, Children, 3.3(ii); E184, 11 and E203, p6); the difficulty of getting Departments to give a mandate and empower and prepare staff to take the necessary risks in E78, p2; the role of 'Halfway Houses' in E9, pp1 & 2; the need to improve and evaluate after-care in E178, 3.4 and E203, pp2–3.

There is support for the idea of a flexible procedure for leaving rather than an arbitrary cut-off at 18 (E110, 2.6(ii); E38, p7). The Children's Family Trust draws attention to the financial responsibility they feel for their children who are leaving care in a time of unemployment and shortage of rented accommodation (E81, VII, 2), and Barnardo's call for mandatory financial support from local authorities for young people leaving care (E149, p21, G(ii)). They also point to the difficulty for child care agencies in deciding when to cut off support from severely handicapped children who need life-long care (*ibid*, G(i)).

NAYPIC provides a client's-eye view of the problems of leaving care (*E39* and *E148, pp8–9*).

Rights of Residents

> Society seem[s], perhaps unwittingly to have come to the conclusion that the players should be withdrawn from the game of life before the match has been completed. Is this actually what we would want to happen, and if it is, then at what point are the players deemed too vulnerable for further play and who is to decide? (E72, p2)

> Difficulties arise not in subscribing to principles but in acting in particular situations. For example, will the person who is determined to make her own way from her chair in the lounge to her own room, in the only way she can manage, by crawling, be permitted to do so when important visitors are in the house? (E159, p3).

Clients must have personal dignity and individuality protected. Essentially this concept is in conflict with community life (E44, C24).

Although 'Rights' do not feature prominently among contributors' Recommendations, they are, as already indicated, the basis of the value system on which the current theory of residential care is founded and are therefore a constant theme of the formal evidence. Their full implications and the conflicts which can arise from them are apparently still emerging. Residents' rights are discussed at some length or listed in E7, p30(i); E29, p4; E32, C3; *E59, Handbook I, pp22–31*; E75, 11 & 12; E88, 4.4–6; E90, 2.4; *E100 passim*; E111, p13; *E116, passim*; E118, Physically Handicapped, p2; *E148 II* NAYPIC *Charter of Rights*; E152, 2.1.4–5; E170, p3; E196, 35–38.

From these references and others throughout the evidence it emerges that the observance of individual rights is by no means as simple as it might appear from some lists. The conflict which is noted most often (and which it is suggested might be helped by mutual discussion) is that between the rights of residents and rights of staff (E66, C2; E118, Elderly, C7; E149, p11, C(iii)). Then there are conflicts between the rights of the individual and the rights of the community— for example over sexual relationships in the Richmond community (E75, 11.1–3, 12.1–2), or the tendency of the young to exercise their rights 'sometimes to the discomfort of their neighbours, fellow residents and caring staff' (E143, 4.5.1). 'No social group can thrive if every member is primarily concerned about their rights' (E38, p8). There are conflicts between the rights of individuals—if residents' control is increased, will those who so choose be able to 'deter or debar new black residents or the employment of black staff' (E130, p3)?

Implicit rather than explicit is the conflict between different rights of the same individual. There are 'the right to discipline, the right of training' (E38, p8) which must often be weighed against the child's right to choice—'the aim is to give pupils a lifestyle that any parent would give their child, eg meals are at defined times' (E154, p8). In homes for the elderly, the right to choice must sometimes conflict with the routine which is important to the confused (E135, Elderly, p4). And the right of the mentally handicapped and the mentally ill to freedom and independence seems sometimes to conflict with their right to care or choice. 'To force residents into "independence" or isolation too early is sometimes to deprive them of the opportunity to make real choices' (E75, 12.7; see also E186, p4).

Risk
The other controversial area concerning rights is 'risk'. It appears to be generally accepted that risks will follow from granting rights to clients, but what they may be is examined in detail only in *E59, Handbook I,*

pp26–29. The ability to make choices, with the concomitant risks, is seen as an aspect of development (E17, C3; E100, 8) and normalisation (E184, 22).

> The question of risk is an important one, because if residents are encouraged to grow, then such growth will entail risks which society at large, employers, families and staff may be unwilling to permit (E66, C4).

Lincolnshire ssd declare, 'The department would support responsible risk taking as long as the decision does not threaten the safety of the other residents' (E135, Elderly, p6), but there is no discussion here or elsewhere of the implications of this for staff. Nottingham sca comments:

> Ours should be a risk taking profession and yet it seems a contained situation is often the only measure of success in the work we do. Judged on this basis we adopt the most restrictive environment in order to at least be safe (E191, p18).

Rights

> The question of franchise involves the rights of residents to have a say over how their home is run, and staff need to be clear about their own limits of discretion and those of residents (E209, p3).

Choice is the right which is most often mentioned. The point is made several times that the basic choices are 'who you live with; who provides you with whatever support you need; where you live' (E100, 9; see also E38, p6; E86, II, p2). If these choices are denied, no choice of furnishing or mealtimes will compensate. It is also clear from much of the evidence that choice of home is usually limited by availability to one or none (E37, 21). On the lesser choices there is general agreement that they should be offered but little information about practice, although it is good to know that at least one home allows budgies (E86, I, c)! naypic is 'alarmed' at the number of authorities who still buy in bulk food, toiletries etc, and reports that a few still use clothing orders, thus depriving residents of choice (E148, p5).

Privacy is the other right which is felt to be important, particularly in relation to residents' rooms. Privacy for the toilet and dressing is urged in E27, p5; E34, p2; E179, p4; E191, p1(b); E195, B, and that of mail and phone calls in E149, p12. There is also a plea that there should be no surveillance by TV monitors (E124, 3.2.5).

Freedom. The 'fundamental right to liberty . . . must be safe-guarded' (E116, p5) and there is concern in the evidence over the current use of secure accommodation and custodial sentences for young people (E116, p5; E118, Children, 7.3; E141, 2.4.6: E175, p13, 2.1). Freedom as well as choice may be thought to be involved in the frequent use of the terms 'dementia' and 'mental illness' without the need to justify them (E29, p4) and 'the use of inappropriate sanctions and controls in private residential care homes and nursing homes' (E186, pp17–18).

Complaints. The need for a 'clearly defined complaints procedure' is mentioned in relation to both children and old people (E76, II, 12.0; E79, pp3 & 9; E116, pp4–5; E141, 6.4; E148, p8; E186, p19, 4) and in both cases the fear of recrimination and victimisation is raised as a difficulty. Access to independent advocates is one suggested solution (which might perhaps be linked to the suggestion that voluntary societies should develop the provision of independent advocates to help old people in care who are unable to manage their own money and have no relatives or friends, E124, 3.3). The role of such an advocate or 'ombudsman' is discussed in relation to the mentally handicapped, especially children, in E186, pp18–19 and to the elderly in E204, pp11–14.

Ethnic Minority Groups

Only a small proportion of the evidence discusses the issue of ethnic minority groups, the rest either ignoring the subject or saying that there is no problem. Contributors who do discuss it, however, often make it a major issue. The question is dealt with in E4, c(e), E6, p3; E8, p2; E23, 17(1–4); E34, p2; E38, p8; E39, p1; E68, p3; E77, p3; E78, p2; *E90, 3.3;* 4.2; E97, p2C; *E113, 8–10;* E119, 5.1, 8.3; E170, p4; E194. Questions to which the Committee is asked to seek answers are posed in E130. The issues are discussed almost entirely in relation to the elderly and children.

The issues common to all client groups include special diets, anti-racist training for staff, the participation of minority community groups and associations in planning, and the recruitment of staff who reflect the racial mix of the local community.

Elderly Evidence of the great increase which will take place in the numbers of the elderly in the ethnic minority communities over the next few years is the subject of *E31* and is dealt with also in E30, p1 and E99, pp7–8. As is pointed out in E90, 3.3 and E99, the elderly are most likely to have language difficulties and to hold firmly to their dietary customs and religious beliefs. There is anxiety that they should be ensured equal access to residential accommodation and uncertainty as to whether this

is best provided separately in view of religious and dietary requirements. The implication for housing needs and capital costs are looked
at in E90, 3.3 and E153, 4.2 and 6.3. An interesting pilot scheme for
Asian elders in Leicestershire is described in detail in *E161*. Fears are
expressed in E158 that special provision for ethnic minorities will lead
to newspaper campaigns against 'Curry on the Rates' (pp7–8). The difficulties are presented from an unusual aspect by Wandsworth SSD
where the staff 'form a majority group mainly of West Indian origin. The
majority of residents therefore have very little reflection of their own cultural background through the staff who care for them' (E184, App A,
p7).

Children   The major worry concerning black children in care is that they
will suffer a loss of identity because of lack of contact with their cultural
background and shortage of young black staff who can act as role
models (E78, p2; E110, 3.2; E113, 10(3); E116, pp6–7; E203, pp4 & 7).

A general point made by Brent SSD is the importance of avoiding
stereotypes—'the term "Asian" embraces several major world religions
and national groups' (E113, 10(1)). Even within groups there are differences of age, education, class background etc and all clients should be
treated as individuals (*ibid*, 10(2)).

CCETSW suggests that black and other minority group workers may
be less likely to be seconded for training (E165, p5; Annexe, p11; see also
E201, C).

There is a plea in E132, B, 11 for recognition that religion as well as
race is an aspect of identity and needs to be treated as important.

Management and Organisation

> If the establishment is to be really effective, the values implicit in its aims
> need to permeate the attitudes of the whole staff team; including the
> management, administration and ancillary staff as well as those directly ful-
> filling tending and social work roles (E111, 62).

The creation of a team spirit based on a shared philosophy and clear
goals appears to be the agreed requirement for good management (E94,
D; E111, 53–67). The fullest discussion of the practical issues is to be
found in E75, 15.1–14, *E88, section 5; E175, pp29–30, 1.1–11* and, for voluntary management, in E183, 5, 10–14. Management training is dealt
with under 'Training' (qv).

Management within the establishment

> All staff should work as a team and should show concern for each other as
> well as their clients. A warm family atmosphere should exist but obviously

there must be an undisputed leader and a degree of discipline as in any happy family (E86, I, D).

Management structures vary considerably across the membership but this makes for a healthy dialogue. ARC insists that this is an area in which intervention would be unwise unless advice and assistance is sought (50, E4).

The officer-in-charge and senior staff are seen as crucial to the shared ethos of an establishment and their role, its importance, changes in it, influences and constraints on it and qualities required for it are discussed in E29, p5; E32, D1; E33, D27; E51, p4; E88, 4.8; E121, p5; E129, p3; E175, p30, 1.10; E181, p1; E197, p5; E200, p2. The effects of the shift duty system on management are discussed in E71, p7 and in E44, D34–35, where a danger is seen of all senior staff attempting to fulfil the same functions (although E191, p4 recommends a horizontal rather than a hierarchical structure). It is suggested that the appointment of a bursar would leave managers to concentrate on professional matters and this suggestion finds support in E67, 5.4 and E137, p8.

The degree of autonomy allowed to establishments is regarded as important (E38, p5; E47; E175, p30, 1.9; E184, 11). Limits on this from statutory requirements, financial constraints and the ethos and rules of the parent body (E32, D2) are thought likely to affect, among other things, the quality of links with the community (E38, p5) and the 'degree of entrepreneurial flair' possible for managers (E137, p7). Management styles and structures need to vary to match the varied tasks of establishments (E111, 55).

There is support for the involvement of residents in management and the setting of standards (E37, 22; E59 Handbook I, 48f; E76, III, 2.5; E105, 3.4; E175, p29, 1.6; E183, 4.9(iii) & (iv)). It is suggested in E66, D1 that the usual management triangle should be inverted with the manager at the bottom seen as supporting the staff, and both together supporting the residents, whose home it is.

Management from outside
The major point made in relation to external management is the need for senior managers to have substantial residential experience and a positive attitude to residential care (E83, D2; E111, 66; E112, 27; E149, p8, A(v); p14, d(i); E169, p6; E191, pp16 & 18).

Visits from managers should be sufficiently frequent and prolonged to give support to the staff and give residents the confidence to express their views and complaints (E29, p6; E111, 63 & 64; E148, p7, 4(iv)). A danger is foreseen that managers who visit too frequently may identify with the feelings of staff (E29), but infrequent visits may cause staff to feel isolated and abandoned (E75, 15.6; E133B, p3). The involvement of heads of homes in Management Teams, and meetings between senior staff of different homes are considered valuable (E71, p8; E80, 7; E175, p30, 1.8; E195, p4, D).

External management is seen as responsible for the setting of objectives and standards of practice, the introduction of innovations, the support of staff and the development of shared philosophies and styles of practice.

Assessment, reviews and care planning

Although there are many brief references acknowledging the importance of assessment, reviews and care planning, the only detailed discussion of their nature and use comes in *E175, pp31–2, 3.1–6*; for young people in *E160, pp6, 7–8*; for medical assessment of the elderly in *E103, Appendix* and for handicapped children in *E186, pp7–9 & 14*.

Further references to medical assessment are found in E20, 5; E60 and E175, p32, 3.2–3. The role of the clinical psychologist is discussed in E146, and multi-disciplinary assessment is recommended in E71, p9 and E175, p32, 3.1. The use of 'halfway houses' for assessment of old people leaving hospital is suggested in E103, p1, 2, and the need to take account of the problems of carers in assessment is pointed out in E96, p3, C. NAYPIC questions the usefulness of assessment centres and asks why families are not assessed rather than individuals (E148, pp6–7).

There is support for the involvement of residents in assessment, reviews and care planning (E33, 29; E68, p2; E76, II, 8.0 & III, 2.6; E80, 8; E118, Physically Handicapped, 15 and Elderly, D.3; E170, p4), although the staff of Malvern Community Home point out that reviews can be somewhat traumatic events and children may prefer to write their contribution (E56, p6). Others suggest that when clients do not wish to attend they could be represented by advocates. The Children's Family Trust regards reviews as a useful tool but are concerned when they threaten a child's security by unnecessarily questioning the permanency of placements (E81, III, 2). Keith White considers them 'potentially destructive in long-term care' and asks, 'Could there not be a right not to have six-monthly reviews?' (E38, p9).

There is some concern that residential staff's 'very clear and sharp appreciation of a client's needs' is not always appreciated by other care professionals (E113, 6), and that, 'An inverse ratio seems to operate in that the person spending most time with a resident is the one whose view is least sought' (E154, p11).

The National Confederation of Registered Rest Home Associations would welcome research into the claim that assessment procedures for statutory and some voluntary establishments are more thorough than those in private care and the identification of models of good practice. It has, however, reservations about 'the vogue for assessment' (E159, p4).

Records and access to files

Again, there are acknowledgements of the importance of good records and recognition of the need to improve them, but no detailed discussion of how they should be kept, apart from E175, pp32–3, 3.7–11.

The subject of access to files evokes more difference of opinion. The general view appears to be that clients should have access (E39, p1 & p2, E67, 4.10; E71, p9; *E116, p6*; E118, Physically Handicapped, 15; E141, 6.8; E175, p32, 3.8; E183, 4.3–5; E201, p2; E203, pp7 & 8). BASW (E175) supports the right of clients to keep their case file in their possession, and NAYPIC (E39) the right of young people leaving care to take their file with them. However, the difficulty of carrying out a policy of access is described in E123, p5, D, and the Richmond Fellowship, while support-ing the policy, points out also the need for security, and reservations are expressed by some of their residents (*E75, 16, 1–7*). Both the Richmond Fellowship and NAYPIC suggest that a member of staff should be present to explain and discuss the records.

Barnardo's describe the difficulties caused by dealing in the same unit with children whose local authorities have different policies on access (E149, p15, D(iii)), and in E80, 8 it is pointed out that access may depend on the agreement of other professions (educational, medical). The evidence indicates that that agreement might not be forthcoming, the RHHI (E33, 30) and the BMA (E96, p5, D) both insisting on the importance of confidentiality. One GP writing to the Soroptomists favours free access, but another correspondent comments that 'people do not always wish to know that the doctor thinks they are deteriorating or a hypochrondriac' (E99, p8).

Administrative and clerical help

The point is made several times in the evidence that care staff are often performing clerical and administrative tasks for which they are not trained and which could be done more efficiently by a part-time clerk/typist. This would free the care staff for more appropriate duties (E7, II, p33; E56, p8; E64, B/D(ii); E76, 5.3; E175, p30, 1.7; E184, 10; E195, p4).

Models of organisation and patterns of care

Patterns of care should be based on assessed need, the concept of 'normalis-ation' and the expectation of the client (E50, E2).

The ways in which buildings can 'preserve the independence, dignity and privacy of an individual but . . . allow for possibilities of social exchange' are indicated in an interesting summary of design criteria for homes for the elderly (*E179*). The writer emphasises, in his conclusion, the importance of attempting to apply these criteria to the upgrading of existing building stock. However, although many old people in Part III accommodation must still be living in large buildings (Lincolnshire, for example, has 3 new compared to 30 old Part III Homes; E135, Elderly, p2), there is very little in the evidence about models of organisation or patterns of care for them. The abstract of Tim Booth's *Home Truths* included as E22 indicates that patterns of care, 'as encapsulated in daily routines and management practices, have no measurable effects on [the residents'] social functioning or their chances of survival'. The evidence of NCVO, however, suggests that where attempts have been made to introduce the principle of 'normalisation' into traditional homes through group living arrangements, there has been a noticeable change in the level of activity and degree of confusion of the residents (E90, p8). Lincolnshire reports somewhat similar results for some residents transferred to a new group home, although other residents were unable to adapt (E135, Elderly, p6).

The majority of the evidence concentrates on new accommodation purchased or designed with 'normalisation' in mind. Here models of organisation and patterns of care are determined by the domestic size of the accommodation and the needs of the client. Two patterns predominate:

The complex, where accommodation may range from ordinary sheltered housing through respite care, hostels, very sheltered housing and residential care to nursing care, with perhaps a day centre, resource centre or other facilities on the same site. Examples of such complexes are given in E4, G, p8; E14; plans for them are described in E8, p11; E95, II; E163, III, pp4–11 and E189, enc p6; and they are recommended in E5, H3; E21; E34, G; E96A; E118, Elderly, B8; E135, Elderly, p9. They appear to be the most popular model of organisation for the elderly or mixed groups in the future, since they offer a possibility of care until death on one familiar site, together with a range of facilities catering for the needs of different residents. However, E212 foresees a possibility of clients being exploited in private complexes (p24).

Core and cluster is the other popular pattern, developed to meet the needs of the mentally handicapped and mentally ill discharged from hospital, but now being used or suggested also for the physically handicapped, the elderly and young people. It is very fully discussed in *E43* and *E151, Pt II, 3.1–4* and more briefly in E3, 3(iv); E26G; E51, p5; E66, G1; E76, 1.4; E149, p15. Its advantage is that it fulfils the requirement of CMH that, 'staff support should be what moves around, not people with mental handicaps' (E100, p5). The 'cluster' includes ordinary houses scattered around a neighbourhood, where staff support can be increased or diminished according to need. This makes possible another requirement of CMH, that residents should have the same tenancy rights as others (E100, 5; see also, E119, 10.3; E183, 4.9 (ii)).

Shared housing or group housing is also mentioned quite frequently and is also discussed fully in *E151, Pt II, 2.1–7*. The houses in core and cluster are in effect shared housing, but shared or group housing can also be a single small project with minimal staffing (E63) or very high staffing ratios (E151, Pt II, 2.6).

Size of Group. There is some disagreement about the size of group which the new policies of 'normalisation' and 'domestic' size require. The National Autistic Society solves the problem simply by stating that any group which is too big to use ordinary domestic equipment (e.g. fridge or kettle) is too large (E154, p17). Other suggestions include 6–8 (E95, Enc 5); less than 10 (E66, A3.1); 10–12 to allow emotional space for disturbed children (E81, p4); and 10–20 as the size preferred by most Soroptomists for the elderly (E99, p3).

Although the great majority of contributors certainly favour small units and Carematch confirms this as the choice of their clients also (E37, 8), there are a few doubting or dissenting voices. RHHI asserts that the reaction against large care homes is ill-founded (E33, 44). Christian Concern for the Mentally Handicapped believes that there are dangers in being too small (discussed in E17, G1), and financial and staffing implications of small units are questioned in E19, 12.1 and E125, p2.

It is perhaps worth remarking that whereas with other client groups there is a sense of excitement about new methods and patterns of work developing, this does not seem to be so in residential child care. Here it is only the therapeutic communities which still seem to feel an enthusiastic commitment to a method of working and a desire to convince the Committee of its value. Innovation appears to be almost entirely in the area of replacing residential care as usually defined by such measures as family centres and fostering (E7). There is no detailed description in the evidence of new patterns of residential care developing for the increasing numbers of adolescents who appear to need it, although there are occasional hints that some agencies may be attempting this.

Staffing

Levels of staffing

> The range of different projects with different objectives is so great that to seek formulae for the 'right' staffing levels is impossible. To base staffing levels on the category of resident is not appropriate, since people with similar problems can have different support needs (E153, Appendix I, 10.2).

In contrast to the NFHA, quoted above, the Social Care Association believes there should be 'national clearly identified guidelines' for staffing levels (E111, 69; see also E92, 2(b)). The difficulty of establishing such guidelines is apparent from the number of factors which the evidence suggests should be taken into consideration. Chief among these is levels of dependency (E77, p3; E95, I, p6; E106, 17.4; E119, 9.8). Others include the differing sizes of establishments (E150, p2, E(i)); the need to give residents individual attention (E80, 9; E95, IV, 5.4) and enable them to do more (E64, C); the need for continuity and consistency (E80, 9); the different needs at different times of day (E118, I, 5); and, covering many of these, the function of the establishment and the resident group (E111, 68).

Examples of existing staff ratios are given, in varying degrees of detail, in E26, E; E27, pp7–12; E32, E(1); E33, 32; E69, pp5–9; E75, 17.4–5; E88, 7.2; E99, IV, p14; E135, Elderly, p8; E154, pp20–25; E160, p9; and a suggested ratio in E71, E1. A number of contributors assert that current ratios are too low (E52, p4; E67, 5.15; E86, I, E; E91, App I, 1.13; E175, p34, 1.2; E191, p14). There are recommendations that within the overall ratios, ratios of nursing (E77, p3) and rehabilitation (E124, 3.2.1) staff should be specified. The need to make allowance for increased leave is pointed out in E66, E1; and the stress of awaiting replacements in E56, p9.

The ADSS recommends the papers on staffing ratios of the Birmingham Group (Social Services Liaison Group Working Party) (E137, p8).

Qualities and Qualifications

> We are unhappy at the increasing emphasis on academic qualifications for staff in residential care homes. Our primary concern is for the right qualities rather than the right qualifications (E17, E2).

> a dangerous form of inverted snobbery which views the ability to provide care as being actively impeded by the obtaining of professional qualifications or educational attainment (E88, 7.13).

> Surely the committee will wish to express astonishment that a nation which requires that all teachers shall be professionally qualified before they are permitted to teach the children of the nation can be content to have the most vulnerable children of a nation served by people many of whom have had little or no training or experience in welfare settings (E137, p7).

Although initially it may appear that there is a great difference of opinion between those who consider personal qualities most important for residential staff (E34, E; E38, p9; E56, p9; E100, 6; E141, 7.2; E170, p6) and those who regard qualifications as essential, the difference is not as deep as it appears. Many of those who insist on the right personal qualities assume that, once appointed, staff will undertake training. Those who place emphasis on qualifications presumably expect that personal qualities will have been assessed in the course of gaining those qualifications. 'Maturity' is the quality most often required; ability to communicate, to relate to a client group, to work in a staff team (E56, p9; E80, 12; E111, 72) are others. Lengthier lists of desirable qualities are in E38, p9; E75, 17.1–2 and E154, pp21 & 23.

There are suggestions that senior staff need to be qualified before appointment (E88, 7.18, (ii); E123, p6); and that posts which require social work skills should be identified so that only qualified staff might be appointed for these (E149, p19). The Social Care Association suggests a system of registration (and de-registration) of approved social care workers (E111, 74).

Recruitment and appointment

> The persistent undervaluing and denigration of the residential sector tends to keep it as a residual service. The consequent low status and morale make it difficult to recruit good staff into residential work. A social work student of mine......heard this comment in her last placement from a qualified (God help us) field social worker. 'They only do residential work because they haven't got the brains to do any other work' (E19, E.1).

Whatever qualities or qualifications may be thought necessary for residential work, to recruit staff who have them appears to be extremely difficult (E88, 7.5; E92, 2(c); E118, Elderly, E1; E149, p16, E(i); E154, p22; E175, pp36–7, 1–7; E189, p2). It is thought desirable to have staff of mixed ages, sexes, race and background, and the problem of recruitment is particularly intractable in the case of men (E80, 10; E99, p9; E123, p5E), who may find the low salary scales a particular problem (E154, p23).

Some evidence urges that residents should be involved in the process of appointing staff (E39, p2; E66, E3; E97, E, p3; E111, 71). There is a suggestion in E66, E3 that the appointment process should be spread over a period of time, and in E71, E3 that the Director of Social Services should be present at the appointment of an officer-in-charge. CCETSW recommends that discussion about training should form part of the selection process (E165, p4), a suggestion echoed in E191, p6.

Stress on staff

As can be seen from the list below, stress on staff is a major and continual theme of the evidence. The causes cited are given in the order in which they were noted down, without any attempt to classify them, as this may give a better impression of the multiple nature of the stresses staff apparently feel.

Seeing deterioration or pain of residents E4, C(d); E32, C(4); E88, 4.9; E128, p4.

Unsocial and irregular hours E24, C; E27, p6; E44, C28; E67, 4.7; E149, p13; E154, p13.

Changing roles and client groups E24, C.

Limited supervision/support E24, C; E44, C27; E67, 4.6; E86, II, p6; E88, 4.11.

Limited peer group support E24, C; E101, C; E154, p13.

Restricted career opportunities E24, C; E149, p13.

Fear of violence ('There is the fear of attack and as strong the fear that a member of staff will snap and assault the resident' E27, p6) E76, 3.2; E149, p13; E154, pp13–14; E205, p5.

Unreasonable or antisocial behaviour of residents E32, C4; E56, p7(i); E101, C; E117, 6; E123, p3.

Lack of time for personal relationships E32, C4; E56, p7(2); E123, p3.

Strain of living in enclosed community E32, C4; E88, 4.9; E38, p8.

The conflict between helping and enabling E32, C4; E44, 29; E67, 4.8; E88, 4.10; E118, Mentally Handicapped, 3.2.

Lack of training E67, 4.5 & 7; E86, II, p6.

Repetitive demands E94, II, p4.

Tidying up after someone else E94, II, p4.

Coping with relatives' guilt E117, 6.

Organisational factors E128, p4.

Increasing concentration of disturbed children E149, p12.

Low status E121, p4; E145, A(i); E146, p4; E149, p13.

Uncertain future of residential care E149, p13.

Poor pay E149, p13.

Increasing mismatch between training and demands on staff E146, p4.

Special stresses of therapeutic environment E160, p10.

Not sharing same views of residential care E195, p7.

Lists of causes, as may have been gathered from the above occur at E24 C; E32 C; E44 C; E86, II, p6; E94, II; E121, p4; E149, pp12 & 16; E154, pp13–14; E172. Stress is suspected of causing 'sickness' absences (E94, Elderly, p4) and leading to defensive institutional patterns of care (E119, 9.5). Suggestions for alleviating it include better supervision, staffing, and pay (E123, 4) and regular staff meetings (E135, Elderly, p8). Other suggestions relate to training (qv) and the keyworker system (qv). And a cheering comment from the voluntary sector reminds us that 'life in a symphony orchestra is highly stressful, but many choose it because of the creative tensions' (E38, p8).

Effects of change
Changing roles and client groups have been listed as a cause of stress and will be mentioned as a reason for need of training. The nature of

these changes, particularly in relation to the elderly (more dependent) and children (more disturbed), and their implications for staffing are examined at length in the *Appendices of E121* and E205. They are discussed more briefly in E19, B2; E24B; E51, p4; E64, A, C, E/F; E71G and E137, p1; E180, 61.13; E209, pp2–3.

Supervision, support and consultancy

One of the answers to the stress and changes experienced by residential workers is said to be increased supervision and support. This is dealt with most fully in *E75, Section 18* and *E169, pp5–6*. A particular need is noted for consultancy from those with 'no line management responsibility' (E41, III, p4; E121, p5; E137, 6; E141, 7.4; E175, 1.8; E201, p2). It is suggested in E38, p9 that staff should be able choose their own consultant.

Keyworker system

> The promising development of the keyworker system owes as much to improving the work satisfaction and contribution of staff as it does to ensuring that resident's needs are met effectively (E32, B4).

The keyworker system is seen as 'the most significant development in residential care for all client groups' (E118, Children, 4.1) and as another means of combatting the stress on staff. Some contributors (E71, E2; E80, 11; E197, p6) point to the confusion over the exact meaning of the term and an attempt is made to define it in E123, p5, E. The concept is dealt with most fully in E95, App.6, 2.4–5, 3.2–4.4 and E160, pp6–7. The only disadvantages of the system that are mentioned are a risk of favouritism, by either resident or staff, and the possibility of it breaking down at holiday time. There is also one obscure reference to 'certain practices seen as threatening eg keyworker systems' (E126). On the other side, there are a great many favourable references to it.

Wages and Conditions of Service

Wages and Grades

> Grades and conditions of service should reflect task expectation. Care staff grades should be as for field workers in the future (E44, 41).

> There should be a single salary grading structure for social care workers in all settings (E111, 86).

> Residential care depends principally upon staff. Underpaid and undervalued, continuity is the exception. This important job deserves adequate pay and a proper career structure, the foundation for any such professional work (E103, 4, p4).

There is virtual unanimity on the need for a better pay structure for residential workers, and most contributors appear to support the policy of parity for residential and field social workers and the transfer of care assistants from manual to RASC grades and conditions. The whole question is studied in great detail in *E152*, a draft report by the BASW Project Group on Parity for Service Conditions. NALGO's evidence is also, of course, crucial and can be found in *E178, 6.1–6.4.4*. The following references were chosen from among a great number because they mention most of the arguments and issues: E51, p4; E67, 5.7 & 12–14; E71, E3; E80, 14; E92, 2(c); E97, E, p3; E118, Children, 5.5; E119, 9.9–10; E136, (b); E138, 7; E184, 12 & 25. The main arguments advanced for the change are that it would acknowledge the parity of the roles involved; that it would make it easier for workers to transfer from one area of work to another; that it would enhance career prospects; that it would aid recruitment of staff; and that it would recognize the need for those working together in local networks to be part of a harmonized service.

Pay and conditions in the private sector receive very little consideration in the formal evidence excepting E152, 7.1.6, but from what is written in some of the case material submitted by the CAB (E58) and in the personal evidence they would appear to merit considerable concern.

The shift system

> The continuing erosions of the eight hour shift can only lead to a decline in the quality of care (E123, p6).

> We believe that proper financial recompense should be made, but that commitment is as important as professionalism, and this may often lead to longer hours than those recommended (E145, D).

In contrast to the view expressed above, E106, 13.4; E142, p6; E143, 4.5.2 and E178, 4.2 consider that the stress of residential work makes shorter shifts and/or shorter working weeks necessary. However, in this evidence the weight of opinion is against them. The concern is mainly that shifts have become too short to allow continuity of care and that 'some systems and processes have developed which appear to have the needs of staff and their domestic arrangements as their primary focus' (E76, III, 2.3). Anxiety about various effects of shift systems as they are currently operated are expressed in E71, D1; E80, 15; E110, 1.7; E118, Mentally Handicapped, 3.2; Children, 5.4; E141, 7.9–10. A suggestion is made in E141 that the DHSS might fund experiments in alternative staffing patterns to see if some of these effects can be avoided (see also E184, 14 & 15). Other suggestions are to move from the 'working week' to the 'working month' for increased flexibility (E68, p4), and to give sabbaticals to make up for long and unsocial hours (E101, II, 2).

Living-in

> One of the biggest differences between types of care is, in my view, not accounted for by client-group, objectives, type of organisation, and training, but by the simple criterion of whether or not the place is the home of the carers/adults/staff... If the adults'...home is the clients' home (as in fostering), nearly every aspect of daily living and experience is different from the place where the adult merely 'works' (E38, p1).

> It is the strongly held view of some staff involved in the residential care of children and young people that the introduction of non-resident staff working a much reduced working week has resulted in bad child care practice (E111, 85).

> Few staff are now required to be resident and most Authorities consider staff will be better able to carry out their role if they are not resident (E121, p6).

Several contributors express the feeling that the industrial model of wages and hours is not appropriate to residential care (E111, 84; E141, 7.8), but others go further than questioning ideas of overtime to assert the need for 'more than a commitment to a job...also an investment in a way of life' (E49, p7; see also E194, pp2 & 3). It is not surprising to find the residential and therapeutic communities expressing such views, but there appears to be strong feeling about the issue in much of the voluntary sector. The Social Care Association writes that 'as residential social work has been "professionalised"...the quality of the experience of living together has been lost' (E111, 50). NCH refers to the recent DHSS Review of Community Homes which found that 93.8 per cent of staff were non-resident and fears that 'the non-residence of the care worker may militate against the best interests of the child' (E141, 7.11). It feels that more research is needed into this. The importance of 'living-in' is emphasised also in *E81, VI, 1–3 and letter*.

However, even amongst voluntary agencies, there are those with the opposite position: 'The pressure of living and working on site led to such pressure on staff that we no longer have any resident staff. Sleep-in night cover is provided on a rota basis' (E17, C4). At the extreme of the spectrum, NALGO finds sleeping-in 'an unsatisfactory form of cheap labour...where overnight cover is necessary it should be provided by a night shift on working duty' (E178, 5.2).

It is probably this issue more than any other that highlights the effect of the different value bases considered in our first section and shows the difficulty in some areas of finding a solution which will satisfy them all.

Trade unions and professional associations

There is not a great deal of interest shown in the subject of trade unions and professional associations, except as might be expected from NALGO and BASW, and even they do not have a great deal to say on the matter.

Comments indicate a feeling that professional associations better understand the feelings of residential workers about their job, but that trade unions are necessary at a time of redundancies and increased likelihood of disciplinary procedures arising from the violence of more disturbed children. The suggestion of a separate union for residential workers 'able to understand the problems peculiar to residential work' is made in E56, 10. Other references to these issues can be found in E41, III, pp6–7; E47, E52, p4(e); E66, E4; E71, E4; E77, p3; E80, 16; E88, 7.16; E94, I, p3; E123, p6; E205, p5.

Training

There is a need for a radical relook at training for the residential sector. This should include the amount of training, the methods of training (location, medium, etc), the content of training, and the transferability of training (E52, p41, E).

Why Training?

Training is the major preoccupation of contributors, being mentioned in their final Recommendations almost twice as often as any other subject. The reasons for this are many. Implicit is a feeling that lack of facilities for training reflects lack of appreciation of residential skills and consequently low status for residential workers in comparison with field workers (E169, p4, d).

Is it right that RSW's, Grade 1, unqualified, are expected to run children's groups, offer bereavement and sexual counselling, practise high techniques in management control and act as a child's advocate in all situations they become involved in? (E83, E2).

It could be argued that the worker in a residential unit requires training even more than the fieldworker in i) the developmental and emotional needs of children and adolescents; ii) the dynamics of attachment, separation, loss, grief and transference (E110, 3.3.1).

The Association of Teachers in Social Work Education 'regards the task of the social worker in residential care as demanding a level of skills as high as that which is required by social workers in other settings' (E185, 3), an opinion supported and elaborated in E205, E.

Lack of confidence in untrained staff is suspected of being the reason why fieldworkers are called in to conduct reviews, and budgets are centrally controlled (E111, 59–60).

Specifically, training is seen as a necessary corollary of moves towards unified pay and conditions (qv) for residential and field workers (*E152, Section 1, 1.1–7; Section 6*), full integration of residential workers within the career structure of social services departments, and transferability of workers between residential and community settings (E195, p6).

> There should be greater changeability of workers between field and residential work facilitated by more joint training (E52, p3, d)

This ability to move between field and residential work is seen as one of the means of reducing stress (qv) (E67, 4.5). The increased confidence and self-knowledge given by training is thought to be another.

Other reasons for the emphasis on training relate to the changing nature of residential work (*E165*, pp1–2; Annexe p19, 3).

> The process of training never ends; it merely changes course to keep abreast of developing trends and looks to areas and ideas previously not explored (E94, I (Children) p3, E). (See also E152, 6.1.16; E169, p4, c)

Training is thought to be particularly necessary for staff in new, more independent living units (E153, 8.1; E186, p5(v)); for the new enabling approach to mental handicap and mental illness (E139, p4; E184, 22 & 23); and for dealing with the more difficult (children's homes) or more frail (homes for the elderly) populations now in residential care (E152, 2.6.5; E175, p10, 1.9.8; E165, Annexe p19; E184, 8–9, 26).

> [Residential Homes] now admit the more difficult and disturbed children. This means that specialist provision is expected of residential workers without adequate training or sufficient numbers of qualified staff (E19, B(2)).

The suggested local networks of care involving residential workers in support and after-care of clients in the community are also seen as a reason for training alongside field workers (E144, p1; E157, 2.4; E165, Annexe pp18–19).

Increased responsibilities and new roles are thought to require specialist training for managers (E104, 4(i); E139, pp4–5; E165, Annexe p18; E169, p3, b; E191, p6; E210, H) and for registration officers/inspectors (E90, p30, 4.9(2); E175, p27, 5.4; p40, 8.7 & 8; E211, J). It is suggested that care staff in special schools should be included in training schemes (E186, p18, 8).

Finally, it is thought that

> in-service and induction training should focus strongly on...underlying values so that staff have the opportunity to develop shared approaches in their work (E100, 6),

such sharing being another antidote to stress.

In-service or full-time?
The development of a shared ethos is one reason why a number of contributors favour in-service training (E92(c); E100, 6; E126; E139, p2;

E147, pp6–7). Another reason is the financial and staffing implications of full-time training (E92, 1(b)–(d); E99 Addendum; E118, Mentally Handicapped, 5.3; E138, (2)).

> The training of residential care workers involves replacement costs not always present with other care workers (E52, p3(c)).

The problems of secondment and training budgets are considered in E184, 6 & 7 and E185, 5.

The CCETSW proposals

Such resource factors underlie the main reservations about the CCETSW proposals for integrated training and a single award. The proposals are generally welcomed (E19, E(6); E67, 4.5; E80, 14; E110, 3.3.2; E123, p6; E136 (b); E149, p19), but there is fear that a three-year course will make it more difficult to ensure that residential staff are seconded for it (E99, Addendum; E121, p6). The size of the problem is clear from the *Manpower and Qualification Survey attached to E139*. One residential worker comments gloomily:

> It will currently take some fourteen years, on the basis of one every two years, for the remaining staff in this unit to achieve qualified status (E136).

These resource factors are seen as a particular problem for the voluntary and private sectors (E99, p9; E152, 6.1.34; E153, Guidance for Registration, p17, 10.11) and it seems that therefore local authorities may have an important part to play in their training (E16, 5, 2–5; E100, 7; E104, 4(ii)). Certainly CCETSW indicates an extremely low proportion of private sector staff involved in CSS training (E165, Annexe p17). It is suggested in E201, F that registration officers should have the power to insist on training for staff.

Current and proposed training packages

Details of current CCETSW approved qualifications are given in E165, Annexe pp4–6. The use of the Open University course 'Caring for Children and Young People' is described in E169, p4, and a projected Open University package to form part of qualifying training in E169, p5. Information on how staff are currently being trained is given in E4, E, b; E26, p1; E86, I, p2. E129, p3; E150, p3, E3; E75, 5.2; 19, 7–13. Training packages or approaches are suggested in E7, II (Elderly), p31; E50, C9; F7; E92, 1(a) & (c); E110, 3.3.3–6; E111, 34; E149, p19.

One contribution expresses concern at the emphasis on modular training (E112, 24–5), but another sees 'a broadly-based modular education in the behavioural sciences' as the way forward (E176, 1).

Content

The Department of Social Studies at Selly Oak College offers a detailed 'framework' of the structure and content of its curriculum (E201, App I). Otherwise, of the actual content of the training from which so much is hoped, little is specified. The RNID hopes for more and better specialist training (E129, p3). Several contributors hope that it will change attitudes to the elderly (E32, G(2); E62). A need for 'activity rather than social work orientated' programmes for child care workers is suggested in E205, p4. ARC comments,

> Most staff currently regard existing courses as archaic, irrelevant and providing insufficient staff development opportunity. If training does nothing else, it must allow for and encourage self evaluation (E50, C(8)).

Further stringent criticism of the content of current courses can be found in E192, 15–17 and E202, pp. 5–6.

The Doubters

Finally two dissenting voices and a cautionary note. 75 per cent of the staff in the homes for the elderly who responded to the questionnaire sent out by Barking and Dagenham SSD considered that they were already adequately trained, 'because our job consists of mostly domestic tasks, you don't really need many qualifications' (E123, p2C). And Masud Hoghughi of Aycliffe School questions 'whether most social work training, as currently practised, is worth the resources that are expended on it' (E131, p6).

CCETSW has doubts about its worth for quite another reason—'the wastage of qualified staff from residential work' (E165, Annexe p10)—and suggests that 'qualification may be seen as a passport out from work that is...intensive, includes unsociable hours and where status and future prospects are relatively low' (*ibid*, p8). (See also E169, p3).

Finance

> I would look forward to a fundamental shift in the allocation of GNP resources taking account of projected demographic changes, rather than merely partial or piece-meal measures. Many professionals will subscribe to the view that present levels of resources for maintaining an increasingly dependent and long living sector of the population are neither adequate or realistic (E6, p3, 3).

> If government does not increase the supplementary benefits significantly soon, a great many residential homes will close down...The whole of the financing of residential care homes is in a mess (E4, F(a)).

This fundamental aspect of care is totally inequitable and unsatisfactory on a national basis. The changes which have taken place in recent years now threaten to impoverish voluntary bodies (E50, G1).

Concern about finance, particularly in relation to capital funding and DHSS benefits and particularly on the part of the voluntary sector, pervades the formal evidence. The main points made are that the level of funding for residential care is too low, that the way funds are disbursed discourages community care or leads to inappropriate patterns of residential care, and that public money is being spent on individuals without assessment of their needs or the quality of care provided. Many of these difficulties are seen as stemming from inconsistencies in the policies of the DHSS, DOE and Local Authorities.

Level of Funding
In relation to capital and revenue costs, the contributors identified a major problem surrounding the transfer of funds from hospital provision to community care. Until the hospitals are closed, the health service cannot afford to release the money, but until the local authorities have money to provide accommodation and care in the community the hospitals cannot (or should not) be closed. This dilemma and the urgent need for transitional funding and improvements to Joint Finance are discussed in E66, F1; E90, p35, 5 & 6; E103, p3; E105, App II, pp15–16; E118, Mentally Handicapped, 6.1; E149, p20, F(i); *E167, p1, 5; p7, 7; pp10–11, 7–11;* E170, p5; E180, 61.20.

Voluntary organisations point out that the use of their capital resources can save public funds (E149, p20), but it is nevertheless very difficult to obtain help for building programmes from statutory authorities (E5, F4). Because of the lack of a close relationship between payment of supplementary benefit and degree of disability, intensity of care required or provision of rehabilitation and day care, many voluntary societies find that they do not cover costs and an enormous deficit remains to be met from charitable resources (E82, 5.1; E177, 5.3; E186, p13(v)). At the same time voluntary homes, like private ones, face the costs consequent on registration (eg the need to enlarge rooms) while remaining subject to the DHSS ceiling (E6; E174; E211, A, pp 1–5). The local authorities are suspected of welcoming the opportunity to shift their responsibilities onto the DHSS and failing to provide all the support possible to the voluntary organisations (eg through 'topping up') (E90, p25; E177, 5.3; E186, p13(iv) & (v)). Some local authorities do not feel that the financial implications of the changed task of residential care are fully appreciated (E88, 8.2) and others point out that true community care may cost at least as much as residential care (E123, p6F; E125, p2). East Sussex (E52) comments that future local authority capital spending is likely to be concentrated on existing homes, while the difficulties of raising the capital now required to meet the standards expected of private homes may restrict growth in the private sector. Further restriction on development may arise because Housing Association Grants and Hostel Deficit Grants are not available for housing primarily built to provide care and staffed to the level which registering authorities may require (E4).

The impact of finance
Taken as a whole, the evidence demonstrates the insidious way in which not only shortage of finance but also the way it is made available can influence the development of services and the quality of life of the individual. Arguments are presentedd that too much money is spent on residential and institutional as against community care, that funding and benefits influence individuals' choices between residential and community care, that they hinder independence (ie they may discourage or prevent severely dependent individuals from leaving hospital, leaving home or working) and that organisations may for funding reasons develop inappropriate forms of care.

Priorities A picture emerges of large areas of expenditure on residential or in-patient care which has a consequence on community care initiatives. This cycle has to be broken with a reduction of in-patient care expenditure whether in hospital or residential care to more money being directed towards community care initiatives (E157, 1.3).

Choice If HMG are going to pay £230 to keep me in a Nursing Home (per week)—which I don't want—then would it not be more humane and sensible to let me stay at home by paying for the Care/Help I would need? (E18; see also E168).

Financial arrangements should neither penalise those who prefer the residential solution, nor force people into residential care against their will. The current hotch potch often manages to do both at the same time (E55, 1.2).

The most effective way to provide choice is to give people the money they require and allow them to buy the services they prefer (Ibid, 2.1).

The way in which finance limits the right of choice is shown in E26, F; E50, G4; E52, p5. E89, p1; E96, B, p3; E99, p4; E153, 9.1–7; E168; E183, 3.3; E186, p10, 1 & 2.

Independence The effect of the current system of support for residents on the degree of independence allowed to individuals can be seen from E10; *E55, 3.1 & 2; 4.4; 6.2 & 3; 8.1–3;* E75, 21.10; E82, 5.2; *E89, App II;* E99, II, p13; E118, II, 16; E140, p1; E151, Part II, 4.8; E153, 6.4; E183, 4.8.

Patterns of Care The way in which both capital funding and revenue funding (including support for residents) are made available affects the development of patterns of care (E3, 3(iv); E16, 7(2); E47, 4.8; E51, p4; *E52, pp4–5; E90, pp24–26;* E153, 6.4; E175, p12, 1.10.5; E183, 4.1, 6 & 7; E186, pp11–12).

Financial support of residents

The rationalising of financial support for residents was the third most popular subject for the contributors' Recommendations.

> DHSS policies currently mean that public money is spent without assessment of need or evaluation of the service received (E52, p5).

The local authorities and medical bodies see the provision of DHSS benefits without assessment as leading to misuse of resources and the possibility of inappropriate placements (E52, p5; E96, B, p3; E157, 2.5). The British Federation of Care Home Proprietors suggest that the DHSS should have trained officers to advise on benefit applications and suitable placements, and maintain contact with clients after placement (E211, B, p3). As noted in the section on the role of the three sectors and the quantity of provision, the overall effect of the present system is thought to be a diversion of funds from the statutory to the private sector and from domiciliary to residential care in a totally unplanned manner.

The evidence contains some very full and helpful material on these problems in *E90, Appendix III, The Long Term Funding of Residential Care*, which looks in detail at four different options; in the *Appendices to E6—Residential Care for the Elderly (Altshul)* and *Board and Lodgings Limits: One Year On*, which describes how the situation arose and what it is at present; in *E55* which examines RADAR's preferred solution; and in *E212* which examines the effect on the growth of the private sector. E90, App III is the NCVO's evidence to the DHSS/Local Authority Joint Working Party on the Long Term Funding of Residential Care (presumably the same as the Second Joint Central and Local Government Working Party on Supplementary Benefit and Residential Care with which the AMA hopes the Committee will collaborate (E119, 10.4) and which is also mentioned in E129, p4 and E70, p3).

There is shorter discussion of the issues involved in E4, F(a); E17, F(1); E26 F; E37, 18 & 29; E50, G3; E75, 21.8–13; E89, App II; E99, II, p12; E104, 6(ii) & (iii); E140; E151, II, 4.5–15.

Other concerns about the payment of DHSS benefits relate to the fact that only those with less than £3,000 capital receive them. This was felt to be unjust in that it could negate the effect of Criminal Injuries Compensation (E99, p6) or careful saving for a 'nest egg' (E104, 6(i)). One contributor suggests that 50 per cent of self-financing clients will eventually reach that £3,000 level and require DHSS benefits (E106, 17.5). Another complains that able-bodied partners may be required by the DHSS to pay excessive amounts to maintain their disabled spouse in care; that a disabled person in residential care with an occupational pension scheme may be unable to use this for the support of their families (E177, 5.5); and that the DHSS 'discriminates' against disabled people over retirement age.

> It does not appear to be the case that it costs less to provide care for a severely disabled person over retirement age than it does for someone under that age (E177, 5.6).

Registration

> The overall result has been very disappointing when we had expected such good things from the Registered Homes Act 1984 (E17, F2).

There is very little praise and much criticism for the Registered Homes Act 1984. The criticism ranges over a wide variety of general issues and specific complaints but an attempt has been made to group them under seven categories.

Effectiveness

> A monitoring system that concentrates on physical facilities rather than the sensitive issues of care has made it possible for bad practice to exist in homes that have passed all the registration requirements (E211, E, p2).

(a) *'Quality of care* is not ensured by registration' (E24, F). This opinion of South Tyneside SSD is supported by E26, F; E33, 40 and E99, p9. Suggestions for remedying the situation include an annual review of all homes in all sectors by senior managers in addition to the basic inspection (E124, 5.3); more frequent inspection; inspection without prior notice; inspection by two people, one specialising in technical matters and the other in care of the residents (E22, 2); better training for ROs (dealt with below); and guidelines concerning staff ratios and qualifications (E44, 47).

(b) *Specific closure powers* were thought to need improvement in E151, III, 1.2, but in E71, F2 the powers themselves were thought adequate and the need to be for good local authority solicitors. In either case, there was concern that de-registered homes could still take up to three people (E73), and it is suggested that homes taking less than four should also be registered and inspected (E159, 7.2.3; E211, E, p7). Another suggestion is that DHSS benefits should be lower for residents in unregistered homes (E36, 2).

(c) *Police records.* It is suggested that a procedure is needed for checking the police records of those caring for vulnerable clients other than children (E67, 6.5; E151, Pt.III, 1.4).

(d) *Distribution of homes.* As already noted in the consideration of 'Quantity' in Section 4, Registration exercises no control over the uneven distribution of private Homes. It is suggested that an Amendment to the Act is required stating that the number of Homes in any area should be related to the needs of the population (E36, 1).

Inflexibility

The Registered Homes Act 1984 was introduced with the best of intentions but was ill-considered and those responsible for its drafting appeared to know little about the various categories of residential homes (E4, B(b)).

Some registration authorities fail to take adequate note of the wide variation in the ways in which homes are conducted and the differing needs of residents. An attempt to enforce uniform or so-called minimum standards is likely to result in a misuse of resources and put quality of life at risk' (E32, B3; see also E211, J).

Dorset Association of Registered Rest Homes asks that requirements should be geared to the type of specialist care being offered and that, in future, acts and regulations for homes for the elderly, for instance, should be differentiated from those for children or addicts (E36). However, most complaints of inflexibility relate to normalisation:

The philosophy of care provided by the Act is in direct contrast to the type of care provided by normalisation theory (E151, II, 4.4).

Ironically, while registration policy is linked to the philosophy of Home Life (independent living, choice, risk taking) many of the registration requirements actually create barriers to putting that philosophy into practice (E153, 7.1).

The theme of the above quotations is developed and illustrated in E25, p2; E26, F(c); E72; E75, 22.4–8; E89, p2; *E90, 4.3*; E93 letter; E125, p1; E147, pp8–9; E151, Pt II, 4.1–4; Pt III, 1.3; *E153, 7.1 & App I, Guidance for Registration, 10.15*; E184, 16.

Inconsistency

It is unacceptable that the quality of life for residents may depend on who provides that service with the biggest provider being exempt from account-ability under the provision of existing legislation (E154, p26).

Another major complaint relating to Registration is that it does not apply to local authority provision. The sentiment quoted above is echoed in, among others, E26, F(c); E70, p2; E94, III, Elderly; E106, 18.1; E122, 2; E129, p3; E137, p9; E149, p21, F(ii); E157, 7.2; E159, 7.2.2; E170, p7; E175, p39, 3; E180, 61.18; E211, E, p7.

The Act is also thought to be applied inconsistently by different local authorities.

Registration has become a nightmare for organisations who, like ourselves, operate in more than one local authority area (E17, F2).

Similar experiences are referred to in E1, p1; E4, F(b); E75, 22.9; E147, p9; E149, p21, F(ii); E211, D, (C) 1 (i).

A national inspectorate

A popular solution to the problems of unfairness and inconsistency is the setting up of a national inspectorate, which some see as needing to be a separate organisation, to allow it to inspect local authority homes as well as private and voluntary ones without prejudice. Suggestions along these lines are found in E4, F(b); E36, 4; E52, p6; E96, p6, F; E106, 18.2; E124, 5.4; E129, p3; E159, 3.2. The Faculty of Community Medicine, however, warns against insisting on the same standards throughout the country: 'It is difficult to envisage uniformity through-out the country being achieved because of variations in the price of property and the availability of trained and untrained staff' (E107, p2).

Registration officers

Another measure which it is hoped might make inspection more effective, more flexible and more just is the training of registration officers.

> Expectations of the legislation. . .have now extended to cover the stimu-lation, development and training of the sector (E52, p5).

> Sadly it is not an uncommon experience to find that the RO is inadequately trained and of limited experience to the extent that he/she cannot fulfil the role of helper and adviser' (E50, C7).

> I think that I was expecting the registration officer to be a kind of homes supervisor and I was hoping to have a discussion at a professional level. I had not expected her to go round turning taps on and off, flushing lavatories and looking inside the cups in the cupboard (E41, III, p7).

The current training and experience of registration officers is questioned in E99, p5 and E159, 7.2 and the variability of their numbers, grade and support in E76, 6.1. The need for this to be rectified is urged in E124, 5.2, E170, p7 and E211, J.

A fear that the political views of registration officers may bias them against private homes is expressed in E45, F; E124, 5.4; and E159, 7.2.5. Another fear is that where a home is for an ethnic minority group, registration officers may have difficulty in accepting different standards from their own (E107, p2).

The financial burden

The cost of registration together with the cost of the alterations demanded (often, as we have seen, considered unnecessary if not actually counter-productive) is proving a crippling financial burden to some voluntary organisations. The local authorities are accused by one of them of exercising 'authority without responsibility' (E4, A(d)). Although not so forcibly expressed, similar feelings can be traced in E32, F1; E41, III, p7; E70, p2; E186, p13(vi) and E211, A & C.

Dual Registration

> The two registering authorities have very different philosophies of care; this can cause serious problems for the proprietor who cannot develop an environment which satisfies both the social services department [and] health authority (E189, p2).

The RNID hopes that the Committee will look at the problems surrounding dual registration (E129, p4). Those expressed in the evidence concern the plea for a relaxation in the rules concerning nursing care, so that it is possible to care for a person who becomes ill without the trauma of a move (E53, p8; E159, 2.2) but also without the necessity for dual registration which can bring in its wake conflict between social work values and nursing methods (eg over control of medication) (E175, pp39–40, 5 & 6; E177, 4.2). In addition, a definition of 'nursing care' is suggested in E106, 13.8 and the need for two separate inspections is queried in E14, p2.

Recommendations
BASW's recommendations in its review of the 1984 Registration Act are given in E175, pp40–41, 8.1–14. Those of the British Federation of Care Home Proprietors can be found in E211, D(C) and E, p7.

Research and Information

Research

> Hopefully all developments for the future will be based on firmly established and assessed need and not the blind following of philosophical thought (E26, G).

The evidence attaches much hope to research (E64, G(i) & H(12); E88, 10.1 and *passim*; E175, p26, 5.3) but gives no detail as to how it may be carried out. Research is required to establish the size and nature of various client populations and the size and nature of the provision they require (E31, p1; E101, A; E103, p1, 2; E105, 2.1 & App II, p17; E112, 39; E154, p1). It is expected to be able to help in evaluation and the obtaining of client views on services (E66, B, 2; E81, III, 6; E118, I, 2 & 3; E175, p22). And it is expected to provide miscellaneous data (eg E112, 53; E165, p4).

Information

Social workers' knowledge of residential accommodation in the private and voluntary sectors is said to be poor and the need of an information system for them is mentioned in E37, 23–24; E75, 2.22; E81, II, 2 and E186, p6(vii). An information network with information about vacancies and suitability is seen as one of the possible off-shoots of coordination between services (E77, p2; E105, App I, p9). To enable the public to make an informed choice in the private sector, Help the Aged suggests that a voluntary body should develop a focus for independent consumer information (E163, Annex). Examples of information services already operating are the Bed Bank Bureau run by Oldham and District Registered Rest Homes Association (E117, 2) and a Directory of Homes in Oxfordshire (E106, 14.1). Carematch suggests that information should be readily available from the homes themselves, from the DHSS and from local authorities (E37, 27, 30 & 31) and the supply of information is suggested as one function of resource centres (E119, 8.1). Carematch is one of a number of contributors who suggest that all homes should produce a brochure explaining their aims and describing conditions in the home (E180, 61.6; E201, C).

Issues Relating to Particular Client Groups

Children

> We believe that, given time, children will respond to consistent love, constant commitment and sensitive understanding of their individual qualities, and will move towards integration as fulfilled people (E81, II, 8).

> Evaluation of quality and effectiveness could best be assessed as rapid through-put, plus extensive outreach and preventive work (E67, 8.10).

> In my opinion, what is required today are specialist units staffed by multi-disciplinary teams, making full use of therapeutic programmes with sensible staffing ratios, in which casework responsibility rests with the prime or key Residential Worker (E136, p2).

The three quotations above with their different emphases on love and commitment, on cost effectiveness and on current social work techniques illustrate the conflict of values which appears to affect residential child care more than other client groups. It may explain why some workers in the child care field are so unhappy with the direction in which they see residential care moving (eg E205).

While Warwickshire is proud of its achievement in closing all its children's homes (E7, I), others see the increasing disappearance of the residential sector as a betrayal of emotionally damaged children who are unable to settle in foster homes. They point to the high rate of fostering breakdowns (E98, 2; E81, VIII, 2; E112, 6; E205, p2); the increasing number of younger children for whom residential accommodation has been sought recently (E141, 5.5; E143, 4.4.3); the use of special schools for 52 week care (E116, p2; *E186, pp14–16*); and the increase in custodial care (E141, 2.4.6; E169, p2). The Principal of the Cotswold Community writes, 'My concern centres on the lack of a coherent national child care strategy. . .I know there are probably thousands of children who are severely disturbed and in need of specialist help. Whether or not they get it seems to depend on the attitude of their particular local authority' (E49, letter, pp1–2).

It is not only those from therapeutic communities who believe that the contribution of the residential sector has been too easily dismissed. The Children's Legal Centre writes that the child's needs may well be met best 'in a small children's home in which they are respected and supported as individuals, without any assumptions about their place in a new "family". Young people are clearly entitled to expect stability' (E116, p2). Stability is, however, thought to be what is lacking in current residential care, which is seen as 'reinforcing or providing a model of disruption and change' (E78, p1). The Children's section of Gloucestershire SSD writes of the effects of short stay care: 'The greater number of movements mean that the atmosphere of the house is more unsettled than in previous years, and it is more difficult to provide security for those young people who need to stay longer in residential care' (E95, Enc 5, 5.5).

What evidence there is from young people, notably through NAYPIC, would seem to confirm a wish for more children's homes and less emphasis on fostering. However, it must be remembered that if the evidence appears to suggest more support for residential care than for fostering, that must be partly because neither foster parents nor successfully fostered children have felt it necessary to write in. The real message is expressed in E101—a need for research on the size and nature of the problem and of the provision required. This might include some attention to the views of parents, whose voice is never heard in the formal evidence.

The main questions which the evidence appears to raise in relation to children are: 1) Has the run-down in residential provision gone too far? 2) Does the residential care which is provided offer sufficient security for disturbed children in view of staff turnover, the virtual disappearance of 'living-in', shift systems and the comings and goings of short stay children? 3) Does it offer sufficient psychological under-standing? ('what now passes for treatment used to be described as "good child care"', E54) 4) How much and what type of provision is needed for older adolescents? 5) What type of provision is needed for the children currently finding their way into custodial establishments and 52-week provision in special schools and for those who are beginning to be provided for in private 'lock-ups'?

The Mentally Handicapped and Mentally Ill

The mentally handicapped and mentally ill are dealt with together since the problems concerning both arise from the speedy discharge of patients from the long-stay hospitals. There is uncertainty over how many have failed to find satisfactory accommodation and how well those who have found accommodation are coping with their new way of life. The evidence dealt with so far has given a favourable picture of services for these two groups since it was in response to their needs that the policy of normalisation and the concept of 'core and cluster' were developed. The accommodation and care described by local authorities and voluntary bodies have been of these newest patterns. But there is another side to the picture which the evidence paints vividly.

> *Lack of preparation.* Although the concept of care in the community was welcomed, the haste and lack of adequate funding and planning with which it has been put into operation has resulted in considerable confusion within the personal social services and inexcusable misery and privation for hundreds of ill-equipped and inarticulate ex-hospital patients (E175, p18, 4.2.3).

> The road to hell is paved with good intentions, to use a well known saying, and this can be said for 'normalisation' of the Mentally Handicapped. The new concept did not prepare either the patients or the carers for the development (E86, II, p4).

> *Lack of Accommodation.* The plight of the mentally ill discharged from long stay hospitals is now a national scandal with patients having been discharged to run down hostels moving out to wander the streets of our cities, the responsibility of no-one. The mentally handicapped may be joining them if facilities are not in place and staff trained before discharge takes place . . .for many of the patients community care may well be seen as the worst option in time (E103, p3, 3).

> There is increasing evidence that the more chronically ill . . .are ending up homeless or in unsuitable accommodation. Many of the night shelters throughout the country are experiencing an increase in mentally ill clients (E105, App II, p12).

> *Lack of social contact.* Integration back into ordinary society is clearly a priority—but not at the expense of personal loneliness and insecurity (E13, G).

> A house in an ordinary street can be more of a stigmatized 'ghetto' than an open community that provides plenty of interaction with the wider community (E105, App I, p8).

Whilst the idea of care in the community is highly laudable, it is often restrictive on the resident or patient themselves as they feel more intimidated and restricted in being able to go out and about in the community than they would in mixing with people with similar disabilities as themselves (E99, II, p11).

Lack of progress. It is much easier to take over and do things for people. Without proper staff training and preparation, this will happen in the small community homes and mentally handicapped people or ill people will become isolated and institutionalized within the community (E139, p4).

We are particularly concerned by the growth of private care for mentally handicapped people which seems to be modelled on that offered in the large hospitals (E29, p3(b)).

The formal evidence as a whole raises a question as to which presents the more typical picture of the living conditions of those discharged from the long-stay hospitals—the description of 'normalisation' and the blue-prints for core and cluster, or the excerpts above and the comments of the COHSE staff in E86, III. What proportion of the ex-patients are in the night shelters and what proportion in 'core and cluster'? Is a high proportion of finance and thought being devoted to a relatively small proportion of the mentally handicapped and mentally ill? NAHA (E167) does not answer these questions but it presents a balanced view of many of the issues involved, neither as gloomy as the quotations above nor as enthusiastic as the pioneers in the new methods of care.

The Physically Handicapped

For the physically handicapped under 65 special problems stem from their relatively small numbers. This makes it difficult for residential care to be provided for them on a very local basis and makes them liable to be overlooked when, as at present, funds are short. Otherwise, they share the advantages and disadvantages in provision described in other sections—new accommodation is particularly well designed for an independent life-style but shortage of funds keeps it in short supply leaving some physically handicapped people without the residential care they want, and others trapped in hospital settings or in homes for the elderly. Their right to choice, freedom and independence is now recognized but there are insufficient domiciliary services available to enable them to live at home and enjoy those rights, and the system of DHSS benefits penalises rather than encourages moves towards independence.

The Elderly

For the elderly also the important issues have been covered in other sections. The major problems are the doubts about the distribution, size and quality of the private sector, the difficulty of diverting resources from residential to domiciliary care and the financial restraints which mean that 'normalisation' for many will mean group living in adapted large old buildings rather than in purpose-built complexes. The only important issue raised by the evidence and not yet mentioned is the discussion over whether the confused should be accommodated separately (E66, A, 4.2; E162, p23; E164; E195, p6). The issue is nowhere discussed in detail but some of the examples of group housing for EMI residents which are described confirm that it is a matter to which serious thought has already been given.

Evidence Submitted

E1	Mutual Aid Homes	E30	Ken Blakemore, Coventry (Lanchester) Polytechnic
E2	Turning Point		
E3	Sense (National Deaf-Blind and Rubella Association)	E31	Dr M R D Johnson, Warwick University
E4	Cecil Houses	E32	Methodist Homes for the Aged
E5	Royal British Legion		
E6	Birmingham Jewish Welfare Board	E33	Royal Hospital and Home for Incurables, Putney
E7	Warwickshire Social Services	E34	League of Jewish Women
E8	Hampstead Old People's Housing Trust	E35	Avon Social Services
		E36	Dorset Association of Registered Rest Homes
E9	Sailors' Children's Society		
E10	Mrs Gwenda Patterson (Surrey)	E37	Carematch (Residential Care Consortium Computer Project)
E11	Hertfordshire Social Services		
E12	Nottinghamshire Local Medical Committee	E38	Keith White, Mill Grove
		E39	NAYPIC (Newcastle)
E13	L'Arche	E40	Grace and Compassion Benedictines
E14	Cottage Homes		
E15	Steve Comerford (Coventry)	E41	West of England Friends Housing Society
E16	Norfolk Social Services		
E17	Christian Concern for the Mentally Handicapped	E42	Alan Grant, Devon Social Services
E18	Ken Williams (Shropshire)	E43	Good Practices in Mental Health
E19	Salesian School, Blaisdon Hall		
		E44	Hereford and Worcester Social Services
E20	Dr Gerard Bulger (Leytonstone)		
		E45	Shropshire Association of Registered Residential Homes
E21	Winchester Society of Friends		
E22	Tim Booth, Sheffield University	E46	Barnet Voluntary Services Council
E23	Waltham Forest Social Services	E47	T M Kinglake, Suffolk Social Services
E24	South Tyneside Social Services	E48	'Home from Home' scheme, Birmingham Social Services
E25	Brothers of Charity Services		
E26	Home Farm Trust	E49	John Whitwell, Cotswold Community, Wiltshire
E27	Ealing Social Services		
E28	Cornelia Schwier (Birmingham)	E50	ARC (Association of Residential Communities for the Retarded)
E29	Oldham Social Services		

E51 Durham Social Services
E52 East Sussex Social Services
E53 WRVS (Women's Royal Voluntary Service)
E54 Peper Harow Foundation
E55 RADAR (Royal Association for Disability and Rehabilitation)
E56 Malvern Community Home
E57 Alzheimer's Disease Society
E58 National Association of Citizens' Advice Bureaux
E59 Leonard Cheshire Foundation
E60 Society of Community Medicine
E61 British Medical Association (Central Committee for Community Medicine and Community Health)
E62 Miss Ilse Boas (Edgware)
E63 Wandsworth Association for Mental Health
E64 Doncaster Social Services
E65 Lincolnshire Family Practitioner Committee
E66 ADSW (Association of Directors of Social Work)
E67 Association of County Councils
E68 Residential Services Advisory Group
E69 Knowsley Social Services
E70 Abbeyfield Society
E71 Sidney G Wilkinson (Ipswich)
E72 Friends of the Elderly
E73 West Essex Community Health Council
E74 Leicestershire Libraries and Information Service
E75 Richmond Fellowship
E76 Cambridgeshire Social Services
E77 Health Visitors' Association

E78 First Key (Leaving Care Advisory Service)
E79 Community Service Volunteers
E80 Mr A B Crosby, Barking and Dagenham Social Services
E81 Children's Family Trust
E82 Shaftesbury Society
E83 Graham Ixer (Barnardo's)
E84 Jeff Hopkins, Keele University
E85 Age Concern Greater London
E86 Confederation of Health Service Employees
E87 National Council of YMCAs
E88 Essex Social Services
E89 ASBAH (Association for Spina Bifida and Hydrocephalus)
E90 NCVO Advisory Group on Residential Care
E91 Association of Chief Officers of Probation
E92 Stockport Social Services
E93 Association of Camphill Communities
E94 Dyfed Social Services
E95 Gloucestershire Social Services
E96 British Medical Association (General Medical Services Committee)
E97 Kensington and Chelsea Social Services
E98 Dr R C Benians, Consultant Psychiatrist
E99 Soroptimist International
E100 CMH (Campaign for People with Mental Handicaps)
E101 Association of Workers for Maladjusted Children
E102 Age Concern Chorley
E103 Royal College of General Practitioners

E104 Servite Houses
E105 National Schizophrenia
      Fellowship
E106 Mrs Griffin, State Registered
      Nurse
E107 Faculty of Community
      Medicine
E108 Volunteer Centre
E109 NAS/UWT—Career Teachers'
      Organisation
E110 British Agencies for
      Adoption and Fostering
E111 Social Care Association
E112 SCAFA (Scottish Child and
      Family Alliance)
E113 Brent Social Services
E114 Young Women's Christian
      Association
E115 Devon Social Services
E116 Children's Legal Centre
E117 Oldham and District
      Registered Rest Homes
      Association
E118 Strathclyde Social Work
      Department
E119 AMA (Association of
      Metropolitan Authorities)
E120 Berkshire Social Services
E121 Convention of Scottish Local
      Authorities
E122 Miss A M Walton
      (Aldeburgh)
E123 Barking and Dagenham
      Social Services
E124 Centre for Policy on Ageing
E125 Trevor Stronach, Father
      Hudson's Homes
E126 Liz Collinson, Southfields
      College of Further
      Education, Leicester
E127 Association of Crossroads
      Care Attendant Schemes
E128 Barnardo's (Training Section,
      Scottish Division)

E129 Royal National Institute for
      the Deaf
E130 Multi-racial Society
      Monitoring Group,
      National Institute for
      Social Work
E131 Masud Hoghughi, Aycliffe
      School
E132 Social Welfare Committee,
      Catholic Bishops'
      Conference
E133 The Holt Children and
      Young Persons Centre,
      Leicester
E134 Mencap Homes Foundation
E135 Lincolnshire Social Services
E136 Ferry Road End Community
      Home, King's Lynn
E137 ADSS (Association of
      Directors of Social
      Services)
E138 SCA Day Care course,
      Birmingham Social
      Services
E139 Local Government Training
      Board
E140 Disability Working Group,
      Leicester
E141 NCH (National Children's
      Home)
E142 National Children's Bureau
E143 Hounslow Social Services
E144 Medvale Adolescent Unit,
      Kent Social Services
E145 St Michael's Fellowship
E146 Greater Glasgow Health
      Board (Department of
      Clinical Psychology)
E147 The Children's Society
E148 NAYPIC (National Association
      of Young People in Care)
E149 Barnardo's
E150 Royal Leicestershire Society
      for the Blind

E151 MIND (National Association for Mental Health)

E152 BASW (Report on Integration of Field, Residential and Day Care Services)

E153 National Federation of Housing Associations

E154 National Autistic Society

E155 Catholic Child Welfare Council

E156 Prince of Wales' Advisory Group on Disability

E157 Elderly Services Team, Birmingham Social Services (Harborne)

E158 Y Rizvi, Birmingham Social Services (Sheldon)

E159 National Confederation of Registered Rest Home Associations

E160 St Christopher's Fellowship

E161 Pilot Scheme for Asian Elders, Leicestershire Social Services

E162 Doncaster Social Services

E163 Help the Aged

E164 Lewisham Branch, Alzheimer's Disease Society

E165 CCETSW (Central Council for Education and Training in Social Work)

E166 Royal Surgical Aid Society

E167 NAHA (National Association of Health Authorities)

E168 Philip Mason (Bordon, Hants)

E169 Child Care Open Learning Project

E170 VOPSS (Voluntary Organisations Personal Social Services Group)

E171 Exeter Council for Independent Living

E172 Spastics Society

E174 Nottinghamshire Residential Care Association

E175 BASW (British Association of Social Workers)

E176 Peter Bevington, Quinta Christian Centre

E177 MS (Multiple Sclerosis Society)

E178 NALGO (National and Local Government Officers' Association)

E179 Martin Valins, Chartered Architect

E180 Hillingdon Social Services

E181 Margaret Buckley (Shrewsbury)

E182 Douglas Banyard (Manormead Nursing Home, Hindhead)

E183 Alcohol Concern

E184 Wandsworth Social Services

E185 Association of Teachers in Social Work Education

E186 Voluntary Council for Handicapped Children

E187 Newmarket Day Centre

E188 Association of Therapeutic Communities

E189 Cooper Care Group

E190 Bob Sapey, Social Worker, St Austell

E191 Nottingham Branch, Social Care Association

E192 Special Needs Housing Advisory Service

E193 J Griffiths, Sefton Social Services

E194 Save the Children (Vietnamese Children's Home)

E195 Supervisory Staff, Homes for Elderly People, Cleveland Social Services

E196 Age Concern (Council of Europe colloquy on the Social Protection of the Very Old)

E197 R Willet, Dudley Social Services

E198 Dianne Willcocks, Polytechnic of North London

E199 Habinteg Housing Association

E200 Nigel Paul Bailey (Ruskin College, Oxford)

E201 Selly Oak Colleges

E202 East Pennine Branch, Social Care Association

E203 Charlie Maynard (Bradford)

E204 Philippa Collins (Fawcett Society Health Committee)

E205 Lorncliffe Children's Home, Calne

E206 Ann Macfarlane, Surbiton

E207 CSV Independent Living Scheme, Islington

E208 Michael Illingworth (Macclesfield)

E209 Community Social Work Exchange Working Party, National Institute for Social Work

E210 Lightfoot Lawn, Portsmouth, Hampshire Social Services

E211 BFCHP (British Federation of Care Home Proprietors)

E212 Mrs A Cawkwell (Hayling Island)

A Message from Gillian Wagner

I have been invited to chair a Working Group which is to review residential care services and make recommendations for changes in the way residential care is provided in future.

I should very much like to hear from people who are living in 'homes' and other places providing residential care, or who have close relatives who are doing so; also from people who are themselves employed as residential care staff. Some questions are suggested below, but please do not feel limited by them in any way.

If you live in a residential home (or have a relative in one):

- How did you come into residential care? How long ago? Has it been a success from your point of view?

- What do you like best about the place where you are now living, and the care which you receive there?

- Is there anything which you do *not* like? or that you would prefer to see changed or improved?

- Are you planning to leave residential care in due course? If so, when? Is enough being done to prepare you for this?

If you work in a residential home:

- How did you first come into residential care work? How long ago? What training have you received?

- What do you like best about your present job?

- What do you find most difficult about your present job?

- What improvements would you most like to see, either immediately or in the future.

Your comments on these or similar questions would be most helpful to the Working Group in its task. Please write to me before the end of 1986, if you can; all replies will be treated in strict confidence.

Gillian Wagner
NISW
5–7 Tavistock Place
London WC1H 9SS   *July 1986*

[221]

Review of Residential Care
Guidelines for those who wish to submit evidence

1. The Working Group, which is committed to completing and submitting its report by the end of 1987, will welcome written evidence from concerned organisations or from individuals who are engaged in providing residential care or have contacts of any kind with residential care services. To ensure that such evidence is taken fully into account, it should be submitted to the Secretary of the Review of Residential Care, at the National Institute for Social Work as soon as possible, and not later than 30 September 1986; please let him know if evidence is unavoidably delayed beyond this date.

2. The Working Group's terms of reference are 'to review the role of residential care and the range of services given in statutory, voluntary and private residential establishments within the personal social services in England and Wales; to consider, having regard to the practical constraints and other relevant developments, what changes, if any, are required to enable the residential care sector to respond more effectively to changing social needs; and to make recommendations accordingly'.

3. Organisations and individuals who wish to put their views to the Working Group may find it helpful to have guidance on the topics about which evidence is being sought: a list is set out overleaf. This does not imply that everyone should seek to cover all of them; and it is recognised that evidence will often be concerned with the needs and interests of particular groups rather than with the residential sector as a whole.

4. The list of topics is not in any sense exhaustive, and the Working Group hopes that both organisations and individuals will write freely on any points which concern them.

5. When the Residential Care Review has been completed, a copy of the evidence received will (unless it was submitted in confidence) be deposited in the library of the National Institute for Social Work, where it will be available for future reference.

May 1986

A. General principles

Why do we need/should we provide residential care services? What is their place within the spectrum of personal social services?

For whom is residential care considered appropriate: of what kinds, and what should it be aiming to achieve?

Types of agency offering residential care: respective roles of statutory, voluntary and private sectors.

Cooperation/coordination between social services, education, housing and health authorities; and between residential care and other types of social service (eg day, field, domiciliary).

Links with the local community; should residential care be administered as part of a network of neighbourhood services, or as a separate sector?

B. Evaluation

How satisfactory is current residential care provision and practice, in quantity and quality? Are costs of placements justified by results?

Are there ways in which resources might be used more effectively? Methods of evaluation; systems for monitoring standards of care.

Examples of innovation and/or good practice.

C. Experience of living and working in residential care settings

of residents: how they enter, participate in, and leave residential care; daily routines and personal care.

of staff: how they define and perceive their work with residents.

clients' rights: choice of life style; personal finance; clothing and possessions.

stresses of living/working in residential care.

ethnic minority groups: special problems facing them, as residents or as staff.

D. Organisation of Care

Styles of management; leadership; roles of management staff within and outside establishments.

Models of organisation; influence of different patterns of care.

Assessment, care planning and review; records and record-keeping, including clients' access.

E. Staffing

Levels of staffing, recruitment, management and supervision.

Specific roles and tasks of residential care staff (eg key worker); basic educational and personal qualifications required for them, and corresponding staff development and training needs.

How are/should staff be appointed? Grades and conditions of service? Role of professional associations/trade unions.

F. Other issues
Financing residential care: capital; revenue; financial support of residents.

Registration of voluntary and private homes: effectiveness and equity of existing system.

G. Future developments
Along what lines do you see residential care developing in the next two decades? Likely size and shape of residential sector. Any new kinds of provision you would particularly wish to see developed?

H. Recommendations
Please list in order of preference the three improvements you would most like to see implemented—as a matter of urgency, as soon as possible? Ideally, in the longer term?

APPENDIX II

A Note on the Committee

The following were members of the Committee:

Gillian Wagner, OBE, Ph D: Chairman
Chairman, Barnardo's 1978–84; Chairman, Volunteer Centre since 1985; President, National Bureau for Handicapped Students.

Jack Hanson, OBE: Vice Chairman (to March 1987)
Director of Social Services, Dorset, 1970–84.

James Atherton
Principal Tutor, Social Work Education Centre, Bedford College of Higher Education.

Chris Beddoe
Director, National Confederation of Registered Rest Home Associations.

Ben Brown
Assistant Divisional Director, Barnardo's London Region (to March 1987); now Social Services Inspector, London Region, DHSS.

Hema Ghadiali
Consultant Psychiatrist in Behaviour Modification Unit, St. Crispin's Hospital, Northampton (to March 1987); now Consultant Psychiatrist for Rehabilitation, South Derbyshire.

Des Kelly
Head of Home, Newlands House, Coventry SSD.

David Lane
Director of Social Services, Wakefield.

Phyllida Parsloe Ph D
Professor of Social Work, University of Bristol.

Malcolm Payne: (from November 1986)
Assistant Director for Development, The Richmond Fellowship (to July 1987); now Head of Department, Applied Community Studies, Manchester Polytechnic.

Patrick Phelan
Assistant Director, Social Work, Royal School for the Blind, Leatherhead.

Consolata Smyth
Sister of the Order of the Good Shepherd; Principal, Duncroft School, Staines, (to November 1986); now in Rome.

Mary Sugden, CBE: (from May 1987)
Principal, National Institute for Social Work, 1982–7.

Martin Weinberg
Principal, Pengwern Hall, North Wales (to November 1987); now Research Fellow, Dept of Psychiatry, University of Manchester.

Mary Wilson
Director of Community Nursing Services, Blackburn, Hyndburn and Ribble Valley District Health Authority (to February 1987); now Director of Nursing Services, PARC Care.

Jane Wyndham-Kaye, OBE
General Secretary, Health Visitors' Association, 1964–84. Since 1986, Chairman, South & West Hertfordshire Health Authority.

Mary Sugden, CBE attended the Committee's meetings as an observer, in her capacity as Principal of the National Institute for Social Work, until her retirement from that post in May 1987, when she was invited to join the Committee as a full member. Her successor at the Institute, **Daphne Statham**, has attended the Committee as an observer, since June 1987.

Sister Consolata Smyth was unable to attend the Committee's regular meetings after her transfer to Rome in November 1986; and **Jack Hanson** resigned as Vice-Chairman, on personal grounds, in March 1987; both, however, contributed to drafting the Committee's final Report and attended the two residential meetings at Cumberland Lodge.

Mr Tony Greaves, Chairman of the Social Services Committee of the Association of County Councils, was appointed to the Committee but resigned in October 1986, having been prevented by the pressure of other business from attending any of its meetings. **Mr Christopher Hayward**, who was appointed in his place, was able to attend only one meeting before he, too, resigned for the same reason in March 1987.

The Committee held 32 meetings between 13th May 1986 and 2nd February 1988. Ordinary meetings were held in London on the second and fourth Tuesdays of each month, either at the National Institute for Social Work or at the Thomas Coram Foundation. In addition, there were four two-day residential meetings: at the University of Surrey and the Royal School for the Blind, Leatherhead on 21st–22nd July 1986; at Pengwern Hall, Rhuddlan, North Wales on 13th–14th October 1986; at Cumberland Lodge, Windsor Great Park on 7th–9th September 1987 and 11th–13th January 1988. Committee members visited a number of residential establishments in Clwyd on 14th October 1986 and carried out a comprehensive programme of visits to residential facilities in Bradford on 9th–10th March 1987, which they followed up by further visits to selected establishments in Coventry, Warwickshire and Birmingham on 27th–28th April 1987.

Printed in the United Kingdom for Her Majesty's Stationery Office
Dd291457 7/88 C20 G443 10170